CRYSTAL MIRROR

Volume IV

May whatever merit acquired by this work bestow endless peace and happiness on all living beings.

Crystal Mirror is the annual journal of the
Tibetan Nyingma Meditation Center,
2425 Hillside Ave., Berkeley, CA 94704

ISBN 0-913546-34-6; 0-913546-11-9 (pbk)
Typeset in Fototronic Garamond and printed by
Dharma Press, Emeryville, California

Articles by Tarthang Tulku were composed or translated by Rinpoche and edited by Paul Clemens and Lawrence Gruber.

Portions of "Questions and Answers" appearing in *Crystal Mirror* are based on a talk given at the University of California Medical Center (S.F.). The entire talk will be published in *On the Way to Self-knowledge: Sacred Tradition and Psychotherapy*, edited by Jacob Needleman (New York: Knopf, 1976).

Photography credits:
Anila Li Gotami Govinda: 191, 192, 196, 215, 217, 218, 227, 228, 229, 231, 232, 234, 245, 246, 249, 250
Peter Ogilvie: 151, 167, 183, 263, 271, 283
Robert A. Miller: 203

The symbols (gnam chos dbang ldan) appearing on pages 156, 161, 170, and 177 are Padmasambhava's seal. Iconographically, they have many outer, inner, and secret meanings which are explained in the non-dual Tantras.

Frontispiece: Śakyamuni Buddha. Above: Amitābha (center), the Buddha of Boundless Life; Avalokiteśvara (left), the Buddha of Infinite Compassion; and Padmasambhava (right), the Lotus-born Guru, who is identical to all the Buddhas of the Ten Directions and the Three Moments of Time. Below: Guru Drag-po (left), the inner manifestation of Padmasambhava representing the male energy which subdues obscurations; Senge-dong chen-ma (right), the secret manifestation of Padmasambhava representing the female energy; three Nyingma Dharmapalas (center), protectors of the Doctrine.

[illegible]

A Word from Tarthang Tulku

FOR MANY CENTURIES, the pure teachings of the Buddha have alleviated much suffering in the world. So in the past year it has been encouraging to see many more people become interested in studying the Dharma. The Dharma is not just a series of doctrines and practices, but a way of life–a learning process that encompasses every possible situation.

Buddha's teaching emerges from his own experience of being human. But we often are blinded by our own confusion, frustration and struggling. We are afraid, or we feel trapped by our karma. The fascinated mind chases after sensations which glitter like rainbows, but we must realize that all grasping is insatiable and futile.

Studying the Dharma means to look at ourselves honestly, with complete openness–not as we would like to be or should be, but just as we are. Our lives are precious and time is precious, so use this present situation, whatever it is, to feel more positive, more balanced, and to live harmoniously with others.

The Dharma is vast and often quite subtle. It cannot be evaluated or appreciated without a willingness and openness to study. We are not trying to escape this world, but thoroughly examining our participation in it. By analyzing the contents and limitations of our own mind, we can gain a knowledge and understanding which no one will ever be able to take away. With sincere study comes clarity and certainty, a broad, healthy point of view, and the solution to doubt and confusion. The Dharma becomes our refuge, our protection, our own home.

The essence of Buddhist teachings can best be understood by internalizing the meaning–not by searching and evaluating from the outside. Over time, the effects and significance of Buddhist practices change and deepen as our minds and hearts become more open. Knowledge is as infinite as the stars in the sky, yet the most valuable, the most useful, the most reliable knowledge is knowledge of our own mind. This is the lasting gift of the Dharma.

The Vajrayāna teachings are the highest expression of Buddhist theory and practice. All aspects of our present situation can be used to understand the mind's true nature. With proper self-acceptance and self-nurturing, we can learn to heal ourselves, and then to encourage others. The ancient transmission of the Vajrayāna includes a wide range of approaches, such as philosophy, psychology, meditation, and ritual practices. All of these topics are vast subjects. In this volume of *Crystal Mirror* we are only beginning to lay the foundation for study and practice. Once we have a useful understanding of the basic teachings, once we have directly experienced the inner freedom that is possible, then further study will come naturally.

Since the Vajrayāna expresses the understanding of the Nyingma lineage, we are presenting the early history of Buddhism in Tibet, as well as the life story of Padmasambhava and short biographies of his twenty-five disciples, who were responsible for the early continuation and spread of the Tantric teachings in Tibet. These articles are not meant to be scholarly, but include what I can remember from my own study, the words of my teachers, and some research with my students. Few materials are available for study, so in the future we hope to present a comprehensive survey of Buddhism in Tibet.

I hope this volume of *Crystal Mirror* will help to make your life easier and give you greater insight into your own process of growth and health. I especially appreciate the encouragement and help of my wife Nazli, the students who collaborated with me in editing the various manuscripts, and everyone at Dharma Press for their hard work and dedication to the preservation of the Nyingma teachings.

May the blessing of Lord Buddha and the Lotus-born Guru inspire you with strength, understanding, and compassion, and may the lineage of Nyingma masters bring you to full enlightenment in the Dharma.

With the blessings of the Triple Gem,

Tarthang Tulku, Rinpoche
Head Lama of the Tibetan
Nyingma Meditation Center

CRYSTAL MIRROR

Volume IV

PART ONE

HISTORY

The Life and Liberation of Padmasambhava

Tarthang Tulku

When Lord Buddha was about to pass into final Nirvāṇa, he said to his followers, "This worldly life is transitory and separation is inevitable. But eight years from now, in the midst of an immaculately pure lake in the northwest land of Uḍḍiyāna, one will appear who is wiser and more powerful than myself. Born from the center of a lotus blossom, he will be known as Padmasambhava and will reveal the teachings of the Secret Mantras to deliver all beings from misery."

YE-SHEY TSO-GYAL, Padma Thang Yig

Padmasambhava, the renowned saint and scholar of the eighth century, became a central figure in the shaping of Buddhism's history in Tibet. Born from the lotus of compassion and revered as the 'second Buddha', he entered this world to enlighten all beings. As his biography relates, Padmasambhava is the manifestation of the mind of Avalokiteśvara, the speech of Amitābha, and the body of Śākyamuni Buddha. All the Buddhas of the Ten Directions and the Three Times of past, present and future are identical in essence and unitively embodied in Padmasambhava. Just as the Buddha's teaching is the same for all but is interpreted variously by those on different stages of the spiritual path, so Padmasambhava appears in different ways according to the receptivity of those seeking liberation.

This account of Padmasambhava's life story operates on many levels. While his origins as well as various episodes in his career are shrouded in mystery, we know that he appeared on this earth as a great seeker and integrator of the Vajrayāna teachings. In worldly matters, such as language, logic, the earth sciences, the fine arts, and even architecture, Padmasambhava was the quintessence of a true 'renaissance man'. In his travels, he exhaustively mastered the teachings of human and 'non-human' guides, practiced austerities to subdue the demons of cupidity-attachment, aversion-hatred and bewilderment-erring, received numerous initiations and appellations, and, at the time of his invitation to Tibet, was renowned as the foremost scholar and Tantric master at the University of Nālandā. Upon his arrival in Tibet, he did not entertain obstacles but instantly transmuted countless manifestations of negativity and, in a short time, safeguarded the Tantric teachings in the hearts and minds of the Tibetan people.

In the grandeur of the mountain highlands, Padmasambhava encountered numerous capricious spirits, personifications of the emotional undercurrent of the entire Tibetan civilization. At once he was faced with the prevailing powers of primitive mythic beliefs, hostile natural forces and wrathful wielders of destructive magic. His first task, therefore, was to provide new explanations for ancient understandings and to demonstrate, in a skillful and unsullied manner, the deepest and most mystic aspects of human existence. He could not ignore the pre-existing Tibetan predilection for magic and the world of spirits, for Buddhism has always recognized that demonic or godlike forms are the expression of our own minds. To subdue wrathful spirits is to tame our own emotionality, and thus the very obstacles to our spiritual progress. To some therefore, the magical acts performed by Padmasambhava may appear to be an ostentatious display of his psychic accomplishments. However, his miraculous acts were in actuality a pretense for something else. By encountering these malevolent demons, he not only transformed their hostile displays into an energetic appreciation for the Dharma, but entrusted to their charge the responsibility of protecting and safeguarding the sacred teachings. Similarly, his words and deeds sent a shaft of fear into the minds of the Tibetans and stirred them with hope, offering to the king and his subjects a dramatic opportunity to express their confidence in him. In this way he carefully prepared them to receive the liberating teachings of the Tantras. Until they sought out the truth in their own minds, the Guru illustrated that they would remain helpless against the demons who inflicted wrath upon the country.

As the dispeller of darkness and the immediate expression of Buddhahood, Guru Rinpoche addresses himself to the consciousness of all beings. More implicitly, episodes in Padmasambhava's biography express meditation experiences through events in the outer world. To some, for example, he may appear as the wrathful deity, Dorje Drolo, fearlessly treading underfoot the ever-deceptive ego and severing karmic entanglements by wielding his three-edged dagger (*phur-bu*). To others he appears as the central figure of a radiant Maṇḍala, an all-discerning friend, refuge and inner guide. By subduing the self-created demons and fascinations of our individual predispositions, he lays bare the apparitional nature of all selfish aims and exposes the mind as utterly pure and ready to receive any content without bias. He challenges every manifestation of negativity with an attitude that each situation in life, regardless of its outward appearance, can prove to be an instruction in truth.

If, in the course of Guru Rinpoche's biography, certain episodes seem ambiguous or are couched in metaphorical language, it is because the essential meaning is revealed in silence, beneath the level of specific language, such that one is left to measure and test the authenticity of his own psychological insights from within the meditation.

On the most inner level, Padmasambhava is not intended to be viewed as a mere historical figure having a psycho-somatic constitution just like ours, for he is no ordinary being. He is like a rainbow—pure, transparent, untouchable and clear. He is all-knowing and all beauty—the Buddhas of the Three Times shine from the pores of his skin. His entire form is pure light in a world of absolute perfection. He sits on a lotus seat of compassion and a sun throne of highest wisdom which resides in the heart of the meditator. From here, the illuminated mind of the Guru fills the Ten Directions of space like the rays of the sun, the embodiment of the Tri kāya: his view is all-embracing, absolute awareness (Dharmakāya), his thoughts are in perfect attunement with every situation, self-lucent (Sambhogakāya), and all his actions the on-going expression of the very nature of the universe (Nirmāṇakāya). Timeless, ageless and deathless, unoriginated, not dependent on externals and without suffering, he manifests through a variety of forms which he assumes at various times—and in this time—to teach the Diamond Path.

Constant and mindful meditation on the pure essence of the Guru destroys all selfish desires, inappropriate qualities and unnecessary delusions, so that one learns to view every situation as the means to attain Buddhahood in this lifetime. Ordinarily, the mind is diffused and wandering, but when this meditation is properly enacted, every form which one sees becomes the body of Padmasambhava, every sound which one hears, the speech of Padmasambhava, and all action, the mind of Padmasambhava.

IN THE LAND OF Uḍḍiyāna[1] lived a wealthy king named Indrabhūti. He was a compassionate king who in times past had freely given his wealth—and even his eyesight—for the welfare of his people. Upon the death of his only son and heir, he was filled with overwhelming sorrow, for famine and drought afflicted the land, the royal treasury was exhausted, and the people were forced to eat unripened grain and flowers. Making offerings of all their possessions, the King and his people prayed to the immortal Buddhas.

Avalokiteśvara saw all this from the Sukhāvatī heaven, and appealed to the Ādibuddha of primordial awareness, Amitābha—from whom all Buddhas emanate—to witness the people's suffering with compassion. Immediately there went forth from Amitābha's tongue a ray of red light, which, like a meteor, entered the center of the Dhanakośa Lake where a lotus blossom spontaneously unfolded. Simultaneously, he emitted from his heart the mantric syllable HRĪ which fell in the shape of a golden dorje into the center of the lotus. There, in a mist of rainbow light, sat the essence of all Buddhas in the appearance of an eight-year-old boy, who was surrounded by Ḍākinīs.[2] Thus, from the heart of the most compassionate Buddha, the Lotus-born Guru appeared in the world to aid all beings.

Indrabhūti, meanwhile, downcast and near despair, decided to risk his life for the good of his people and set out to obtain a wondrous wish-fulfilling gem from the Nāgas who dwelt beneath the waters of the ocean. After a hazardous but successful journey, the Nāgas greeted him with offerings of precious stones, while the Goddess of Azure unveiled a brilliant blue gem. With this auspicious gem safely concealed in his garments, the King uttered a wish, and his blind left eye immediately opened.

Returning from the palace of the Nāgas, the King beheld a five-colored rainbow hovering over the Dhanakośa Lake. There he discovered the young boy—whose body shone like the sun—sitting on the pollen bed of an enormous lotus. Believing this shimmering sight to be a dream, the King asked the child who he was and from whence he came, and the boy replied, "I have no parents, but am born spiritually, the gift of Amitābha and Avalokiteśvara. As foretold by the Buddha, I have come to aid all beings and reveal the doctrine of the

Inner Mantras." Hearing this, the King completely recovered his sight and joyfully enthroned the youth as his son and heir, naming him Padma Jung-nay ('Lotus-born'). Thereafter, in the land of Uḍḍiyāna, vapor arose from the sea, clouds formed in the sky, rain fell, flowers blossomed and fruits ripened; all depression and fear lifted from the hearts of the people.

When the Lotus-born grew to maturity, Indrabhūti, who had now grown old, arranged Padma's marriage to a beautiful princess from Siṃhala[3] and crowned the young prince King of Uḍḍiyāna, Padma Gyal-po ('Lotus King'). Secretly, the King presented Padma with the wish-fulfilling gem, saying, "This will satisfy all your wants." But the prince returned it replying, "Whatever I behold is my wish-fulfilling gem," and, requesting the king to extend his opened hand, instantaneously produced another gem. But Padma's attainment of the heights of worldly power and sensuous enjoyment quickly led him to realize the illusory and unsatisfactory nature of all things. Recalling the Great Renunciation of the Buddha, he decided to renounce his home and kingship, saying, "This worldly life is transitory, the activities of Saṃsāra are endless, and separation is inevitable. Since this is the law of the world, I will fix my thoughts on attaining liberation." Soon, however, it happened that Padma was held karmically responsible for killing the wife and demon son of a minister and was banished into exile without worldly possessions. Thereupon he freely took up the life of a yogi.

Seeking the Teachings

Wandering among the eight famous cemeteries (cremation grounds) of India, Padma practiced meditation without distraction. Then he proceeded to the Cool Sandalwood cemetery near Bōdh Gayā.[4] Using corpses for his seat, he entered into deep Samādhi and continued meditation for five years. Peaceful Ḍākinīs often visited him and gave him many empowerments and oral instructions. For food he took the offerings made to the dead, and for clothing, the shrouds of the corpses. In each of the eight cemeteries he received ritual practices (*sādhana*) from the guardian Herukas (wrathful male deities) and Siddha Masters (accomplished yogis), who hold the secrets of enlightenment. While meditating for many years in these cemeteries, Padma traveled through space to different realms and world-systems, requesting instructions in the esoteric teachings. Through constant practice he acquired mastery over all the restless and destructive forces of nature and was named Dorje Drag-po ('Indomitable Wrathful One').

Then Padma walked to Bōdh Gayā multiplying his body so that it appeared like a vast multitude of yogis, and thus astounded the crowd of onlookers. When asked by the people who he was and what guru he followed, Padma replied, "I have no guru, but am the Self-born Buddha." Yet seeing that these people and those of coming generations would need spiritual guidance, Padma disciplined himself in the three yogas of body, speech and mind, and continued to study with teachers in both human and non-human realms. For he desired to find a doctrine capable of being explained in a few words, which, when applied, would prove immediately effective, just as the Sun, once it has risen, immediately gives heat and light.

Journeying to the country of Padmāvatī, Padma mastered the art of healing, learning diagnoses and an innumerable variety of remedies. In the land of Ragala, Padma met an old, white-haired man, the Friend-of-All, and asked him, "Old man, what is your knowledge?" And the old man replied, "In teaching language and writing, I have no rival in the world beneath the sun." "Then," Padma said, "kindly teach me language and writing," and so he learned Sanskrit, the language of the gods, and many other dialects–all together 360 languages and 64 forms of writing. Thereafter, he mastered the arts of the lapidary and the potter and became skillful in all crafts. In this way, Padma proceeded, receiving whatever instruction he requested.

From Ānanda he received an account of all the Sūtras and commentaries that had been recorded in writing. From Guhyabuddha he received the Mahāyoga Tantras, from Śri Siṃha the Tantras of the Supreme Heruka, and from Garab Dorje the Dzog-chen (Mahāsandhi) teachings, the highest of the Tantras.[5] Visited by Bodhisattvas from other realms, Padma learned all that was known concerning astrology, philosophy, logic, physics and the combined wisdom of all other worlds. His next teacher was an ordained Ḍākinī who manifested before him one hundred Peaceful and Wrathful Deities and transformed him into the syllable HŪṂ. Then she initiated him into the Hayagrīva Maṇḍala, empowering him to overcome all conflicting spiritual beings and mental forces. Thus having practiced the outer, inner and secret traditions of the Tripiṭaka, and having received the precepts, explanations, initiations and empowerments of the Tantras, Padma became a complete master of all existing knowledge. Before him, the incarnation of the mind of the Buddha Amitābha, there spontaneously appeared the Maṇḍala of the Unity of all Buddhas and Bodhisattvas. Externally he appeared as a brown-robed monk, but inwardly he was master of the Supreme Secret Mantras.

Then Padma attained the yogic arts of clairvoyant seeing, hearing, feeling, smelling and tasting, by practicing austerities which assisted his development of breath control and the resultant 'psychic heat'. Having acquired knowledge as limitless as the sky, Padma journeyed to a cemetery where the Tantric deity, Mahākāla, dwelt. There, resting his back against a Stūpa adorned with precious gems, he taught the Mahāyāna and Vajrayāna teachings to the Ḍākinīs. Having traveled far and wide, in India he was called Nyi-ma Od-zer ('Ray of the Sun'), and in Nepal, Lōden Chog-se ('the Transmitter of Wisdom to all Worlds').

Travels throughout the World

Padma then journeyed to the land of Zahor where he preached the Dharma and gave instructions in the Mantrayāna to the King's daughter, Princess Mandāravā. However, the people became scandalized, believing that a monk was cohabiting with a woman, and reported this to the King. The King became enraged, confined his daughter to a pit of thorns, and condemned Padma to be burned alive. But the Lotus-born Teacher, in full command of all natural forces, transformed his cremation pyre into an immense lake[6] surrounded by a burning ditch. In the center of this lake, an ivory-petalled lotus supported a child of eight, whose translucent body glowed with the purplish color of seashells. The King, rubbing his eyes, saw the whole sky haloed with iridescent lights and, repenting his error, offered Padma the throne, naming him Padmasambhava ('The One Born from a Lotus').

Then Amitāyus ('Buddha of Boundless Life') came in a vision to Padma and Mandāravā as they were meditating in a cave, and, placing the urn of boundless life on their heads, rendered their bodies luminous, and henceforth immune to illness, old age and death—the immortal essence of the Buddhas. Thereupon he constructed the Maṇḍalas of the Wrathful Deities and demonstrated the effective methods of doctrine and conduct, whereby one may, step by step, attain Nirvāṇa.

Stainless as a diamond, the Guru then returned to his birthplace, Uḍḍiyāna, and appeared in public with his woman disciple, asking for alms. But the royal ministers recognized him saying, "This is the former prince who abandoned his wife and then murdered the minister's son. What catastrophe will he now bring upon the country? He aspires not to good, but to crime." All the ministers agreed. So loads of sandalwood and measures of oil were assembled, and the couple was committed to the flames. But even after twenty-one days, the smoke from the pyre had not dispersed. With all his ministers the King visited the site and beheld an enormous lake, with the entwined couple dancing in the center of a blossoming lotus, radiantly enhaloed in rainbow auras. Humbly, the King of Uḍḍiyāna asked for blessings and teachings, and Padma replied, "The three worlds[7] are like a prison house. Even though you are a wise king and possess every material comfort, you cannot escape the material and sensual attachments which cause you frustration and mental suffering. But knowledge of temporal impermanence and the inevitability of death will guide you to honor this precious life, abandon worldly illusions, and teach you to govern your mind." Thus saying, Padma became known as Dorje Dro-lo ('The Eternal Comforter

of All Beings'), and stayed in Uḍḍiyāna for thirteen years, instructing the populace in the outer, inner and secret mantric formulas. Many of these people became successful practitioners and later passed away in a brilliant rainbow light, leaving behind no physical trace.

Padmasambhava traveled throughout India and Nepal giving instructions in the Mantrayāna. He also journeyed throughout this world and to higher realms—to South India and Lanka (Ceylon), Indonesia, Burma, Central Asia, parts of China and Russia, Afghanistan, Persia, Egypt, Africa, to various mystic lands such as Śambhala and Sumeru, and to many other realms. In all these lands he subdued fierce mountain gods, barbaric cannibal spirits, and demons of pestilence and plague. To all dark planetary forces he brought the harmonious influence of the Dharma, and in those tormented by mental anguish, emotional instability and lack of confidence, he dispelled the causes and manifestations of bewilderment, dissatisfaction, frustration and negativity, and cultivated equanimity.

In Southeast Asia, in the copper-colored land of Zang-ling, a Tīrthika (non-Buddhist) king had him bound and thrown into the river. But Padma flew up into the sky, dancing in the air, and converted the ruler and his people. Thus he became known as 'Vajra Garuḍa', or 'Diamond Bird'. Another Tīrthika king poisoned him to prevent the teaching of the Dharma, but the Precious Guru transmuted the poison in his body into purest radiant light.

Once, at Nālandā Mahāvihāra, the renowned Buddhist university, the Buddhist scholars were being challenged in philosophical debate by powerful proponents of opposing doctrines and said among themselves, "Although we can defeat them in controversy, we cannot overcome their occult powers." Thus, making many prayers and offerings, the Buddhists invited Padmasambhava. The next morning at dawn, Padma arrived at the palace, coming down through the branches of trees like a great bird, and emanated four personalities resembling his own, while he himself remained seated in meditation. Quickly challenging dualistic arguments, he convinced his opponents to doubt their own views. In the next competition, the non-Buddhists magically produced leaping flames of fire, whereupon Padma touched the earth. At once, a lotus blossom appeared and a wide swash of sun-bright flame jumped from the pollen bed, rising beyond sight into the sky. Thus quelling all doubts concerning the supreme nature of the Buddhadharma, Padma became known as Seng-ge Dra-dog ('The Lion-Master of Wisdom').

Padma also traveled to Nepal where, at that time, many natural disasters–earthquakes, storms and floods–plagued the land, destroying both animals and harvests. While meditating in Yang-le-shod grotto, he assumed the wrathful manifestation of Vajrakīla (rDo-rje Phur-bu) and, through the intensity of his concentration, bound by promise eight different classes of conflicting and disruptive forces to protect and defend the Dharma in Nepal. Through his activity, Padma transmuted the obscuring powers of bewilderment into a stream of peaceful existence and exemplified the unerring integrity and compassion of all Buddhas.

The Advice of the Bodhisattva Abbot

The work of perfecting mankind is guided by three Bodhisattvas called the Lords of the Three Families: Mañjuśrī, Lord of Wisdom, Avalokiteśvara, Lord of Compassion, and Vajrapāṇi, Lord of Mystic Power. In order to bring the Dharma to the plateaus of Tibet, they appeared as three early kings of that land. Avalokiteśvara manifested as Song-tsen Gam-po, the first Buddhist king of Tibet, whose two queens, a Chinese and a Nepalese princess, were emanations of merciful female Bodhisattvas. Mañjuśrī appeared as King Tri-song De-tsen, and Vajrapāṇi as King Ral-pa-can.

Tri-song De-tsen, eager to spread the Buddhadharma in his kingdom, invited from India the learned scholar and gentle Bodhisattva, Śāntarakṣita, and placed the construction of the 'Self-created Temple' of Samye[8] under his direction. One auspicious morning, the King, robed in white silk, took a golden pickaxe smeared with unguents and dug to the depth of one cubit, whereupon three oils oozed up from the earth, one red, one yellow, and one white. Spreading this chrysm over his face and anointing his head, the King proclaimed, with great joy, the coming of the Buddha's Doctrine to the Land of Snows. Thus were the foundations laid for the building of Samye Monastery.

The priests and shamans of the Bön-po religion, however, did not wish to relinquish either their governing social status or their cultural heritage. They firmly resisted the intrusion of new and different teachings, and called upon the wrathful Nāgas who destroyed by night what had been constructed during the day, restoring all the earth and stone to its original places. Realizing that social insurrection and chaos would ensue if Śāntarakṣita remained, Tri-song De-tsen reluctantly requested him to depart. But the Abbot replied, "I have endeavored to perfect the spirit of a Bodhisattva. If gentleness cannot prevail, we must rely upon one who is learned in the five classes of knowledge and before whom all negative forces tremble and become powerless. At this moment, the Doctor from Uḍḍiyāna, Padmasambhava, resides near the Diamond Throne of India. All your hopes for the people of Tibet will materialize if you invite this incarnate Buddha of the Three Times."

Padma Is Invited to Tibet[9]

And Siddharāja, after traveling around India,
came to King Tri-song De-tsen with this news:
"In the Indian land, the crowd of Paṇḍitas
is like the crowd of stars, without number.
The one who among them all has proven himself the best
is Guru Padmasambhava,
who resides in a cavern of the Lofty Schist Mountains.
Born not sexually but by spiritual projection,
he is a renowned incarnation."
The King was moved to great joy by these words
and he dispatched three messengers:
to Khri Gzir of the village of Sba, to Māradharṣaṇavajra,
to Śākyaprabha of the Chim clan, and

to the military count, Lion-of-Fame;
to all four he sent gold dust and golden bowls
to be borne to the Diamond Throne of India.

The four lotsāvas crossed the Indian plain.
To King Sūrya they presented a measure of gold dust,
a golden bowl and a message;
to the great ceremonial Paṇḍita, one measure;
to Padma of Uḍḍiyāna, one measure and a golden bowl.
The Great Guru graciously received the royal gifts.
Then the envoys spoke: "The King of Tibet, Tri-song De-tsen
has decided to found a residence for the faith,
a monastery of meditation,
but the Spirits are obstructing him.
We invite you to consecrate the blessed soil,
and to secure, preserve, and defend the Buddha's doctrine;
we beseech you to show yourself well-disposed."
The Great Saint of Uḍḍiyāna looked with condescension
on this request, and in the earth-male-tiger year,
on the fifteenth day of the winter midmoon,
under the sign of the Pleiades, he set out on his way.
By new moon he had reached Nepal.
Then Padma, the Doctor of Uḍḍiyāna, spoke:
"Carrying out the task of conversion, in the end I will arrive.
The Spirits born sexually must hold their peace.
You, the lotsāvas, go on ahead!"
And he dispatched them in advance, endowed with his
protective blessing.

The Great Saint of Uḍḍiyāna spent three lunar months in Nepal.
After loading with benefactions the Nepalese Vasudhara
and many other beings in Nepal,
he hid a treasure in the monastery of Ekāra.
Then, in the grotto of Yang-le-shod, Asura and other grottoes,
in the monastery of Sankhu and other Nepalese monasteries,
at the crag called Mighty Soil, and in many roundabout places,
he hid a thousand other treasures.
Then, on the first day of the first summer moon,
having decided to continue on his way, he dreamed
that the trees of India and Nepal were pointing
their crests toward Tibet,

that all the flowers facing Tibet opened new blossoms,
that the Paṇḍitas of India and Nepal beheld dreams
with mysterious portents,
that the sun and moon rose together in Tibet,
and, the Law of India having been transferred in its entirety to Tibet,
that this barbarian region was newly bedecked with monasteries.

At this, the Ḍākinīs of all four orders cried out graspingly:
"The Guru is leaving for Tibet. Postpone such a declaration!
Diamond master, treasure of thought,
teaching the treetops, is that a method?
The flower corollas, do they have a south?
The Paṇḍitās' nightmares, are they a method?
Once the glorious Maṇḍala has gone, there will be
forthwith a relapse into the cycle.
The Guru is departing. It is as though
the unshakable unmoving sky were leaving.
Increate infinity of the four elements,
the Guru is leaving and will not remain.
Immense spontaneous benefaction for beings,
we beg the Guru not to depart, but to remain."
Thus they spoke. The Master answered:
"Oh, conspiring Ḍākinīs, listen to me!
At the instigation of the summer season, fruits swell with juice.
Besought by those in need of conversion, pity springs up.
Having seen the law of Karma, I do not have the time to linger.

The Garuḍa, wings outspread, is soaring.
For me, benefits and happiness are mere ornaments of the past.
The time has come to benefit others impartially.
Mother and sister Ḍākinīs, may the Dharma befriend you!"

Having spoken thus, he arrived at Mang-yul [the border of Tibet].
There, in the presence of the Nepalese woman, Śākyadevī, he predicted:
"After the lapse of more than two hundred generations,
in the districts Purang and Mang-yul,
a king, Threefold-Aid, will rise from among your descendants.
In Kashmir, three noble brothers from Turkestan will be famous.
In Nepal, from the interior of the Ekāra monastery
will be made manifest the hidden Holy Law of Uḍḍiyāna.
In the town of Lad-lar, the monastery Virtue and Renown will appear.
If poor folk lay down body and life for the Dharma,
their confidence will prove to be a substantial pillar."
He spoke, and Śākyadevī, the Nepalese woman,
placed her trust in the master Who-Will-Mold-the-World.

Clairvoyantly, the Great One from Uḍḍiyāna
now deemed that the time had come to effect
conversion through the force of deeds,
and he went to Lake Nyimakhud in Nepal.
Seven royal envoys met him there, to entreat him once again.
Ākāśagarbha headed the delegation, accompanied by
the chief of Dab Mang, Lion-of-Light-from-the-Gods-Above,
a man from Dab, Kru Zinga, one from Cogro,
Guardian-of-the-Noble-Formulas,
Māradharṣaṇa of the Na-nam clan, Putrasī of Sa,
and finally the minister Who-Looks-the-Tiger-in-the-Face.
"He has vanquished Mang-yul. How was that possible?
His investigation embraces everything, he scrutinizes essential Truth.
He brings about the festival of increasing joy by means of the Dharma.
Through his fortune-binding benediction
he plants hope within one's mind.
Thanks to him the human race follows the holy Dharma."
Conversing thus, and carrying the inscribed roll and the gold dust,
they reached their destination.
From this side of Nepal, facing India,
they gained access to the Great One of Uḍḍiyāna, Padmasambhava,
and handed over the inscribed roll together with the King's presents.

Thereupon the Guru sent the seven intercessors
ahead of him, to Samye.

The Great One from Uḍḍiyāna, after mounting to the sky,
remained in the central plain of Mang-yul for three lunar months.
In high places and low, wherever he chose, he hid a treasure.
And Tri-song De-tsen, King of Tibet, forthwith
dispatched posthaste Śrīkūta of Skaba,
Māhadharṣaṇavajra and Nāgadhvaja of Cogro, bearing gold.
On their way they talked day and night, wearing themselves out.
And when the Guru's Ḍākinī-guardians invited them to express a wish,
the three couriers, overwhelmed with fatigue,
begged to be conveyed as far as Mang-yul's central plain.

After admitting them to audience, the Master asked,
though he already knew, "Who are you?"
"We are Tibetans, come with an invitation for the Guru."
They greeted him, offering a measure of gold dust.
"Are these presents from the ruler of the Town-of-the-Deceased?"
And he threw the gold to the farthest limits of Mang-yul and Nepal.
But he saw that the loss affected them painfully, and said,
"Hold out the flaps of your cloaks!"

And he filled them with earth and pebbles.
When, one by one, they opened the flaps and looked,
all was gold, silver, turquoises, and precious stones.
Filled with complete confidence,
they conceived great respect for the Saint.

Padma Subdues the Demons of Tibet

Then, in the autumn, Padmasambhava came to the castle of Mang-yul.
A Fury of the region of Zhang-zhung, Jamun the Eminent Enemy,
thought she could crush the Guru between two stone mountains.
But he rose up in the sky, and the humiliated Fury
offered the heart of her life.
Her secret name became Debt-of-Turquoises-and-Diamonds,
and the Guru gave her a great treasure to protect.

Then, on the Plateau of the Sky, he reached the Black Castle.
The White Ḍākinī of the glaciers
thought a thunderbolt would destroy him.
But the Guru, surrounding her with one finger,
swept her away into a lake.
The terrified apparition fled as far as the lake of Pal-mo Pal-thang.
At once the water began to boil, her flesh dropped from her bones,
and the Guru, hurling the Vajra, blinded her in one eye, whereupon
she rose above the surface and uttered this supplication:
"Face of the Master! Oh, Vajra! Strength-of-the-Death's-Heads-Rosary!
I swear I will do no more harm. This thought comforts me.
What else could I do? I yield, I approach as the Guru's vassal."
Thus she gave the heart of her life while he bound her by an oath.
Her secret name became the Unfleshed Turquoise-and-Diamond Lamp,
and he committed a great treasure to her care.

Then he came to Oyug-bremo,
where twelve Earth Goddesses each released a thunderbolt
and tried to crush him between the mountains.
But the thunderbolts turned into charcoal, the Goddesses'
strength failed to crush him, and they were exorcized.
The twelve of them, together with the twelve Tutelary Ladies
and the twelve From Above and From Below,

offered the heart of their lives.
The Guru bound them by oath and to all of them entrusted a treasure.

Then he pushed on to the fort called the Bird's Nest of Oyug.
The great layman, Protective-Good-Vajra,
appeared amid a retinue of three hundred and sixty brothers.
Padma bound them all by an oath and left a treasure in their care.
Then, when he came to the valley of Sham-po,
Sham-po appeared, a white yak the size of a mountain,
with mouth and nostrils exhaling whirlwinds and snow tempests.
Using the iron-hook mudrā, the Guru seized him by the muzzle,
bound him with the mudrā of the noose, chained him
with the mudrā of the shackles,
and, with the bell mudrā, flogged him body and mind.
When the great white yak offered the heart of his life,
the Guru bound him by oath and entrusted him with a treasure.

To test the Guru, the Spirit of the Argalis Plateau
took on the guise of a white reptile and blocked his path.
The head reached the district of the Uighurs,
while the tail coincided with the Sog River of Kham
and Gyer-mo-thang.
With a staff the Guru transfixed the serpent
through the middle, saying,
"You are the King-Dragon Chalk-Color,
king of the Gandharvas with the Five Hair Coils.
Depart, and prepare yourself to make a circular oblation!"
The Spirit fled to the ice-cold snows, but the snows melted
and, when the greenish ice had given way,
the black mountain peak could be seen.
The Spirit could withstand no longer, so he served a Gaṇacakra
(food offering) decked out with dainties
and, changing into a child with a turquoise hair net
and a turban of white silk, he did obeisance and circumambulated.
He gave the heart of his life and, having been bound by oath,
he was given one hundred treasures to watch over.
His secret name became Vajra-of-Great-Power.

Then, on the Northern Plateau, the Guru came
to the valley of Phan-yul.

Those insolent Northerners, the Ting-lo-man Visages,
gathered together the storms of the arctic regions
and loosed them on the Guru and his following.
Those who were with him became thirsty, so he attracted a cool breeze.
Then, guiding a fiery wind, he melted, like sun on butter,
one of the Ting-lo-mans and bound him by oath.
When all of them had given the heart of their lives,
he entrusted a treasure to their care.

Then, at Lang-drom of the Heavenly Blue Juniper Trees,
he entered the Maṇḍala of the Supreme Perfect Meaning
and reached Attainment. On the midnight following the seventh day,
fright and anguish reigned. And when he looked,
the leaders of the army of Māra, their banners
unfurled, were imploring him.
"Oh, Guru! Now we are terrified. Forgive us!"
They gave the heart of their lives, and were bound by oath.
Thereupon he placed a treasure into their keeping.

Then he came to Kham, to the place called One-Legged-Musk-Deer.
There he bound by oath all the Cyclops and the other The'urang.
After that he halted at the crag, Lion of Kham.
The being called Impure-One-Born-from-Slate,
an old man with a monkey's amice as headgear,
put his head on the Guru's chest,
stretched his feet toward Gyer-mo-thang in Kham
and raised his hands to the peaks of Mount Kailāśa
and to Lake Manasarowar.
Ten milliard millions of Non-Human-Beings,
utterly unimaginable, hastened thither,
letting fall like rain weapons of every kind.
The Guru took on the fearsome aspect of the
five classes of Angry Deities
and, together with their leader Born-from-Slate,
all these Genies were tamed.

Then he reached Mount Chubo and Kharag,
where he bound by oath all the Mamos and all the Senmos.
Then he came to Silma in Tsang,
where he bound by oath all the Manmos and all the Lhasmans.
At the spring of Gempa he obtained the submission of all the laymen.

At the sands of Rabka, he mastered the Spirits of all eight classes.
In the speckled vale of Roha, he tamed the Ladies of the Epidemics.
In the black valley of Rong-rong, he subjugated the Ogres.
In Malgro, he bound by oath the Dragon tribes.
At Phugmo-of-the-Turquoises, he bound by oath the Phorgyuds.
At the Seashell-Color-Vermilion-Rock,
he bound by oath the Perfume Eaters.
On the snowy peaks of Mount Kailāśa,
he subjugated the twenty-eight asterisms.
In the cavern of the Hidden-Elephant,
he concealed yet another treasure.
At the Stargo glacier, he subjugated
the eight great planets and other satellites
and concealed twenty-one treasures.
At the Blue glacier, the Genies prepared a concentric oblation,
offering all the victuals and wealth of the universe.
In this glacier and at the lake of the Stargo glacier,
the Guru hid yet other revelatory scriptures.
At Lobo, he bound by oath the nine Danma sisters.
Called by the Genie Pūrṇabhadra, he bound him by oath.
Called to the glacier of the Genie of the Peaks,
he bound the Genie by oath.
Called by the Genie of the Heavenly Mountain, he bound him by oath.
And to each of them he entrusted a treasure.

At this juncture a repeated message arrived from the sovereign:
"The time has been fixed for our meeting
in the Tod-lung-grambu Park.
Triumphant and powerful king as I am,
I have dispatched many legates to you;
now only I myself have yet to come."

Yet for one more winter and one more lunar month,
the Guru resided on Mount Khalabrag.
Binding by oath the crude Spirits of the Mountaintops,
he entrusted to them a treasure.
Then he sojourned at the park of the Hemiones, at Zul-phug.
After taming demons, planets, and the Damri gnomes,
he gave a treasure into their keeping.
Then he dwelt for a whole spring in the Lofty Schist Mountains,
subjugating the Gongpos of the Ja ravines, and the Damri at Sosha.

Padma Arrives in Tibet and Encounters the King

Then Padma came to Lhasa, to the Tod-lung pleasure park.
The king, who had taken up his abode on the bank of the Brahmaputra,
sent Bhadradeva and Nāgaśrī as ambassadors
with five hundred iron-clad horsemen to escort them.
Now, at the time of this encounter at Tod-lung Zong-pa-mia,
the heat was oppressive and neither water nor tea was available.
But the Great One from Uḍḍiyāna, Padmasambhava,
laid his staff on the Tod-lung well.
"Bhadradeva! The water is gushing out. Hold a basin under it!" he said.
And the spot was called Divine-Water-of-the-Basin.[10]

After that, in the Double-Castle in the park
along the Brahmaputra's bank, he met the ruler himself.
The King of Tibet stood forth in the midst of his mercenaries—
one might have thought it the quivering radiance of a brood of pigeons.
And the two queens appeared, surrounded by their ladies,
in dazzling attire, iridescent as tents made of samite.
For welcome there were dances with drums, dances with songs,
dances with masks, and harmonious dances.

Padma, the Great One from Uḍḍiyāna, thought to himself:
'I was not born from a womb, I was born by apparition;
the King was born from a womb: by birth I am the greater.
At this instant the Law of Uḍḍiyāna lays hold on his kingdom.
This King of defiled Tibet is great through his paternal lineage.
But who are we, he and I? Plunged in darkness is his mind;
I am learned in the five realms of knowledge,
Buddha in a single lifetime, exempt from birth and death.
Out of necessity he invites me here.
Formally, this King came to greet me.
Shall I or shall I not return his greeting?
If yes, the majesty of the Doctrine will be slighted.
If no, since he is the King, he will be angered.
Yet, however great he be, greet him I cannot.'

And King Tri-song De-tsen thought to himself:
'I am sovereign over all the black-headed peoples of Tibet.
The Bodhisattva Abbot has already greeted me.
The Guru must greet me too.'
So, loath to extend the first greeting, he stood there hesitant.

Now the Guru sang his greatness and nobility:
"'The Buddhas of the Three Moments of Time passed through the gate
of the vagina.
Theirs are knowledge and merit, heaped up thrice innumerable.
But I am the Buddha Sprung-from-the-Lotus.
Mine are the counselings in the lofty concepts of the Dharma.
I possess the precepts of the Tantric Scriptures.
I explain exhaustively, clearly distinguishing all the Vehicles.

"'I am Padmasambhava the Holy Doctrine.
Mine are the counselings for assured ascension in the Dharma.
Externally I am a brown-robed Bhikṣu,
Within, yogi of the Supreme Secret Mantras.

"'I am Padmasambhava the Stūpa.
Mine are the counselings of attentiveness of mind, the theory
and practice of the Scriptures,
an intuition higher than the heavens,
more precise than the wheaten meal of retribution.

"I am Padmasambhava the Lama.
Mine are the counselings that illuminate and measure the Causal Data
of the Doctrine.
In the book of the World and of Nirvāṇa
I explain the direct sense and the sense transcendent.

"I am Padmasambhava the Friend-of-Good.
Mine are the counselings that classify failings and virtues in keeping
with the Teachings.
I don the mantle of the fivefold sciences.
I am the vessel of the Five Perfect Beings.

"I am Padmasambhava the Doctor.
Mine are the counselings of Man-become-Buddha.
I know solitude within inspection and tranquillity.
Effortlessly I deliver the 'Great Perfection' and its themes.

"I am Padmasambhava Lofty Meditation.
Mine are the counselings on contemplating the Doctrine outside
the time of repose.
In Nirvāṇa's circle of Victory
I am peerless in espousing or refusing the meditations that lead
to apotheosis.

"I am Padmasambhava Master of Mantric Formulas.
Mine are the counselings for evading the apotheoses
within the Doctrine.
On the table of divination, appearing in white and red,
I shall enumerate retribution's choices.

"I am Padmasambhava the Reckoner.
Mine are the counselings of the three indivisible holy vows.
To men laid low by the sickness of the five poisons
I bring the immaculate Teaching as balm.

"I am Padmasambhava the Leech.
Mine are the nectar of the Law, the counselings
that cure one of death.
And, apart from their apparition,
I raise up images identical with the gods.

"I am Padmasambhava Maker-of-Gods.
Mine are the counselings of the Holy Luminosities on the Level
of Essence.
Concerning equanimity, that chart of the mind,
I interrogate the scripture that has no words to bear the meaning.

"I am Padmasambhava the Scribe.
Mine are the counselings of the unwritten Teachings.
To men born on the four continents
I expound archknowledge by means of the knowledge
of the Three Moments of Time.

"I am Padmasambhava the Astrologer.
Mine are the counselings of the Way that converts everyone
on his own path.
Surging up as the enemy of the five poisons, of the five evil Geniuses,
I am floodwater at the heart of the five branches of learning.

"I am Padmasambhava the Sorcerer.
Mine are the counselings of the Dharma that transmutes
the five poisons.
I do not bid farewell to pleasures, I take them with me on the path.
I exult in the fivefold knowledge of the positive.

"I am Padmasambhava the Bön-po.
Mine are the counselings of the Doctrine that awards
ill-fortune and luck.
I bear happiness to the six orders of beings.
I have bent to my service Gods and Rākṣasas of the eight classes.

"I am Padmasambhava the King.
Mine are the counselings of the Dharma possessing authority
in the Three Realms.
I embrace and shake profound Karma, profound cycle of causality.
I accomplish every action, subjugating the mind itself.

"I am Padmasambhava the Minister.
Mine are the counselings for entering into the Dharma,
whatever one's past deeds.
I watch over the ultimate outcome of desires.
I contemplate the Three Jewels without averting my gaze.

"I am Padmasambhava the Queen.
Mine are the counselings of the Buddha at the hour of death.
I protect the undertakings of those who have great confidence.
I make happy the subsequent life of man.

"I am Padmasambhava the Lord.
Mine are the counselings of the Doctrine that scrutinizes and
pronounces upon error.
With the Bodhisattva's compassion as a blade,
I have slaughtered inimical heresy and doubt.

"I am Padmasambhava the Hero.
Mine are the counselings of the Doctrine that treads underfoot
the hostile cycle.
Having assigned the heritage of the three gifts,
firmly within the Doctrine I establish blessed sons.

"I am Padmasambhava the Aged Man.
Mine are the counselings of the Doctrine that with its finger
touches old men.
I escort and guide the three monastic vows.
I travel the ways of celestial happiness.

"I am Padmasambhava the Aged Woman.
Mine are the counselings of the Doctrine whose imperious finger
points at old women.
I gird about me the armor of threefold patience.
I vanquish inimical misery and error.

"I am Padmasambhava the Young Woman.
Mine are the counselings of the Doctrine that halts fourfold Māra.
I don the adornments of the three zeals.
I give myself as spouse to all beings.

"I am Padmasambhava the Adolescent.
Mine are the counselings of the meaning, both relative and absolute,
of the Doctrine.
I storm the fortress of the threefold ecstasy.
In places of every kind I like to play.

"I am Padmasambhava the Child.
Mine are the counselings of the Doctrine that imposes silence
on the denunciation of offenses.
I see by means of the threefold eye of understanding.
I suck the milk of the unitary knowledge of Śūnyatā.

"I am Padmasambhava the Little One.
Mine are the counselings of the ecstasy of the Doctrine
that rouses one from sleep.
While in the Three Realms the transitory being dies,
I evoke that glorious Yoga, Receptacle-of-the-Knowledge-of-Life.

"I am Padmasambhava the Deathless.
Mine are the counselings for the diamond life of the Doctrine.
I am not dependent upon the four external elements
nor do I set up a dwelling for the internal body of flesh and blood.

"I am Padmasambhava the Unoriginated.
Mine are the counselings of the Great Seal of the Doctrine.
My diamond body will never wane.
For my mind, in Awakening, is perennial lucidity.

"I am Padmasambhava the Ageless.
Mine are the counselings of the Doctrine that assuages suffering.
He who once sensed his arrow-straight body yields to sickness.
He whose presence was a splendor, through accident loses it.

"I am Padmasambhava Who-Knows-No-Sickness.
The counselings of the Great Perfection of the Doctrine are mine.

"And you, King of barbarian Tibet,
King of a country without virtue,
uncouth men and ogres surround you.
You rely upon famine's serfs,
neither joy nor good humor is yours.
As for your queens, Rākṣasī in human shape,
beautiful purple ghouls surround them,
sandalwood, turquoise, and gold adorn them,
but by love and charm they are abandoned.
Since you are King, your lungs swell.
Great is your power, your liver is well-satisfied.
Sceptre in hand, you stand high and haughty.
But I, Sire, will not greet you!
And yet, in accordance with my conjoined vows,
Having come to the heart of Tibet, here I stay.
Great King, witness, have I come?"

He spoke, turned his hands and, springing up from his finger
a miraculous flame seared the king's garments.
King, ministers, courtiers could not withstand him.
Bowing in unison, they gave greeting as though swept by a scythe.

Padma Translates the Sūtras and Tantras

Padma purified the ground to lay the foundations for the temple at Samye and then assembled all the subjugated demons and spirits. Men worked by day and nonhumans by night, while the Guru sought

to restore the wealth of the King's treasury. For three nights, Padma sat in deep meditation and enjoined the Nāgas to become friends with the King of Tibet. Whereupon a large serpent emerged from the lake and stirred the water, flooding the shores with waves of gold.

When the temple was finished, Padma emanated one hundred and eight simultaneous bodies and scattered blossoms throughout the one hundred and eight shrines of the temple. At once, all the sacred images came to life and strolled around the temple discussing the Dharma. The sky filled with spontaneous music, flames of fire leapt from the heads of the wrathful guardian deities who faced the four directions, and healing nectars rained from cloudless skies.

But Tri-song De-tsen, fearing that this Great Master of the Elements would depart, addressed the Guru saying, "Over the years, my grandfather and parents built one hundred and eight temples throughout the Himalayas. Some of these areas are so remote and

difficult to reach that many have now fallen into disrepair. And the teachings, scattered far and wide, have never been gathered in one place. I will have built Stūpas, written commentaries, and erected temples to no avail if, once you are here, the sacred texts of the Sūtra and Tantra cannot be brought to Tibet and completely translated."

The King, therefore, sent off a caravan of young Tibetan translators to learn Sanskrit in India from renowned teachers and to carry back the sacred texts of the Dharma. And, though old, Śāntarakṣita remained in Tibet to introduce the Sūtras and philosophical commentaries of the Hīnayāna and Mahāyāna and to train the first native-born Tibetan monks. Then, at the appropriate time, the lotsāvas and paṇḍitas gathered in the central hall of the lofty Samye Monastery. Guru Padma, free of the stain of birth and sprung from the lotus stalk, who understood perfectly the meaning of all the Sūtras and Tantras, and who, having been summoned to Tibet, converted the whole land, sat cross-legged on a golden throne in the center of the temple. He was joined by the Tantric scholar and master from Kashmir, Vimalamitra, who comprehended completely the Three Baskets (Tripiṭaka) and the external and internal Mantras. Then the entire assembly of 800 scholars began the monumental work of translating, without a single omission, the Buddhist scriptures and texts from the languages of Sanskrit, Pāli, Gilgit and Chinese into Tibetan. Together with the learned lotsāva Vairocana, who knew twenty-one languages, Padmasambhava translated the general and esoteric ritual Tantras and revealed the special Mantra teachings of the Vajrayāna. Not even India, it has been said, could match the heights of enlightened activity that flourished at that time in Tibet.

Padma Initiates His Close Disciples and Departs from Tibet

Many disciples matured in their understanding of the texts and practices and sought out the Precious Guru who was practicing Sādhanā (yogic meditation) in solitude on the upper slopes near Chim-phu above Samye Monastery. King Tri-song De-tsen, Ye-shey Tso-gyal, the translator Vairocana, and others, each offered the Guru a ten-ounce gold-piece, shaped as a lotus flower, and asked him for initiation into the Maṇḍala of the Unity of all Buddhas (*bDe-gshegs-'Dus-pa'i dKyil-'kor*). During the ritual ceremony, each of the disciples tossed a flower into the Maṇḍala and thus invoked the wrathful deities (Herukas) who guard the entrances to the inner circle. Identifying thoughts, feelings and perceptions fully and actively with Guru Rinpoche, the disciples integrated their consciousness with one of his many manifestations.

Then Padma released to twenty-five close disciples the essential oral instruction, the precepts which give complete liberation from Saṃsāra. For seven years they meditated before achieving the level of one-pointedness of mind through which they expressed many uncontrived and miraculous demonstrations. The King sat absorbed in Samādhi, Ye-shey Tso-gyal resurrected a man from the dead, Nam-khay Nying-po could ride on the rays of the sun, and Vairocana attained clairvoyant insight, gaining access to all knowledge in the three moments of time.

Padmasambhava remained for a while among the Tibetan people, meditating in various caves, cemeteries, gardens and groves, and on various mountains in the Land of the Snows. Realizing that mankind was not yet ready to receive some of the highest Tantric teachings, the Precious Guru composed many scriptures which contained the essence of his teachings. At a cave near Chim-phu, several miles north of Samye, these texts were transcribed by his disciples in an abbreviated, codified script which could only be understood by those who were properly prepared. These teachings, or Terma, were then carefully wrapped and concealed in caves and temples, at the bottom of pools and in the cracks of rocks—and also in the Guru's Mind.[11] Knowing that the Buddhadharma would be misinterpreted by those who were not enlightened, the Uḍḍiyāna Teacher predicted that these same twenty-five disciples would later return as Tertons, incarnate emanations of the Guru, to recover these treasures from their hiding places and to interpret the abbreviated script for the understanding of whoever required instruction.

When at last this work was completed, the Master of the Mantrayāna predicted the specific time and place of the Terma discoveries, the name of each Terton, the disciple to whom the teachings would be given, and the number of people who would become enlightened throughout the Himalayas and the world as a result of their efforts. Then for twenty-one days, at Tha-duk (Multi-colored Dragon), he once again explained the outer, inner and secret teachings, and finally commanded the King and his people to practice diligently and to protect the Dharma in the future. In addition, he advised them on a variety of subjects such as farming, law, the organization of society and principles of enlightened government.

A vast throng of people then escorted the Lotus-born Guru to the Gung-thang-la Pass on the border of Tibet (Mang-yul) where he made his final gift to the people—the Thirteen Precepts which remove all obstacles to the continuation of the Tantric lineage. Giving them his final instruction, Padma said, "May all future generations who cannot now meet me read this exposition of my spiritual practice and self-liberated existence in this world, obtain a clear view of its significance, and live according to its implied command, becoming perfect in all things." Thus exhorting the people to aspire to Buddhahood, Padma mounted a winged horse which appeared from out of the sky, and, rising upwards in a mist of rainbow radiance, he vanished on the rays of the sun.

From Tibet, Padma flew to the southwest land of the untamed Rākṣasas and liberated them from the frustrations of samsaric existence. There, on the summit of the Copper-colored Mountain, he now dwells in a celestial palace. Completely compassionate, the Unoriginated Selfless One, Padmasambhava appears in this earthly world as a Bodhisattva, a Ḍākinī and a Wrathful Deity, as Mantra and as Art, as Teacher and as Buddha. The many names and legends which surround him are inexhaustible. From now until the end of all suffering, his manifestations labor effortlessly that all beings may finally rejoice in the ultimate realization of Buddhahood.[12]

Notes

1. Uḍḍiyāna (Oḍḍiyāna, U-ḍi-an or Urgyān) corresponds, perhaps, to an ancient territory northwest of Kashmir, but does not necessarily refer to a specific geographic location in our world system.
2. Ḍākinīs (Tib.: mKha'-'gro-ma, 'sky-walker') are goddesses or accomplished yoginīs who travel in both the sky and in the heights of pure awareness. Together with their male counterparts, Ḍākas, they exemplify the Buddhist teachings of Śūnyatā.
3. Usually identified with Ceylon.
4. Bōdh Gayā, or Vajrāsana, the place or position in which the Buddha sat when he attained enlightenment.
5. Ānanda, Guhyabuddha (or Buddhaguhya, Tib.: Sangs-rgyas gsang-ba), and Śri Siṃha are early Indian masters, and Garab Dorje (b. 55 A.D.) is the first of the rDzogs-chen lineage in human form. The rDzogs-chen Nying-thig, or Absolute Perfection teachings, were delivered by the Buddha Vajradhara to the Indian Paṇḍita Garab Dorje who left them to his pupil, Śri Siṃha, from whom Padmasambhava received them.
6. Today, Lake Rewalsar, between the rivers Byas and Ravi in northern India, is still venerated by pilgrims as the site of Padma's miraculous transformation.
7. The world of desire (kāmadhātu), form (rūpadhātu), and the formless (arūpyadhātu).
8. Samye is situated about thirty miles southeast of Lhasa at an altitude of 11,500 feet.
9. The following three cantos (LIX–LXI) appear in the celebrated Tibetan account of Padmasambhava's life story (*rnam-thar*) *Padma Thang Yig*, which was discovered in the mid-fourteenth century and whose authorship is attributed to Ye-shey Tso-gyal. G.-C. Toussaint translated the Tibetan into French (*Le Dict de Padma*, Paris: 1933), and Kenneth Douglas, the French into English. Tarthang Tulku (Ed.), *The Life and Liberation*

of Padmasambhava, Copyright 1975 Dharma Publishing, unpublished manuscript.

10. Visitors to this place still claim that water flows out of solid rock in a stream with a diameter of about one inch approximately eight feet above the ground.

11. Through the discovery of these revitalizing scriptures (*gter-ma*), the Nyingmapa constantly regenerate their tradition. "In Tibet the principle of continuing revelation takes three forms: the rediscovery of texts and holy objects (*sa-gter*) buried by Padmasambhava and his colleagues for revelation at a future time, the spontaneous appearance of teachings which were concealed in the Guru's Mind for propagation by future emanations (*dgongs-gter*), and instructions passed on by manifestations of gurus and tutelaries in visions (*dag-snang*)" (*see* E. Gene Smith, Preface to *The Autobiographical Reminiscences of Ngag-dbang-dpal-bzang*, Gangtok: 1969). Terma hidden in the Guru's Mind are accessible only during profound meditation, when the clouds of mental obscurity have been dissolved and the structure of being is clearly visible. Terma found in natural phenomena may be discovered by the sudden spontaneous bursting open of a rock disclosing a cipher key (see *The Legend of the Great Stupa*, Berkeley: 1972).

12. Longer accounts of Padmasambhava's life and teachings may be found in the following:

Dudjom Jig-dral Ye-shey rDo-rje, His Holiness. *gsang sngags snga 'gyur rnying ma ba'i bstan pa'i rnam gzhag mdo tsam brjod pa legs bshad snang ba'i dga' ston* [*rNying-ma'i chos-'byung*, The History of the Nying-ma-pa], Kalimpong: 1967.

Evans-Wentz, W. Y. (Ed.). *The Tibetan Book of the Great Liberation*. London and New York: Oxford Univ. Press, 1954.

Tarthang Tulku (Ed.). *The Legend of the Great Stupa* (Trans. Keith Dowman). Berkeley: Dharma Publishing, 1973.

Tarthang Tulku (Ed.). *The Life and Liberation of Padmasambhava* (Trans. Kenneth Douglas). Berkeley: Dharma Publishing, unpublished manuscript.

Toussaint, G.-C. (Trans.). *Le Dict de Padma* (*Padma Thang Yig MS. de Lithang*). Paris: 1933.

The Twenty-five Disciples of Padmasambhava

Tarthang Tulku

During the time of Tri-song De-tsen
many followers of the Vajrayāna appeared
who could walk in the sky,
cause water to flow from rocks,
and who spread the teachings and practices
of the Uḍḍiyāna Guru, Padmasambhava.

GEORGE ROERICH, Blue Annals

Just as the teachings of Lord Buddha were passed on with great care from master to disciple, the Tantric teachings were successfully transplanted to Tibet in the eighth century by Padmasambhava. During the subsequent suppression of Buddhism in Tibet (*see* "Buddhism in Tibet"), these twenty-five disciples preserved the oral instructions and Tantric texts through their spiritual and clan lineages. They thus form the first generation of Nyingma practitioners which has continued in an unbroken lineage for twelve centuries down to the present time.

Upon Padmasambhava's arrival in Tibet, word was secretly spread among the King's ministry that a superior Master of the Vajrayāna had come to instruct others in the Way of the Diamond Path. Soon the Lotus-born Guru attracted many followers who showed their sincerity by engaging in the practice of his teachings. Eventually there appeared those who demonstrated superior capacities and to them the Guru gave private instructions and taught advanced forms of meditation and ritual Sādhana. Realizing the richness and profundity of the Dharma texts from other Buddhist countries bordering Tibet, many of these disciples

Pad-ma Jung-nay

began to systematically translate a number of essential volumes of the Sūtras and Tantras.

At a significant moment in their relationship, the disciples approached the Guru and offered him ritual gifts representing the three actions of body, speech and mind. As Padma himself relates in the *Legend of the Great Stupa:*

> While I was practicing Sādhana in solitude on the upper slopes near Chim-phu, above the monastery of Samye-ling, King Tri-song Detsen . . . and others of the twenty-five disciples, came to me and presented offerings of gold and other precious gifts, entreating me to unfold the Maṇḍala of the Unity of All Buddhas. After I had disclosed the Maṇḍala, I gave them initiation.

The original thankas of the 25 disciples are courtesy of the Tibetan Nyingma Meditation Center. The line drawings appearing herein may not be reproduced in any form without written permission.

Thereafter, each of the twenty-five disciples perfected a particular aspect of Padmasambhava's teaching which stimulated special meditative abilities. Each disciple, then, has come to be known by a specific gesture, as illustrated by the traditional line drawings in the following section. The accompanying biographies are also intended to provide convenient points of entry into the drawings, for each pictorial metaphor draws our attention to the unitive character of the mind and its external manifestations—something which is neither easily expressed nor experienced.

The lives of the twenty-five disciples provide us with rich examples of properly motivated activity—an aspiration for enlightenment unhampered by pretenses. To enter the Maṇḍala of the dynamic presence of the Guru, each of the disciples made a 'sacrificial' offering of his body, speech and mind—symbolized by casting a flower into the center of the Maṇḍala. The primary purpose of such an offering is to present to one's Guru a gift whose price is beyond measure. To enter a Maṇḍala, either physically or as a totally internalized visualization, is a very significant act. One's entire being—one's thoughts, feelings and perceptions—are fully and actively engaged. Rather than make the pursuit of enlightenment into some idealized, future project, the meditator chooses to give of himself completely here and now. Nothing is held back. Without this basic willingness to surrender all our evaluations of who we think we are and what we think is possible for us, genuine lived freedom is impossible.

For this reason, many Buddhist teachings focus attention on the deceptive nature of desire. Desire can either painfully entrap us in self-centered craving, or it can lead us to recognize our bodily limitations and thus yearn to exchange this world for some illusion concerning the 'infinite' and 'transworldly'. Entry into the Maṇḍala, however, demands the death of *all* desire, and this death permits the birth of an appreciative commitment to the intensity of life just as it unfolds.

'Entering', then, is not possible without 'offering'. Entry into any of the stages of Buddhist development involves the taking of vows by those who are guided by the motivation to attain enlightenment in this lifetime. This vow is not something we must carry out with a blind sense of duty, but rather the natural outflow of a firm commitment to be true to who we *are*, rather than to any selective biases concerning our 'development'. If we must have a 'view' at all, only an enlightened one will do.

This aspiration for enlightenment, which evokes the transfiguration of all generally frustrating constituents of Saṃsāra, is further illumined by a living exemplar, the Guru-as-Reality, who, as the embodiment of the enlightened consciousness, is uncompromisingly awake and compassionately active. At the moment of initiation, each of the disciples accepted as their exemplar one of eight guardian Herukas who elucidate various aspects of the mind of Guru Rinpoche. While our timid personalities are normally confined to the realms of fiction, the wrathful deities, or Herukas, are not similarly constrained to some fictional 'beyond'. They stride over all boundaries and thrive on the nourishment of all circumstances. Their power derives from their fierce practicality, their immunity to the seductiveness of inauthentic uses of body, speech and mind. Their bodily action—the spontaneously kept commitment to reality—suggests the nature of the very advanced Sādhana practiced by the twenty-five disciples. Similarly, by means of this internal transformation, their speech expresses the essential quality of Mantra, which communicates the intrinsic value of life present in every situation. Through Mantra, the mind becomes relaxed, concentrated and fully appreciative, envisioning all manifestations of body, speech and mind as essentially perfect.

Calling upon a 'tutelary deity' or inner guide awakens within us our own deep connections with this enlightened consciousness. For example, propitiation of Hayagrīva (the wrathful aspect of Amitābha, Lord of Speech) empowers the initiate to subdue the impure mental forces of passion-lust. Propitiation of Vajrakīla (the wrathful manifestation of the 'fearless' Amoghasiddhi) severs the roots of karmically inherited dispositions constituting the personality stemming from envy-jealousy, and eliminates feelings of separateness instigated by insecurity, fear and self-condemnation. To call upon one's Heruka is, therefore, to bring the enlightenment of the Guru—who spans all circumstances—into a meaningful relation with the immediate events of one's own life. This process of integration produces a new vision and fresh perspective whereby the individual apprehends the world around him and all that it contains as a total presence—a harmoniously interrelated field seen as the embodiment of absolute being.

Padmasambhava's followers accomplished this integration to such a degree that their actions appeared to be 'magical' to those unwilling to believe that such spontaneous and inspired activity might constitute an appropriate norm for everyone. Their display of paranormal powers or abilities, such as drawing water from rocks, indicates that beyond a rational system of conceptual interpretations, there exists a level of reality where an unprejudiced awareness operates freely within the open, undefined parameters of immediately lived experience. Once this underlying awareness was discovered and developed, the disciples recognized the material world as neither fixed nor solid. By contemplating the transitoriness of all phenomenal existence, they learned to penetrate material substances—such as passing through rocks—as easily as they could penetrate the most subtle regions of mind itself. Neither magicians nor metaphorical 'deities', the disciples manifested the effects of their direct realization through their subsequent activity in the world. The line drawings depicted here, then, only point in a symbolic way to this realization and represent mere drops in the ocean of possibility.

I have compiled these short biographies from the Tibetan accounts of Dudjom Rinpoche's "History of the Nyingma," Kong-trul's "Encyclopedia" and from my own memory based on the teachings of my guru, Jam-yang Khyen-tse Lo-dro. These twenty-five disciples—and their disciples—are also responsible for a great number of the early translations of the Sūtras and Śāstras which appear in the Tibetan Tripiṭaka, as well as many original and compiled works appearing in the collection of Nyingma Tantras known as the *rNying-ma'i rgyud-'bum*. Even today many scholars are not aware of the sizeable contribution by early Nyingma translators such as Vairocana, Ka-wa Pal-tseg, Ye-shey De, Cog-ro Lu'i-rgyal-tshan, Ma Rin-chen-chog and others, so I hope it will be useful and informative to introduce their names to the West.

Throughout the centuries, many great 'precious masters' (*rin-po-che*) from all the schools of Tibetan Buddhism have benefitted from the preservation and oral transmission of Nyingma meditation practices and initiations. May the memory and subtle power of this ancient and direct lineage now be planted and shared with all people, fulfilling Padmasambhava's prophecy that the teachings of the Vajrayāna would one day bloom throughout the world.

[1] *Tri-song De-tsen (mNga-bdag rGyal-po Khri-srong lDe'u-btsan)*

As Tibet's most powerful King (c. 755–97 A.D.), Tri-song De-tsen extended his territories well beyond the Tibetan frontiers and maintained political influence over one-third of the known world. But nothing could satisfy him more than fulfilling his desire to unify the teachings of the Buddha in the Land of the Snow-capped Peaks. So he invited the Bodhisattva Śāntarakṣita to instruct the Tibetans in the meaning of the Sūtras, the practice of the sixteen moral precepts, and the basic mental trainings of Mahāyāna Buddhism. Convinced of the

Tri-song De-tsen

superior value of the Buddhist teachings, Tri-song De-tsen then invited the Uḍḍiyāna Master, the renowned Padmasambhava, who brought with him the inner teachings of the Tantras and the oral instructions of the Mantrayāna. Guru Rinpoche then initiated the King, as well as other advanced disciples, into the Maṇḍala of the Unity of all Buddhas, wherein the King offered a golden flower to Chem-chog Heruka in the center of the Maṇḍala.[1] Through his practice of Sādhana, the King integrated his behavior and awareness with that of Hayagrīva and awakened into Samādhi.[2]

Tri-song De-tsen carefully studied the texts which Śāntarakṣita had brought to Tibet and was determined to translate the Indian texts and teachings into Tibetan. For this reason he sent well over a hundred Tibetans to learn Sanskrit in India. These later returned carrying numerous sacred texts and were accompanied by scores of Indian Paṇḍitas. Then, joined by such masters as Vimalamitra[3] and Vairocana, they translated innumerable volumes of Sūtras, discourses and Tantras in the Great Hall at Samye.

The King, however, whose clan of De belonged to the ancient Bön tradition, found it increasingly difficult to justify to his ministers the presence of the Indian teachers and scholars. The royal family of ministers, who performed specialized religious, social and political functions, were therefore intimidated by the authority and prestige given to the King's Buddhist guests. They accused the King of being tricked by the Indian magicians who, they claimed, had cleverly depleted the royal treasury in order to build Samye monastery. "Of what value," they asked, "are the Buddhists? They waste our resources and make food-offerings to their wrathful deities which are never eaten." Rather than relinquish their power, the King's ministers persistently counseled him against the Buddhists, saying, "You are a Bön-po and the Bön is a venerable tradition. There is no reason for you to invite these Indian teachers and threaten the social order in Tibet." Even the foreign relatives of Tri-song De-tsen's queens opposed the Indian Paṇḍitas and demanded their departure. Not knowing how to resolve this conflict, the King was advised to sponsor a debate to determine which group was more worthy to direct the religious activity of Tibet. The Bön-pos, thinking that they possessed the most eloquent and intellectual speakers, and convinced their psychic capacities were significantly advanced, thus publicized the debates widely.

When the debates were scheduled to take place, the Buddhist disciples of Padmasambhava, who had been meditating in caves and in the surrounding mountains, gathered together near Lhasa. In a place called Drag-mar Rin-zang, a tent made of cotton was erected. Many Bön pos and Buddhists were present, and overseers from each party were appointed. Thereupon, Tri-song De-tsen said: "Everyone observe, which is true and which is false, which has the greater magical powers. Once and for all, Bön-pos and Buddhists must contest their skill." And thus the contest began.

The Buddhist disciples were prepared. Their intense practice had nurtured and stabilized in them a deep understanding that all appearance arises and remains within an open horizon of possibilities, and, with limitless freedom, they displayed myriad signs of their spiritual development.

> The teacher Padma hung his cloak over the rays when the sun
> rose in the morning.
> The Bodhisattva Śāntarakṣita threw a thunderbolt into space
> which stayed there for a day.
> Nam-khay Nying-po left his rosary hanging in mid-air.
> Pal-gyi Seng-ge drew rainbow figures in space.

Gyal-way Lo-dro caught wild animals and milked them.
Sog-po Ha-pal made tigers, leopards, bears, and brown bears
as tame as dogs.
Ma Rin-chen Chog sat cross-legged in space.
Ka-wa Pal-tseg cut off his head and put it back again.
Vairocana's swift-footedness equalled that of a bird.
Gyal-wa Chang-chub stood a vase in mid-air.
Kon-chog Jung-nay sat in a bonfire without being burned.

After this amazing display of skill, the King summoned all of his ministers and said, "Since this holy Buddhism is good for both the here and hereafter, I urge you to follow Buddhism. . . ," and thereby ruled for the Buddhists to remain. The Bön-pos, in their books, also claim to have performed a number of marvelous signs, but, as the King wanted to practice Buddhism, they had no choice but to concede. At that time, many Bön-pos became Buddhists and henceforth the twenty-five disciples of Padmasambhava were recognized as true masters of the Mantrayāna.

Tri-song De-tsen, who was regarded as an incarnation of Mañjuśrī, received Padmasambhava's complete teachings and became Guru Rinpoche's direct successor, passing on the Dzog-chen instructions called *sLob-dPon Chen-po Pad-Ma'i bKa'-Srol.* He wrote commentaries on the Sūtras, practiced the Tantric teachings, and meditated in the awareness of perpetual Samādhi. In subsequent years, scholars and translators arriving from India brought many precious relics and jewels. With these, Tri-song De-tsen initiated the work of restoring the 108 Stūpas which had been constructed throughout Tibet in the time of Song-tsen Gam-po. Thus, under the direction of Tri-song De-tsen, the Doctrine spread across the country like daylight at dawn.

[2] *Ye-shey Tso-gyal (mKh'-'gro Ye-shes mTsho-rgyal)*

Ye-shey Tso-gyal was Padmasambhava's closest disciple and mastered the Guru's complete teachings. In the Initiation Maṇḍala, her flower-offering fell upon Dorje Phur-bu (Vajrakīla) who revealed to her the intrinsic awareness (*ye-shes*) which is radiant with all positive qualities. Originally one of Tri-song De-tsen's young queens, she received the name 'Tso-gyal', which means 'The Conqueress of the Lake', from Padmasambhava. One day, Ye-shey Tso-gyal came upon a young man who had just died, and, out of heart-felt compassion for his mother, restored him to life. Thereafter, wherever she traveled, she liberated many sentient beings from the misery of the lower realms.

Ye-shey Tso-gyal

Ye-shey Tso-gyal often conversed with Guru Rinpoche, asking him many questions and writing down his words. In this way, she requested the essence of the Tantric teachings. Then, with an unfailing memory, she transcribed his teachings and reduced their meaning to symbolic form in a codified script known only to the inner circle of initiates. She prepared these texts, or Terma, on special yellow parchment, some of which were abbreviated to one page while others contained many folios and were much more extensively detailed. Hundreds of these texts were then carefully wrapped, immune to the hazards of weather and natural deterioration, and hidden away for safekeeping in specific locations designated by Padmasambhava.

After Padmasambhava's departure from Tibet, Ye-shey Tso-gyal collaborated with Sang-gye Ye-shey to transcribe many more volumes of Guru Rinpoche's instructions, including Padma's biography, *Padma Thang Yig*. She frequently traveled throughout Tibet and Nepal, encouraging the people there to cultivate the intention to attain Enlightenment, and taught them the Vajra Guru Mantra. She is said to have lived on this earth for over 200 years and was revered as an incarnation of Sarasvatī, the female Bodhisattva of learning and eloquence. She never died, but disappeared in a radiance of rainbow light to join Padmasambhava on the Copper-colored Mountain. Because she is identical with Padmasambhava, all initiations, Terma masters, and siddhis come through Ye-shey Tso-gyal. Through her continuous compassionate activity, she awakens awareness in the hearts of those who recite the Vajra Guru Mantra and who practice the teachings of Guru Rinpoche.

[3] *Vairocana (sPa-gor Lo-chen Bai-ro-tsa-na)*

Vairocana was one of Padmasambhava's most gifted disciples. He was born into the Pagor clan in Zangkor near Lhasa and practiced meditation in caves, unattached to the extremes of misery or happiness. It is said that, at age eight, he left the imprint of his foot imbedded in a rock at sNe-mo as a sign of his spiritual attainments. One of the original seven monks (*sad-mi*) trained by Śāntarakṣita, Vairocana was sent to India by Tri-song De-tsen and, while there, studied with the master Śri Siṃha. Secretly, during the night, the master delivered to him the Tantric doctrines of the Ati-yoga, writing them out with goat's milk on a white cloth. Śri Siṃha told him, "If you hold the cloth over smoke, the letters will become quite visible, but you must carefully guard the secret teachings." When Vairocana returned to Tibet, he became one of the most respected translators of his time, carefully wording the Tripiṭaka and Prajñāpāramitā literature with precision and insight. Afterwards, in close communication with Padmasambhava, he edited the eight Nyingma Tantric Sādhanas, including the cycles of Vajrakīla and Hayagrīva.

When Guru Rinpoche initiated him into the Maṇḍala of the Self-same Nature of All Buddhas, Vairocana cast his golden flower on Drag-nag Heruka (Mod-pa Drag-sngags). Thereafter, he practiced meditation ceaselessly and received many private teachings and advanced practices. Through contemplating that the nature of phenomenal existence has no origination and no characteristic marks, Vairocana became inseparable from the Mind of Guru Rinpoche, who said to him, "As I am, so are you."

Cherishing and utilizing the spontaneous appearances of the

Vairocana

mind's projections, Vairocana mastered the three classes of Mahāsandhi precepts (*Man-ngag rDzogs-pa-chen-po*) as handed down by the Ācār yas Śāntigarbha, Hūṃkara and Vimalamitra: (i) the mental class (*sems-sde*), unveiling the apparitional nature of phenomenality; (ii) the class of relativity (*klong-sde*), or 'vastness teachings', removing all mental judgments through meditation on Śūnyatā thereby revealing the mind effortlessly free in itself; and (iii) the precept class (*man-ngag-gi-sde*), or 'direct methods' of the Nying-tig, which is based on the philosophical system of the Mādhyamika and which provides the 'fulfillment instructions' for the practice of the Mantrayāna.

After meditating for many years in Kham, Vairocana carried the Tantric teachings to China. His unclouded devotion and faith opened his inner eye and enabled him to see both the formed and formless as the manifestation of unoriginated awareness. In the nineteenth century, he reincarnated as the renowned Kong-trul Lo-dro Tha-ye.

Sang-gye Ye-shey

[4] *Sang-gye Ye-shey (gNubs Sangs-rgyas Ye-shes)*

Born in the fertile region of Nub in western Tibet, and initiated by Padmasambhava into the Maṇḍala of the Wrathful Herukas, Sang-gye Ye-shey cast his golden flower upon Yamantaka, who reveals the impermanence underlying all phenomenal existence. While he was practicing the Mantrayāna teachings in the secluded caves above Samye Monastery, he visualized Yamantaka and Mañjuśrī, when, suddenly, all the deities of the Yamantaka Maṇḍala spontaneously appeared before him. Through his practice of the Vajrakīla Sādhana, he pierced the restrictive nature of common appearance, and could shatter rocks with a touch of his *phur-bu*; thus he became widely known as a great Siddha. Absorbing into his body the rays of the sun and moon, he discovered within himself the light of transcending awareness.

During the suppression of Buddhism under Lang-darma, Sang-gye Ye-shey traveled across the Himalayas seven times to visit learned teachers in Nepal and India. There he studied and translated Mahāyāna Sūtras and Nyingma Tantras and imparted the oral teachings of Guru Rinpoche. His practice reached full maturity when he mastered the three unsurpassable yogas, Mahā, Anu and Ati. So successful and fearless was he that one day the King Lang Dar-ma, hearing of the great 'magic man', invited Sang-gye Ye-shey to his court. "What sort of power do you have?" he asked. "Show me your power." So Sang-gye Ye-shey accepted the challenge. Pointing his finger toward the sky, he chanted a mantra, and suddenly a huge scorpion, larger than a yak, stood balanced on his fingertips. Lang Dar-ma looked stunned, but Sang-gye Ye-shey was not yet finished. "Look," he said, and from the scorpion (a swallower of evil) came a thunderbolt that pulverized the nearby rocks into sand. The demonstration was sufficient to terrify Lang Dar-ma, who pledged not to disturb the long-haired, laymen followers of the Mantrayāna (*sngags-pa*).

Sang-gye Ye-shey is one of the more important lamas of the Nyingma tradition. Together with Ye-shey Tso-gyal, he compiled many of Guru Rinpoche's teachings and preserved innumerable texts in his private library during Lang Dar-ma's short but violent reign. He lived for 113 years and, following his death, his disciples continued to transmit the Tantric teachings, especially the practice of the Vajrakīla Sādhana.

[5] *Gyal-wa Chog-yang (Ngan-lam rGyal-ba mChog-dbyangs)*

Born from the Nam-lam clan near Pal-yul (E. Lhasa), Gyal-wa Chog-yang was one of the Bodhisattvas trained by Śāntarakṣita. Respected for his purity as a monk, he offered the flower of his body, speech, mind and action into the Maṇḍala of the Herukas, becoming identical with the Horse-headed One, Hayagrīva. By way of illustrating this spontaneous coemergence with his tutelary deity, he was often heard neighing like a horse from the crown of his head. Thus he dissolved all karmic inclinations by practicing the meditation which is beyond speech, the object of no-thought, the 'horse of non-action', which neither comes nor goes. Through perfect understanding of the inseparability of form and formlessness, he radiated the light of original

Gyal-wa Chog-yang

awareness represented by Amitābha and was able to transmute his body into a raging fire. During his life, Gyal-wa Chog-yang performed many services for King Tri-song De-tsen and learned to blend every action into the path of immediate, lived freedom.

[6] *Nam-khay Nying-po (dGe-slong Nam-mkha'i sNying-po)*

Offering a flower in the shape of a golden heart, Nam-khay Nying-po entered the Initiation Maṇḍala of Yang-dag Heruka, who unites the non-discursive knowledge and spontaneous action of the Buddha. Having translated and practiced the Mantrayāna teachings and the Mahāsandhi (rDzogs-chen) realization, he could ride, in the sky of intrinsic awareness, on the rays of the sun.

One day in early spring, his nephew asked him for some seeds to plant because the farmers' supply was gone. Nam-khay Nying-po re-

Nam-khay Nying-po

plied, "If the farmers have no seed, where can I, a yogi, find some?" But taking some small rocks, he instructed his nephew to pulverize them and then plant the granules. Soon, many varieties of flowers, plants and vegetables could be seen sprouting from the ground.

Accustomed to flying wherever he traveled, one day Nam-khay Nying-po's string of beads fell from the sky into a certain valley. When his fingers, in picking up the beads, touched the earth, five fragrant flowers appeared, and from the center of the flowers emerged five Ḍākinīs who, in turn, erected five Stūpas which exist to this day.

It was not uncommon for his disciples to bring him food offerings and ask for his blessing. But on one occasion, he gave them tiny stones which later turned into precious turquoise, empowering each of them with the sky-like realization.

Nam-khay Nying-po practiced meditation for a long time in the rocky southern mountains of Bhutan and finally left this world embraced in a rainbow of light.

[7] *Ye-shey Zhon-nu (gNyags-lo Ye-shes gZhon-nu)*

Born in Yar-lung, trained by Śāntarakṣita, and taught by Vairocana's disciple Uda, Ye-shey Zhon-nu mastered the Sūtras and Tantras and transcribed many early translations and Nyingma teachings. At his birth, two black moles in the shape of a double-dorje appeared on his throat, signifying his complete detachment from the self-seeking and pride of worldly existence. He was initiated by Padmasambhava and en-

Ye-shey Zhon-nu

tered the center of the Maṇḍala, propitiating Chem-chog Heruka and drinking the pure water of spiritual instruction. One of the early leaders of the Nyingmapa, he manifested many psychic powers. Once when he was staying in a cave at Yar-lung with Gyal-wa Chog-yang, Ye-shey Zhon-nu manifested himself as a crow to see if Gyal-wa Chog-yang would recognize him. Another time he projected himself as a baby camel and playfully pranced around the meditation cave. But both times

Gyal-wa Chog-yang immediately realized who it was and warmly greeted his friend.

Ye-shey Zhon-nu was taught the Vajrakīla Sādhana by Vimalamitra. His study of the Phur-bu tradition heightened his unwavering awareness and, at his touch, healing nectars flowed from rocks. He is most commonly known as Nyag Jna-na Ku-ma-ra and was widely recognized as a master translator and practitioner of the Tantras.

འབྲོག་མི་དཔལ་གྱི་ཡེ་ཤེས།

Pal-gyi Ye-shey

[8] ***Pal-gyi Ye-shey*** *('Brog-mi dPal-gyi Ye-shes)*

Born into the clan of Brog near Shantag, Pal-gyi Ye-shey studied and translated the Nyingma Tantras assiduously, particularly the *Ma-mo Bod-tong*. In the unfolding of the Initiation Maṇḍala, his flower fell on Lha-med Heruka. When the full Maṇḍala spontaneously appeared before him, all restless tendencies of body, speech and mind were consumed in the great fire of intrinsic awareness. With a fiery glance he destroyed self-created obstacles and released both human and non-human spirits from the lower realms of suffering and depression, teaching them watchfulness and attention to immanent death. He practiced meditation on the peaks of snow-encrusted mountains and trained many accomplished disciples and lamas.

Pal-gyi Seng-ge

[9] *Pal-gyi Seng-ge (rLangs dPal-gyi Seng-ge)*

Born from the clan of Lang, Pal-gyi Seng-ge's father was the Bodhisattva, Shang-chig De-kor. At age eight, he traveled throughout the mountains and subdued many wild demons in Uḍḍiyāna at the invitation of Ling Gesar. One of the 108 lotsāvas who were sent to India, Pal-gyi Seng-ge became the heart-son of Guru Rinpoche. Through his earnest practice of the *'Jig-rten mChod-bstod* (Praise of the World) Sādhana, he understood the interrelation of causes and conditions and surrendered completely the neurotic craving which accumulates frustrating Karma. On one occasion he visited the lower realms and liberated many human and non-human beings from the bewilderments of clouded judgment. A layman, Pal-gyi Seng-ge fathered three sons from two wives and passed on the Tantric teachings through his clan lineage. For a long time he practiced meditation in the Himalayas near Bhutan, offering to all the nectar of spiritual instruction.

རྡོ་རྗེ་བདུད་འཇོམས།

Dorje Dud-jom

[10] ***Dorje Dud-jom*** *(rDo-rje bDud-'joms)*

Dorje Dud-jom was born into the clan of Tsarung and one of Tri-song De-tsen's ministers when Śāntarakṣita and Padmasambhava arrived in Tibet. One day, as he was meditating in a completely dark cave, he could see in a vision that the construction of the temple at Samye was nearing completion. He somehow managed to emerge from the sealed cave through a small chink in the rock, leaving behind a large passageway which can still be seen today. During his initiation into the Unity Maṇḍala, his flower fell on Jig-ten Cho-to Heruka *('Jig-rten mChod-bstod*). While practicing the Vajrakīla Sādhana in the mountains near Samye (Hepuri), he cut off thoughts at the root and demonstrated his attainment by sticking his *phur-bu* in a rock. By allowing the self-existing Mind to assume its natural state, he could walk in space as free as the wind, traveling to other continents with the speed of a moment's thought. In later life, he returned to Tsarung, at the red rock called Bird's Nesting Place, where he translated many Tantric texts and communicated the Mantrayāna teachings to the lineage of his clan. Through his control of breath and mental events, he passed from this life, having realized the relative, ungraspable nature of all things. He later reincarnated as a terton, and in recent times as Jam-yang Khen-tse Wang-po.[4]

Ye-shey Yang

[11] *Ye-shey Yang* (*sLob-dpon Ye-shes dbyangs*)

Ye-shey Yang was one of eight manuscript editors who transcribed Guru Rinpoche's private inner teachings. While deep in meditation, he understood the arising and vanishing of thoughts in the sky-like expanse of mind, and his awareness extended beyond space and time to the realm of no-thought. In this lucidity of Mind-itself, he traveled throughout space to the realm of the Ḍākinīs and received the eloquent ciphers appropriate to the recording of the Termas. Following Padmasambhava's directions, he concealed many of these oral teachings—direct manifestations of the Guru's Mind—in various secret places such as rocks, deep pools, caves and the sky. Sometimes called Van-de (Bhande), or teacher, he was known and respected for his clear, exact expression. He released himself from all worldly entanglements and resided for a time in the forested mountainsides with Sog-po Ha-pal. One day, he flew up into the sky and disappeared.

༄ གྲུབ་ཆེན་སོག་པོ་ལྷ་དཔལ།

Sog-po Ha-pal

[12] ***Sog-po Ha-pal*** *(Grub-chen Sog-po lHa-dpal)*

A layman metalsmith, Sog-po Ha-pal was physically very powerful, working cross-legged in the traditional fashion with a crude bellows and a charcoal fire. He was befriended by Ye-shey Zhon-nu who delivered to him the Tantric texts and their oral commentaries. Through practice of the inner Sādhana of Vajrakīla, he purified the analytical powers of his mind. Three times, while sitting in front of his meditation cave, he subdued the prideful enemies of his own thought creations. With fierce mastery of ignorance and illusion, he fearlessly restrained even wild tigers. He lived outdoors in the forests along running mountain streams until he passed away.

Ye-shey-de

[13] ***Ye-shey-de*** *(sNa-nam Ye-shes)*

Na-nam Ye-shey De was one of the three great early Nyingma translators.[5] A master of the Vajrakīla Tantra, he realized the illusory character of all phenomenal appearances and cut the cord of mind-made karmic conditioning, leaving him free to soar in the sky like a bird. He was ever sensitive to the subtle nuances and precise shades of meaning in the hundreds of texts which he translated, and, like Long-chen-pa, comprehensively studied all the Nyingma Tantras and Sādhanas. This scholarly monk was born into the clan of Jang (Byang) and was called, from early times, Van-de Ye-shey De. Throughout his life he exhibited many psychic powers, and from his teachings the Na-nam Phur-bu lineage continues the practice of the Vajrakīla Sādhana to this day.

Pal-gyi Wang-chug

[14] *Pal-gyi Wang-chug (mKhar-chen dPal-gyi dBang-phyug)*

The brother of Ye-shey Tso-gyal, Pal-gyi Wang-chug accompanied Padmasambhava wherever he traveled in Tibet. As a son emulates and imitates his father, Pal-gyi Wang-chug discovered in his practice the essential meaning of Padma's instruction and became known as the 'heart-son' of Guru Rinpoche. Uniting Mantra and Mudrā, he holds aloft the mystic dagger (*phur-bu*) and subdues the illusory objects of phenomena with the blade of discriminating awareness. Simply by raising the *phur-bu*, he could direct feverish heat waves toward his enemies, pacifying them at once and eliminating every obstruction to complete spiritual understanding. An invulnerable lay master (*sngags-pa*), Pal-gyi Wang-chug traveled throughout Tibet, often accompanying Ye-shey Tso-gyal. Wherever he went, he communicated the oral teachings (*bKa'-ma*) of the early Nyingmapa.

Tse-mang

[15] *Tse-mang* (*lDan-ma rTse-mang*)

Born in Kham in Dan-ma, Tse-mang fashioned the elegant handwritten calligraphy of Tibetan script. A precise Sanskrit scholar, he translated and edited the footnotes to Padmasambhava's texts, perceiving their intended meanings through the insight of his understanding.

Many manuscripts discovered by Terma masters were written by his hand and are still preserved in Tibet. Tse-mang was able to recite with perfect recollection the Sūtras and Tantras for days at a time and thus attained the clarity of the non-dual mind, unobscured by the distinctions of time and space. Having studied the Tantric texts, he practiced many Sādhanas and passed a quiet life in the forests and mountains.

Ka-wa Pal-tseg

[16] ***Ka-wa Pal-tseg*** *(Lo-chen sKa-ba dPal-brtsegs)*

At an early age, the lotsāva Ka-wa Pal-tseg was recognized by Padmasambhava as the reincarnation of an Indian Mahāpaṇḍita, purposely born in Tibet in order to translate the texts necessary for the successful transmission of Buddhism. Born in Pembo north of Lhasa, he was one of the seven Bodhisattvas trained in the Sūtras by Śāntarakṣita and became one of the three most influential translators at Samye. Under Padmasambhava's guidance, Ka-wa Pal-tseg studied the Tantric teachings and attained a state of peace, composure and harmony whereby his range of vision was not only widened but perfectly cleared. Able to see both the past and future, he received the powers of telepathy and clairvoyance and thus inherited the all-encompassing knowledge which is devoid of the habit-forming thoughts which cloud the insight of pure awareness. In addition to his many translations, Ka-wa Pal-tseg wrote significant commentaries which were incorporated into the Tantric texts. His printed style of calligraphy became popularly imitated in all of Tibet, and through his lineage many Nyingma Tertons discovered hidden treasures.

[17] *Pal-gyi Seng-ge (Sud-pu dPal-gyi Seng-ge)*

Born from Tri-song De-tsen's clan and a student of the Bön tradition, Pal-gyi Seng-ge was sent by the King to invite Padmasambhava to Tibet. After investigating the many branches of learning available in Sanskrit texts, he returned to Tibet to become one of eight renowned scholars.[6] Following Padmasambhava's instruction, he practiced the Shin-je, Ma-mo and Phur-bu Tantras (Father, Mother and Non-dual Tantras), thereby transcending subjectively experienced negative energies and karmic forces.

Through his practice, Pal-gyi Seng-ge acquired many siddhis. One time, he wished to cross a wide, swift-running river. Touching the water with his *phur-bu*, the river parted and exposed a passageway, allowing him to walk on the river bed to the opposite shore. Another time, placing his *phur-bu* on a rock, he walked directly through the stone to the other side. And once, at Chim-phu near Samye, when he displayed the Vajrakīla Mudrā, the river began to flow upwards. In jest, he often referred to his birth among the Bön-pos and would say, "I am descended from the heaven-clan, out of the sky!" He took an active part in the decoration of Samye temple, and on the East side he built an enormous white Stūpa. Then, after he had sunk a long wooden pipe into the soil, a rich butter-oil oozed up from the earth which he distributed to everyone for their tea.

For many years he practiced meditation in various caves, and his

Pal-gyi Seng-ge

clan lineage generated many successful masters and monks. Larger biographies of Pal-gyi Seng-ge and many of his translations are still available and preserved in Tibet.

[18] *Gyal-way Lo-dro ('Bri rGyal-ba'i bLo-bros)*

Originally one of Tri-song De-tsen's administrators, Gyal-way Lo-dro traveled to India and there became a monk, learning Sanskrit and studying with Huṃkara, one of the Eighty-four Mahāsiddhas. From Padmasambhava he received the oral teachings which grant freedom from all samsaric tendencies and bestow the inner elixir of youth. Through meditation on the unitive nature of the Mind which encompasses all realms and embraces all inhabitants, Gyal-way Lo-dro rescued his mother and many others from the death-realms of the Yamarājas and

Gyal-way Lo-dro

turned their corpses into solid gold. These treasures he stored in caves and statues where various Tertons later discovered them. Through his propitiation of Yan-tag Heruka, he acquired the revitalizing faculty of longevity and lived in the forests and mountains, practicing the teachings and transmitting them to others for over 300 years.

[19] *Khye-hu Chung-lo-tsa* *(Grub-chen Khye'u-chung Lo-tsa)*

Recognized as an incarnation of an Indian Mahāpaṇḍita, Khye-hu Chung-lo was born into the clan of Brog and learned Sanskrit without effort at an early age. Padmasambhava instructed him in many esoteric Tantric teachings, and through his practice he became widely known as an all-encompassing master of the Mantrayāna. He immediately com-

Khye-hu Chung-lo-tsa

prehended that which is beyond the domain of discursive thought, and, like the sky, freed himself from all limitations through unclouded devotion and faith. By means of gestures and finger *mudrās* he was able to attract and catch flying birds and teach them the transient nature of all phenomena. A layman, or *sngags-pa*, he lived in the warm fertile valleys of eastern Tibet and later reincarnated at Kha-thog as the Terma master Ter-chen Dud-dul Dorje-ling-pa.

[20] *Ten-pa Nam-kha (Dran-pa Nam-mkh'a)*

Ten-pa Nam-kha was present at the debates between the Bön-pos and Padmasambhava's disciples and indicated that a person who had attained realization had no need to make any distinction between the

Ten-pa Nam-kha

Bön-pos and Buddhists. Rising up in the sky, he struck the moon and sun together like a pair of cymbals. "There is no need," he said, "to introduce distinctions into the shining knowledge of the mutual sphere of sentient beings." Revered by the Bön-pos as a manifestation of their founder, Ten-pa Nam-kha thereupon cut off a lock of his hair with a gold razor and was initiated into the circle of the Mantrayāna by Padmasambhava. Afterwards, he meditated in the woods and mountains and developed the completely awakened state, free from the agitation of phenomenal forms. Through gestures and *mudrās* alone, he tamed the wild yak of the northern plains and taught many other beings roaming in the realms of restless existence. He is said to have collated many advanced Buddhist texts, particularly the 'mental teachings' (*sems-sde*) of the Dzog-chen. Thereafter he disseminated the translations, commentaries and oral teachings of Guru Rinpoche and later reincarnated as a Terton.

འོ་བྲན་དཔལ་གྱི་དབང་ཕྱུག །

Pal-gyi Wang-chug

[21] ***Pal-gyi Wang-chug*** *('O-Dran dPal-gyi dBang-phyug)*

Pal-gyi Wang-chug was a lay disciple of Padmasambhava and received many private teachings. A learned translator, he entered the Maṇḍala of the Wrathful Tantric Deities, cutting himself free from the formation of illusive thought constructions. Through his practice of visualization, he transmuted all negative and emotional obstructions and entered the stream of non-duality, immersing himself within the great river of spontaneous knowledge. His clan still preserves and practices the oral teachings of the Kama lineage.

[22] ***Rin-chen Chog*** *(rMa Rin-chen mChog)*

Born from the clan of Ma in central Tibet, Rin-chen Chog was trained as a monk by Śāntarakṣita and was initiated into the Mantrayāna methods and practices by Padmasambhava. Viewing the material world as a crystalization of thought-form, he meditated in various caves without food and transformed the rocks into edible nectar. As a translator of Sūtras and commentaries, he fully comprehended the teachings of Nāgārjuna and partook in the historic debate at Samye (c. 792–94) with the Chinese master, Hoshang (Hwa-shang). He studied extensively with the Tantric master, Vimalamitra, who instructed him in the Māyā cycle of Tantras and who passed on to him the *Guhyamūlatantrika.* Rin-chen Chog was recognized as one of eight

Rin-chen Chog

scholarly masters and was responsible for translating the Mahāyoga Tantras, which include eighteen major texts, the root of which is the *sGyu-'phrul gSang-ba sNying-po.* During the course of his life, he wrote over 250 commentaries on the works of Padmasambhava, Vimalamitra, and

Buddhaguhya, which contain the essence of the Dzog-chen Ati-yoga teachings.

After the death of Lang Dar-ma, Rin-chen Chog traveled east to Kham and taught the Mahāyoga Tantras to Tsu-gu Rin-chen Shon-ne who carried on his methods of explaining the Tantric teachings. These have been preserved to the present time in the tradition located at Kham (sGyu-'phrul Khams lugs-ma). One of the most important Nyingma teachers, Ma Rin-chen Chog reincarnated a number of times and rediscovered the esoteric treasures of the Terma.

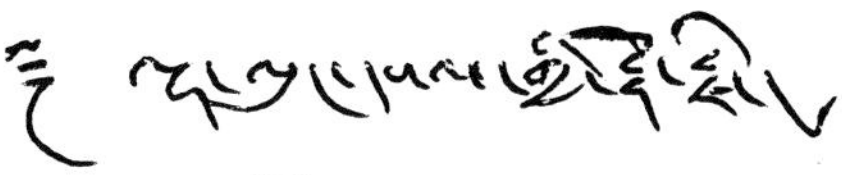

Pal-gyi Dorje

[23] *Pal-gyi Dorje (lHa-lung dPal-gyi rDo-rje)*

Pal-gyi Dorje was born near Lhasa (bDrip-kyi Kar-mo Rong), but moved to the eastern frontiers where he served to protect the border of China and Tibet. Soon he was overcome by sadness at the impermanence of all existence and, hearing about the great Buddhist teachers at Samye, set out with his two brothers for central Tibet. There he studied with Vimalamitra and was initiated by Padmasambhava in the oral teachings of the Mantra tradition. After Guru Rinpoche left Tibet, he wandered throughout the mountains, stopping only to meditate in various caves. One day as he was meditating on a mountain peak, a sudden wind carried him up into the sky far away to a beautiful secluded mountain, and from that time on he was found to possess many extraordinary powers. Thereafter, allowing his mind to rest without discursive thought, he was able to pass freely through rocks and fly from mountain to mountain wherever he wished.

Some time later, while Pal-gyi Dorje was meditating in a cave at Yer-pay-lhay Nying-po, reports of Lang Dar-ma's suppression of the Buddhists reached him and he set out to liberate the body of this mad King from the commission of further crime. Dressed in black and riding a white horse which he had covered with charcoal, Pal-gyi Dorje arrived in Lhasa and found the King attending a ritual dance. Joining the dancers he waited for the right moment, and, with compassion, let fly the fatal arrow and fled, washing off his horse in the nearby Tsang-po River. Then he continued to East Tibet where he again lived in the mountains performing Sādhanas for the sake of all suffering beings. After a long life of solitude, his body became transformed into a rainbow of light, and he disappeared.

[24] *Kon-chog Jung-nay (Lang-gro dKon-mchog 'Byung-gnas)*

Kon-chog Jung-nay was born at Shang Tha-neg (North Black Horse) with the name Lang-dro-nam and became an influential minister under Tri-song De-tsen. A close follower of Padmasambhava, he received instruction in the 'vastness teachings' (Dzog-chen Nying-thig)–the immediate experience of Being-in-itself. In deep relaxation of body and mind, he contemplated the indivisibility of appearance and nothingness–just as wind is not separate from air–and discovered within his mind the realization which is all-encompassing like the sky. With lightning and thunderbolts he directed the wrathful dagger of his clear perception to liberate both humans and non-humans from anxiety and timidity. At life's end, the body of this layman translator became an

Kon-chog Jung-nay

expanse of light. Through his lineage of Tha-nuk Dor-ma-pa, he later incarnated as the Terma master Ratna Ling-pa.

[25] *Gyal-wa Chang-chub* (*La-gSum rGyal-ba Byang-chub*)

One of the eight self-mastering scholars of Tibet, Gyal-wa Chang-chub received the Mantra teachings from Padmasambhava and became an exemplary monk and lotsāva. Just before his departure from Tibet, Padmasambhava gathered together all the disciples at a place called Tha-duk, or 'Multi-colored Dragon'. There he counselled them for twenty-one days, giving them many final instructions in the practice of Sādhana–ritual offerings, Mantra, visualization, meditation on Samādhi, and many other spiritual exercises and techniques. At this

Gyal-wa Chang-chub

time, Padmasambhava initiated Gyal-wa Chang-chub into the All-encompassing Maṇḍala (Khan-du Jeh-tog), wherein Mind-as-such, without birth and death, remains seated on the throne of unchanging Dharmakāya.

Female Disciples

In addition, Padmasambhava's inner circle included fifteen female followers and the five Ḍākinīs: Ye-shey Tso-gyal, Mandāravā of Zahor, Śākyadevī of Nepal, Kālasiddhi of India, and Tashi Khye-dren of Mon-tsa-og (Bhutan). In thankas, Mandāravā is usually depicted to the right, and Ye-shey Tso-gyal to the left of Guru Rinpoche.

Mandāravā. Daughter of the Zahor king, Mandāravā was regarded by everyone as an incarnate goddess. The entire village, as well as forty royal suitors from the kingdoms of India, Persia, Turkey and China, admired her pleasing, captivating features. But thinking over her past lives, she decided to follow a spiritual path. Exercising his prescience, Padmasambhava discerned that the time had come to instruct Mandāravā and flew on a cloud from the Dhanakośa Lake to Zahor. There he found her on retreat with her followers and instructed them in the Mantrayāna teachings. The King, however, was outraged. Misunderstanding Padma's seclusion with his daughter, he decreed that she be tossed into a dark pit, without sight of the blue sky, and that Padma be burned at the stake. Stripped naked, Padma's hands were tied behind his back, a rope was placed around his neck, and he was bound to a stake and wrapped in oil. Thus was he set aflame, and the smoke hid the sun and the sky. But all the deities and Buddhas came to Padma's aid, and he transformed the pyre into a rainbow-enhaloed lake, in the middle of which he sat on the pollen bed of an enormous white lotus.

Under Guru Rinpoche's guidance, Mandāravā renounced all worldly attachments and practiced meditation. On one occasion, Amitāyus appeared to them as they were meditating in a cave and placed on their heads the urn of boundless life, the nectar of immortality. Thereafter Mandāravā traveled throughout the border regions of northern India and into Tibet. Never dying, she manifests in many places at different times to teach the way to liberation.

Śākyadevī. When the queen of Nepal died in childbirth, the king abandoned his young daughter at the queen's gravesite. There she was fed and cared for by monkeys. Her hands were webbed like the feet of a duck, and her body displayed the marks of a goddess. When she was grown, Śākyadevī was discovered in the cemetery by Padmasambhava and became his enlightened consort. Filled with the stream of the Guru's instruction, she alleviates all suffering due to fear, doubt and worry.

Kālasiddhi. Born in India, Kālasiddhi's parents were weavers. When her mother died, her father was convinced that the child would not survive and carried them both to the cemetery. Mandāravā, manifesting as a tigress, came upon the child in the cemetery and, with deep compassion, fed and instructed her. Padmasambhava later initiated her into the Maṇḍala of Vajrasattva, in whom all the Peaceful and

Wrathful Deities unitively merge. On Padmasambhava's departure from Tibet, Kālasiddhi requested him to preserve the teachings, and during her life she concealed many Termas throughout Nepal and Tibet, finally passing away in a mist of light.

Tashi Khye-dren. Born at Mon-tsa-og near the Nepalese border of Tibet, the Ḍākinīs assisted Tashi Khye-dren's inner awakening by activating her ability to recall her past lives. Journeying to southern Tibet, she met Ye-shey Tso-gyal who guided her to Guru Rinpoche, and thereafter she became the consort of his enlightening activity. Tashi Khye-dren manifests as the tigress ridden by Guru Dorje Drolo ('The Changeless Comforter of All Beings'), and together they wrathfully stride over all obstacles to enlightenment, liberating sentient beings from emotional and intellectual bewilderment and revealing the all-pervasive path of the Dharma.

During his stay in Tibet, Padmasambhava also initiated fifteen female disciples who practiced the Dorje Phur-bu and Chem-chog Sādhanas:

She-nam-za Sang-gya-tso, radiant in self-awareness, became a body of effulgent light.

Sel-kar Dor-je-tso surrendered herself, like a plant on a river, to the stream of devotion.

Tshom-bu-za Pe-ma-tso, harmonizing body, breath and mind, discovered unchanging bliss.

Mal-gon-za Rin-chen-tso dressed in radiant clothes of rainbow light.

Rub-za Don-drib-ma, subduing the twelve protectresses, accomplished whatever she wished.

Sud-bu-za She-rab-ma memorized the Sūtras and Śāstras with little effort.

Yar-rag-za Cho-kyi-dro-ma receives praise in the heaven realms by all those who study her teachings.

O-ce-za Ka-gyal-ma, whenever in doubt, conversed with deities.

Zem-za lHa-mo, whenever hungry, received nectar from the heavenly realms.

Bar-za lHa-wang-ma, understanding liberation, illumined the Dharma for others.

Cho-rog-za Chang-chub-ma transformed herself into fire, water and wind.

Dro-ma Pam-ti-chen-mo, free from attachment, traveled in the sky of awareness like a bird.
Rong-man-za Tshul-Khrim-dron transmuted rocks into sustenance.
Kha-za Pal-zhun-ma, exhibiting the *phur-bu*, liberated countless beings.
Trum-za Shel-man, showering flowers in celestial space, inspired many visions.

At Chim-phu near Samye, fifty-five enlightened meditators, free from desire, passed into space, their bodies vanishing like mist. At Yer-pa and She-bou-ri, one-hundred-and-eight meditators, free from attachments, assumed bodies as subtle as rainbows. And at Sel-trag, thirty laymen and twenty-five women, free from duality, entered the radiant light of pure being. All of these, and uncounted others, attained Enlightenment in one lifetime and were the direct disciples of Padmasambhava.

Notes

1. Heruka. Often depicted as a wrathful deity, Herukas represent the activation of the positive qualities of Mind. The eight Herukas, or tutelary deities, mentioned in the biographies of the twenty-five disciples, illumine various aspects of Guru Rinpoche made manifest in meditation. Chem-chog (Che-mchog) Heruka appears in the center of the Maṇḍala.

2. Hayagrīva (rTa-mgrin) is called the 'Horse-headed Lord' and represents the wrathful manifestation of Avalokiteśvara. He is one of the tutelary deities of the Maṇḍala and represents clear discernment. *The Blue Annals* records that "The king especially propitiated Hayagrīva. On three occasions the neighing of a horse was heard, and many people heard it." *See* George N. Roerich (Trans.), *The Blue Annals* [*Deb-ther sngon-po* by 'Gos lot-sa-ba], 2 vols., Calcutta, 1949, 1953, pp. 106–07, for a description of the eight Nyingma Tantras.

3. Vimalamitra was the chief translator of the Tantras among the five hundred Indian Paṇḍitas who came to Tibet during the early propagation of Buddhism. He studied with Śri Siṃha for twenty years and is said to have been two hundred years old when invited to Tibet. There he translated over fifty-two volumes and various texts on the Dzog-pa Chen-po. Some of these works are still found among the collection of mystical treatises of the Nyingma school known as *rNying-ma'i rGyud-'bum* (34 vols.) which includes the profoundly deep instruction known as *sNying-gi Thig-le*. Thus, through Vimalamitra come many important Nyingma teachings. He is said to have attained a radiant rainbow body, and Long-chen-pa is considered to be one of his incarnations.

4. Jam-dbyangs mKhyen-rtse dBang-po (1820–1892), together with Kong-sprul bLo-gros mTha'-yas (1813–1899), were two beacons in the nineteenth-century cultural renaissance which was known as the Eclectic Movement (Ris-med) in Eastern Tibet (sDe-dge in Kham). Khen-tse collected, refined and unified all the major spiritual lineages and traditions from among the old (rNyingma) and new (gSarma) Tantra schools. His collected works total over fifty volumes and include many Tantric initiations and Sādhana practices.

5. The other two are sKa-ba dPal-brtsegs and Cog-ro kLu'i rGyal-mtshan.

6. These eight translator-scholars are: gNyag Jna-na Ku-ma-ra (Ye-shes Zhon-nu), Ka-ba dPal-brtsegs, Cog-ro kLu'i rGyal-mtshan, gYu-sgra sNying-po, Vairocana, Nam-mKha'i sNying-po, rMa Rin-chen mChog, and sNa-nam Ye-shes (Ye-shes De).

Buddhism in Tibet: The Early Chronicles

Tarthang Tulku

More than one thousand years after Buddha had passed into Nirvāṇa . . . there were five sons of the king called Sarba, son of King Kusala of Magadha in India. The youngest son, at birth, had turquoise blue hair; his hands and feet were flat; his eyes closed from below upwards. They said to each other: "He is not like (one who has had) previous incarnation." So putting him into a copper box, they threw him into the River Ganges.

Between Nepal and Tibet an old man of Tibet picked up the box from the bank of the river and opened it. When he looked, there was (in it) a beautiful splendid boy. (When the child) became sixteen years old, seeking the lofty and good (place) of the land and considering the snowy Sambu mountains . . . he came, saying: "I shall settle (here)."

A man of Tibet, meeting him, asked him: "Where do you come from?" (The youth) pointed upwards, (and the man) said: "This child has a destiny from heaven—our Tibet has no king." (So) he raised (the youth) on his neck and carried him away. He was the first Neck-seat King of Tibet.

ERIK HAARH, The Yarluṇ Dynasty

The above quotation is but one version of the mythical origins of the Tibetan Royal Dynasty comprising over forty kings and covering a period of fourteen centuries. For a Tibetan of the fifth century B.C., the world hosted a number of divine beings who became archetypal models for all significant human activity. The religious influence of 'mythic' figures such as Na-tri-tsan-po (gNya'-khri-btsan-po), or the 'Neck-seat King', closely parallels that of the historic figure, Padmasambhava, who employed various 'miraculous acts' in establishing the Buddhist tradition in eighth-century Tibet.

The Tibetans of pre-Buddhist times believed that the forces of wind and water, tides and quakes, personified heavenly powers which, whether wrathful or benevolent, inspired their homage and reverence. Bound to a world of superstition, they believed their kings were divinely empowered, and so traced their ancestry to heavenly realms. As long as the king served as intermediary between the world of man and the world of the gods, man and the mysterious powers of a seemingly impersonal nature might abide in harmony. That the first Tibetan king was *not* of divine origin, but descended from the royal Indian dynasty known as the Licchavīs (Li-tsa-byi) of the city of Vaiśālī, necessitated a radical departure from many ancient cosmological notions.

Followers of the native religion of Bön held that their ancestral inheritance represented a progressive descent, of aeonic duration, from the heavenly spheres. Concurrent with this was the still popular belief in animism whereby demons and other aboriginal powers who dwelt in the obscure recesses of the country possessed the relentless capacity to unleash earthquakes, floods, and other 'natural' catastrophes. Consequently, the myth and legend of Tibet's earliest history reflects a dramatic world—a world impregnated with an atmosphere of joy and grief, of anguish and exultation.

Wherever there is mankind, there is myth. Mythic knowledge does not necessarily depend on man's sense of historical continuity, but on the interpenetration of his psyche with the external world of sensuous forms. The mythic world directly intervenes with human activity because it stems from a world view whose primary interest is practical. More than mere 'speculative knowledge', myth and legend provide man with intuitive insights which not only provide protection from sickness, death or misfortune, but which simultaneously unite him—in his search for total being—with his deepest aspirations. This mythic world may be seen by the scientific-minded as 'ready-made', a symbolic world unique to a specific culture, but which serves no practical purpose. Contemporary man may wish only to take a pragmatic—and hence prosaic—interest in his mythic past, yet to do so would be to overlook the sustaining power which mythic knowledge provides for contacting the potential underlying his own existence.

The macrocosm and the microcosm are not seen as two mutually exclusive domains, but rather coexist within man as a felt unity. In his sense of pure beingness, man is not delimited by deterministic laws, nor by society, nor by the will of some god—he makes himself what he is. In this way he is radically free. This sense of freedom is exemplified in the person of Padmasambhava.

Just before Padmasambhava's journey to Tibet, King Tri-song De-tsen was caught in an imponderable dilemma. With the acceptance of the new religion of Buddhism, the people were gradually forsaking their ties to the old religion of the Bön, and with it, the king was forced to relinquish his god-like status. No longer did he pose as the shamanistic protector of his people against the aboriginal deities that threatened to overrun Tibet with diseases and epidemics. When these forces were unleashed to express opposition to Padmasambhava's arrival, the Great Guru subdued them once and for all, thus reestablishing the preeminence of the king and demonstrating the efficacy of Buddhist practices to transmute negative forces into the supremely positive. Without destroying the ancient traditions, he revitalized the old cosmic order by delegating to the demons and malevolent spirits the responsibility of guarding the new religion. Then, by constructing Samye monastery in the shape of a Maṇḍala, Padmasambhava presented to the Tibetans a new symbol for an entire cosmos, which ultimately finds its source within each individual.

Our story begins approximately seven centuries after the arrival of Na-tri-tsan-po into Tibet, describing an incident that occurred to his twenty-eighth successor, King lHa-tho-tho-ri: the appearance of a mysterious chest provides a natural link between the ancient Bön belief in the sacral status of the king and the introduction of Buddhist ideas . . . by way of a Sūtra book and other articles of a genuinely Buddhist origin.

THE YEAR 333 A.D. marks the dawning of the Sacred Doctrine[1] and the beginning of Dharma history in Tibet. In this year something extraordinary came into the view of King La-tho-tho-ri,[2] who, in his seventy-ninth year, was residing at the summit of the Palace Yam-bu-la-gang[3]—a chest, appearing to descend in a ray of light, fell from the sky. When the King raised the lid, he found two Sūtra books,[4] the Six-syllable Mantra, OṂ MAṆI PADME HŪṂ, a golden Stūpa,[5] and a Wish-fulfilling Gem with its base cast for impressing.[6] The texts, however, were written in a language that neither the King nor his ministers could read, and, since they had fallen from the sky, it was first thought that the chest and its mysterious contents were the gift of a Bön sky god.[7] In a dream, the King received a prophecy which revealed that the significance and meaning of this magnificent gift would not be known for five generations. Nevertheless, these objects were honored as something portentous and very precious.[8] Through their powerful influence, the King was rejuvenated into a youth of sixteen, lived to be 120, and his whole kingdom flourished. To this day, King La-tho-tho-ri is revered as an emanation of the Bodhisattva Samantabhadra.[9]

King Song-tsen Gam-po: The First Great Flourish

The fifth successor to the throne[10] following King La-tho-tho-ri was one of the three most famous and popular kings of Tibet. Song-tsen Gam-po[11] was recognized as an incarnation of the Bodhisattva Avalokiteśvara. When his father died in the year 582, he ascended to the throne at the young age of thirteen. Two years after his coronation, out of a deepening respect for the Buddhadharma, he sent an emissary to southern India to obtain a most valuable statue of Avalokiteśvara. He also sent his loyal minister, Gar,[12] to the court of the Indian king to acquire two priceless statues of Śākyamuni Buddha (*Jo-bo*). These sacred images were formed out of four alchemical metals, adorned with precious jewel inlays, and had been fashioned in India when the Enlightened One was just a young prince.[13] The Indians, however, had previously given these priceless statues away–one to Nepal and the other to China. Thus, in the first century B.C., along the many winding routes from Bodh Gayā and Magadha to Nepal and on to China, these famous statues were venerated by wayfarers, caravan leaders, kings, and noblemen alike, and became early precursors of the northward migration and future blossoming of Buddhism in Tibet.

In order to facilitate relations with China and Nepal, and to acquire these most valuable images, King Song-tsen Gam-po decided to initiate familial relations with the kings of these two bordering countries. The King of Nepal[14] readily agreed to the marriage of his daughter, and as dowry, Princess Ṭhi-tsun[15] brought with her the prized statue of Śākyamuni, as well as images of Akśobhya Buddha, Maitreya the coming Buddha, and a magnificent sandalwood statue of Green Tārā.[16] Several years later (641 A.D.), the king initiated a second marriage, this time with the Princess Wang-co, [17] who was the daughter of Emperor Seng-ge-tsen-po,[18] and whose grandfather was the first emperor of the T'ang Dynasty.[19] But securing this marriage proved more difficult, so the King sent his Minister Gar to the Imperial Palace with one hundred officers to deliver the King's proposal of marriage.

Song-tsen Gam-po with his two queens, Thi-tsun (left) and Wang-co (right)

Concurrent with this, the ruler of the T'u-yu-hun[20] had also proposed marriage to the imperial princess. Upon receiving word of this, Song-tsen Gam-po sent his army of over 200,000 troops to the Kokonor region. The ruler of the T'u-yu-hun, frightened by the presence of this enormous army, readily retracted his request. Then, continuing to demonstrate that Tibet possessed a very powerful militia, the King garrisoned an army in China, which terrified the inhabitants of Szech'uan province by their mere appearance. The army held the city of Sung-chou (Sung-pan) captive until the Emperor would agree to the marriage of his daughter. The Emperor, however, being a man of dignity, let the customs of his country take their course, and insisted instead that his daughter be won by the most talented suitor. Therefore, Minister Gar was forced to undergo a number of trials and contests of skill before he could claim Princess Wang-co for Song-tsen Gam-po. As a wedding gift, the Emperor presented to the king the highly praised, jewel-bedecked figure of Śākyamuni. Delighted by the news, Song-tsen Gam-po journeyed to the Tibetan border to receive the princess who arrived there escorted by a company of Chinese troops. After the princess and the precious statue of Jo-bo had been placed in the hands of the Tibetan army, the royal procession journeyed to Lhasa. Upon their arrival at the Palace of Mar-po-ri,[21] great festivities and rejoicing climaxed the marriage celebration.

During this period, many Dharma texts had already found their way into Tibet, but unfortunately there was no one who could read them or explain their meaning. Recognizing this, the King invited many great translators (*lotsāvas*) from India, Nepal, China, and even Kashmir to journey to Lhasa, to reside in his Mar-po-ri residence and translate these newly acquired scriptures.[22] Also about this time, Thu-mi Sambhoṭa,[23] an incarnation of Mañjuśrī, was returning from his mission to Kashmir and northern India. The King had ordered him to devise a Tibetan alphabet suitable for translating the Buddhist texts brought from India. With the aid of two Indian scholars,[24] Thu-mi constructed an alphabet on the model of the Sanskrit alphabet prevalent in the areas he visited. He also supplied Tibet with its first systematic and written grammar.

Following the success of Thu-mi Sambhoṭa's work, King Song-tsen Gam-po went into relative seclusion for four years, pretending to study the texts which Thu-mi provided.[25] However, being an incarnation of Avalokiteśvara, the King readily understood the meaning of the texts and so spent this time in perpetual Samādhi. Meanwhile, the two princesses, having come from Buddhist countries, greatly revered the Dharma and exerted much influence on the King to assimilate the practice of the Vinaya (disciplinary) texts which Thu-mi had translated into the social mores of the Tibetan people.[26] Following this advice, the King instituted a legal code of sixteen moral virtues[27] and established punishments for such transgressions as murder, theft, and adultery. The Chinese princess also convinced the King that the habit of painting one's face red and wearing animal skins during ceremonial occasions was unkingly.[28] On their own initiative, the two princesses sought to further the development of the Buddhist religion by building two temples during the period their lord was in semi-seclusion.[29] Needless to say, there were many disputes between the two queens. Ṭhi-tsun, since she was the first to pass the lintel of marriage with the King, strove to show her precedence over the beautiful Wang-co. Ṭhi-tsun's influence was further enhanced because she was two years older than the young King, who at this time was only sixteen.

When the King returned from his retreat, he assumed the responsibility of 'Protector of the Doctrine'[30] and taught his favored ministers and noblemen the meaning of the religious texts.[31] He also instructed his people in the practice of the Avalokiteśvara Sādhana, as well as methods of meditative concentration and even the art of healing. Wishing his dominion to be the citadel of the Buddhadharma, he initiated the construction of 108 temples throughout Tibet. At the advanced age of eighty-two, after ruling for sixty-nine years, the King disappeared, together with his two queens, as they joined together in embrace with the eleven-faced statue of Avalokiteśvara.[32] The three of them are said to have vanished—or coalesced—in this embrace, and thus ascended to Tuṣita heaven, 'The Abode of Joy'.

Just before he passed away, the King wrote an inscription on a copper plaque prophesying that in five generations a great-grandson of his would appear: this child will bear the surname of 'De' and usher in the Golden Age of the Dharma. This plaque, which was stored in the King's private treasury to be preserved for future times, marks the end of the first great flourishing of Buddhism in Tibet.

King Tri-song De-tsen: Fulfilling a Prophecy

In the years following the death of Song-tsen Gam-po, members of the Gar family established a mighty Tibetan army which was commanded by the King's successor, Mang-song Mang-tsen. The Tibetan army became exceedingly powerful and displayed an invincible unity, for its commanders always deliberated with care before engaging in any battle. The Chinese, despite many attempts to secure the ill-defined Sino-Tibetan border regions, were repeatedly repulsed in their offensives against the aggressive Tibetan army, and, needless to say, the Tibetans were both feared and admired by the countries and protectorates bordering Tibet.

After the passing of five generations, a minister discovered an inscribed copper plaque in a rocky ravine. This was the very plaque which Song-tsen Gam-po had hidden away many years ago. Thinking the plaque greatly significant, the minister presented it to his lord, King Thi-de-tsug-ten. Upon close inspection, the King surmised that the plaque, and the surname of De mentioned on it, referred to him and took it upon himself to fulfill the prophecy as detailed on the plaque. Without delay, he constructed many new Vihāras (temples) and invited scholars from bordering countries to advance the Doctrine in Tibet. However, despite the energy he invested in trying to carry out this prophecy, the King was most unsuccessful in his attempts to propagate the Dharma–the scholars were reluctant to come and made excuses having to do with ordination requirements.[33] With the birth of his son, the King was once again heartened, for this new heir to the throne promised to be a likely candidate to marry a daughter of the Emperor of China.[34]

To ease the political tensions between China and Tibet, as well as create greater religious affinities between the two countries, both the Emperor and Princess Chin-ch'eng-kung-chu accepted the offer of marriage. But the young Tibetan prince met a most untimely death, murdered by a jealous heretic minister who wished his own son to marry the Chinese princess. The princess had already begun her journey when she learned the tragic news that her would-be spouse was dead. Nevertheless, she continued to the Land of Snows, and, upon arriving, so charmed the King by her beauty that he at once proposed marriage. Through this union was born the famous monarch, Tri-song De-tsen.[35]

When his father died, Tri-song De-tsen received the crown, but not all too comfortably, for now a terrible non-Buddhist minister by the name of Ma-zhang[36] found this period of interregnum most convenient for planting seeds of conspiracy against the Buddhist royalty. Being an avowed enemy of the Doctrine, Ma-zhang was already plotting to deport Buddhist monks and turn the vihāras into butcher shops. Apparently he would attempt anything to seize control of the throne.

Tri-song De-tsen

But Ma-zhang's terror did not last, for as soon as the young King came of age, he displayed an extraordinary mind. His presence alone was enough to impede Ma-zhang's attempts to seize control of the dominion. With the assistance of his mighty army, the young King soon controlled over one-third of the then-known world, trade and opulence spread throughout his dominion, and the bitter disputes among bordering countries ceased.

Tri-song De-tsen realized that this period of peace and prosperity would be most beneficial for propagating the Buddhadharma. Far from being regarded as uncultured or barbaric, Tibet was now looked upon with honor and respect. Without delay, he sent envoys of soldiers and stone masons into China, not only to demonstrate to Emperor T'ai-tsung the power of the Tibetan army, but also to ask his assistance in promoting the Dharma. As a gesture that had religious as well as political significance, the King ordered his men to build many stone pillars and religious monuments throughout China to signify their mutual spiritual concord.

The King could not trust some of his noblemen for fear that heretics might still be secretly present in the council, so he sent two of his most faithful ministers, Sang-si and Sal-nang,[37] to the Imperial Court to ask the Emperor for advice on matters of religious import. When these two noblemen, traveling with a small army, finally arrived at the royal palace, they entered the Imperial Court and were met by a practitioner of the 'meditation of mystic absorption' (*dhyāna*). This master was endowed with great prescience of mind and indicated to the ministers that a certain Indian Upādhyāya (professor of spiritual concerns) would be capable of establishing the Buddhadharma in Tibet. He went on to say that the oracle expressed great favor and that the Doctrine would surely blossom in Tibet. But, he said, this would only occur by means of a highly gifted and compassionate master.

On their return from China, the two ministers brought with them one thousand *bam-pos*, or doctrinal compositions each of which contained 300 metrical verses (similar to *kāvya*). However, they were still uncertain about the safety of Buddhist scriptures, and fearing further agitation by Ma-zhang's underground of non-Buddhists, secretly delivered the *bam-pos* to the King, who read them only in private.

After consulting with Tri-song De-tsen, Sal-nang then journeyed to the neighboring land of Nepal and there met the revered Master of Discipline, Abbot Śāntarakṣita, who was then eighty-one years old. Śāntarakṣita consulted with this worthy minister for many hours and heartily confirmed the necessity of establishing the Buddhadharma in Tibet. Returning to Tibet, the royal minister indicated to the King that the Upādhyāya appeared genuinely concerned and that he would most assuredly come to Tibet carrying the Sacred Basket of the Doctrine.

The King, however, feared the safety of his loyal minister Sal-nang and began making secret plans to render powerless the deposed but treacherous Ma-zhang. With the assistance of court astrologers, the King tricked Ma-zhang into willfully entering a tomb of the dead, for Ma-zhang, being a Bön-po and hence a believer in omens, was convinced that this symbolic act would in some way help him to accomplish his aims. Consequently, Ma-zhang himself gained the status of the 'living dead' and was forced to live out his existence in a prison-like graveyard with no chance to escape, his only sustenance the food brought to the tomb as offerings to the spirits of the Bön royalty buried there.

Tri-song De-tsen then launched a thorough investigation of Śāntarakṣita and, finding him to be a most honorable teacher free from fault, sent an emissary accompanied by troops to escort the noble Upādhyāya to the Palace at Lhasa. For fear that the non-Buddhist underground might still be active, care was taken not to publicize the Upādhyāya's arrival. Several great scholars and translators were assembled at the Palace, and to these Śāntarakṣita first expounded basic Buddhist philosophy and ethics.[38] As this teaching threatened the power of the indigenous Bön spirits who presided over Tibet, they rose up and provoked many catastrophes, such as severe lightning, hailstorms, earth tremors and famine. Thunderbolts struck the stone pillars of the Palace at Mar-po-ri which was carried away in a flood. As a result, certain Bön-pos became increasingly hostile, especially because the Abbot represented a powerful, well-established Indian tradition which could seriously threaten the political, social, and economic position enjoyed by the royalty who used the shamanistic Bön religion as a means to further their own aims.

The Bön-pos were not the principle nemesis to the introduction of Buddhism into Tibet, but rather those unsympathetic families of ministers who saw Dharma as a threat to their power and political ascendancy. The history of the Bön-pos illustrates many virtuous acts on the part of its adherents, and the powers which the Bön priests possessed were often used for such praiseworthy acts as healing or bringing forth rain.[39] It is said that some of the disciples of Śāntarakṣita were formerly members of the Bön, as their family roots extend back to

Śāntarakṣita

the legendary Bön clan of the Zhang-zhung. The Bön-pos also claimed that Śāntarakṣita was born in Zhang-zhung, making him their lineal son. From this, it is evident that the Bön-pos took every opportunity to use whatever elements of early Buddhism they found useful to nourish their own tradition. Not only did Śāntarakṣita rebuke the Bön-po claim, but he exposed the shamanism of the Bön-pos as vastly different from Buddhism, rejecting it as a wasteful and dangerous use of higher forms of energy.

The Bön-pos were divided into a number of sects, with the two major distinctions between the 'white Bön' and the 'black Bön'. While the white Bön-pos performed 'virtuous magic' and eventually adopted the ways of Buddhism, the black Bön-pos became increasingly hostile to the Dharma and sided with the non-Buddhists who attempted to overturn the Dharma by means of 'black magic'. Tri-song De-tsen had family connections with the Bön-pos and so was more sympathetic to them than Śāntarakṣita.

After witnessing the hostility caused by his presence, Śāntarakṣita said to the King, "Do not be dismayed, I shall go to Nepal! The Bön spirits are surely displeased at my presence and my powers are not sufficient to subdue them. Some spiritual force of superior capabilities is needed to subjugate the many non-visibles[40] and mountain spirits[41] who defy the Lamp of the Doctrine and who play upon the wrathful nature of men's minds. However, Oh Great King, in the country of Uḍḍiyāna[42] there resides a great and learned Bodhisattva who is more than human. His name is Padmasambhava, the Lotus-born. Only through the gift of his exemplary compassion and power of *mantra* will these demons, manifestations of man's collective mind-projections, be completely transmuted. Invite this Master to Tibet, and the Dharma will most certainly succeed."

The Journey of the Lotus-born Guru. With these words, Śāntarakṣita departed and Tri-song De-tsen did not wish to make public the invitation he had sent to Padmasambhava. Thus he declared to his ministry that Śāntarakṣita's final instructions had actually come to him as a revelation in a marvelous dream. Secretly, though, an envoy was dispatched carrying flowers, incense, and many sackfuls of gold-dust to greet the renowned Ācārya who was called 'the Lotus Born'. When the envoy presented the offerings, Padmasambhava scoffed at their significance and threw the gold in the Ten Directions as though it were worthless. The King's representatives were most amazed by such an unexpected act and began to doubt the authenticity of this Indian teacher. But Padmasambhava, who knew full well the value of the gold and how heavily the people were taxed under the King's regime, reached down and took a handful of earth. After giving each of them a lump, he transformed the earth into gold right before their eyes! Thereafter, this territory became known as the 'gold country', for it was found to contain rich deposits of gold ore. After leading the King and a few of his noblemen to a large body of water, Padmasambhava then summoned Ma-dros, the great Nāga King and ruler of the aquatic underworld.[43] As a sign of friendship, the Buddhist King offered the Nāga King fourteen kilos of gold which were carried on the backs of twelve mules. Thereafter, Guru Rinpoche and the King's royal envoy journeyed to Samye[44] where a monumental residency would soon be established.

As the Great Guru approached the Tibetan border, the demons and non-visible spirits began to unleash thunderbolts, hailstorms, powerful winds and blinding snow. After much harrassment, these fearful beings finally succeeded in blocking the road through a canyon, making progress impossible. So, Padmasambhava sat down in meditation and, through the power of his Samādhi, converted the evil demons into protectors of the Dharma.[45] On the Khala Pass near Western Tsang, he encountered twelve earth-like goddesses who began releasing thunderbolts like arrows and who tried to crush him between the boulders, but as soon as the Guru raised his hand, their thunderbolts turned to charcoal and their strength failed them. These female spirits became known as the twelve guardian goddesses[46] and, being completely converted, were entrusted with the guardianship of the Doctrine. On his way to Samye, Padma journeyed toward the northern upland and there subdued the spirits of the Thang-lha as well as other non-human forms.[47]

Meanwhile, the Ācārya Śāntarakṣita had returned to Lhasa with his crew of stone masons who were already gathering the materials that would be needed for the future temple at Samye.[48] However, once these were collected, the masons experienced great difficulty in keeping together the stones for building, for what was humanly acquired by day, non-humans scattered in many directions by night.[49] Consequently, Śāntarakṣita knew that he would have to wait for the arrival of the Great Guru to perform the exorcism of these demons before any real progress could be made.

When Padmasambhava arrived in the Tamarisk Garden at Red

Rocky Pass, several miles from Lhasa, a cortege of welcomers greeted him with flowers, songs, dances and drums. As the young King appeared to be inflated with pride, consumed by the magnificence of the occasion, the Guru brought him to his senses by projecting fire from his fingertips, singeing the King's robe. The King immediately responded by prostrating before the Guru, and the whole assembly followed his example. Padmasambhava then blessed the small temple that was situated there and invited all the statues to join in the celebration. The statues, in turn, became animated and began dancing and feasting. That night, the temple was emptied of both statues and humans, and in the morning the enlivened statues were discovered eating food and voicing their opinions concerning the Doctrine. The Great Guru then announced publicly, "There is much work to be done if Samye Temple is to be completed soon." So, escorted by the King and Śāntarakṣita, the Compassionate Guru set out for Samye.

The Maṇḍala of Samye Temple. Upon arrival, Padmasambhava announced that all of the demons, spirits, and other malignant non-humans (*asuras*) must be called forth, for their assistance would be needed in constructing Samye. The King was naturally appalled by such a suggestion, but his doubts were relieved as soon as the Great Guru completed a potent exorcism. When the propitiation[50] rites were over, Padmasambhava indicated that the fearful non-humans were subdued and the demons would assist in the building of Samye monastery. After blessing all those in attendance and consecrating the grounds, the Guru initiated the assembly and work began. As humans labored by day and non-humans by night, the great temple at Samye[51] carried the epithet of *The Eternal Self-Created (svayam-bhū) Temple of Samye*. The plan for the temple and its many outlying complexes was so extensive that it took five years of continuous construction to complete.

Padmasambhava chose for the temple a location thirty-five miles outside of Lhasa, some two miles from the north bank of the Yaru River. Its plan was most elaborate, modeled after the design of a *maṇḍala*. The central temple represented Mount Sumeru (Ri-rab)[52] and surrounding it were four major and eight minor temples, which signified the twelve continents, while two additional temples represented the sun and the moon. A lofty wall, nearly two thousand yards in circumference was built to surround these sacred grounds, with gates at the four cardinal points marked by Stūpas (*mchod-rten*) painted in four colors; and on top of this wall were erected 1,080 small Stūpas.

Extending out from the main temple were four smaller temples, which connected the four sides of the main temple with exotic cloisters. Throughout this exquisite structure stood statues and images made of pure gold or other precious metals and richly adorned with jewels and fine silks from China. Envisioned by Guru Rinpoche long before his arrival at Lhasa, this was the design of one of the most monumental temples ever to be constructed.

When Samye Temple was complete, Padmasambhava and Śāntarakṣita announced a great celebration and imparted their blessings to everyone. And during this celebration many wondrous things occurred. Not only did music come from the sky, but also fruit and beautiful scented flowers fell from the heavens, while shimmering rainbows appeared everywhere. The people joyously began to dance, and the golden statues in the temple became life-like, joining the merriment outside. Even the sun and moon rose conjointly.

After the completion of Samye Monastery and its complex of temples, Śāntarakṣita commented to Padmasambhava, "We now have a number of fine temples, but no sacred relics to place in the Stūpas. What should we do?" The Guru then replied, "I will ask King Tri-song De-tsen to send his 'magic army' to India to seize the precious Buddha-relics (*mkhan-rgyud*) so that they will be preserved for future times."

It is said that in Bodh Gayā, when the Buddha died, his body was divided four times, producing eight sets of 'body-relics' which were subsequently stored in eight different locations in Magadha (northern India) by the King of this area. When the officers of Tri-song De-tsen's army arrived in Magadha, they were informed that the relics which they had come to acquire were carefully preserved in sealed urns placed within a large Stūpa containing a weapon-like mechanical contrivance designed to prevent anyone from entering the Stūpa. This weapon was said to contain very sharp blades that revolved like a windmill, prohibiting anyone from entering the chamber. At this time, the powerful Tibetan army, containing over seventeen million men, was marching through northern India and marking its progress by constructing iron pillars. The Indians, frightened by the appearance of the Tibetan army, fled to East India and elsewhere, leaving the priceless treasures unguarded. For those few who remained, King Tri-song De-tsen left his shoes at the door of a temple, tricking those who gathered there into thinking that he was inside. The Indians, fearful of even entering the temple, remained outside for many hours anxiously awaiting the King's appearance. Meanwhile, Tri-song De-tsen was secretly informed that this marvelous bladed weapon was powered by the waters of the Ganges located several miles away. So, after exploring the banks of the river, the army discovered the point of connection between the river and the distant machine and proceeded to obstruct the flow of water at that location. This enabled the officers to enter the Stūpa and seize the many priceless treasures stored there. This historical event brought much merit to King Tri-song De-tsen, for the acquisition of these relics of the Buddha signified that Samye Monastery and, indeed, all of Tibet was now the new citadel of the Holy Doctrine.

Concurrent with these events, translations were made of the many Sūtras and Śāstras that had been brought from India. For this enormous task, the King invited a number of Indian lotsāvas, including Dharmāloka, Ratnasena and others.[53] The Ācārya Dharmakīrti[54] was also invited to consecrate the newly arrived texts whose content would later form valuable sections in the Tibetan Tripiṭaka. The basic texts of the very important *Guhya-mantra-tantra*[55] were also translated. During this period of fruitful translation, many monks, seven of whom were among the first group of Padmasambhava's disciples, were trained and ordained.[56] These ordinations marked the institution of the first Saṅgha in Tibet. As major emphasis was placed on the disciplinary codes (Vinaya) observed in the monasteries, this community reflected the Hīnayāna Saṅgha as it existed in India. Tri-song De-tsen was very pleased with such a rapid emergence of the Buddhist community and knew that this overwhelming success was due to Guru Rinpoche's blessings. Even many of the King's ministers, especially those from the honorable Gar family, became monks, and in a very short time, the community grew to over three hundred fully ordained monks. The King, desiring the very finest education for his newly-founded community, sent Vairocana to study in India under the great masters of the Mahāyāna and Vajrayāna. After completely mastering the Great Perfection Doctrine,[57] Nam-gyi-nying-po[58] and Yan-tag Heruka practices, Vairocana returned to Tibet as a most accomplished translator and siddha.

During the long period of Padmasambhava's stay in the Land of Snows, his mastery over the many forms of mind-energy enabled countless numbers of men to be guided to the enlightenment-path. Wherever he journeyed, he spread the guardian-light of spirituality indicative of a mind totally liberated and free. Those who had the good fortune to receive instruction from Guru Rinpoche not only became important receptacles of the Oral Transmission, but also found enlightenment in this one lifetime. To lay people and monks alike, Padmasambhava imparted the teachings of the higher Tantras.[59] To some he transmitted the precious Vajrakīla (*Phur-bu*) instructions; and to others he explained the meaning of many written doctrines, including his own treatise, *The Garland of Philosophical Views*.[60]

As a result of the great diversity of teachers, scholars, and translators that journeyed to Tibet from other Buddhist countries, many doctrinal approaches emerged. As long as the authenticity of these divergent positions could be substantiated, they were accepted as genuine Buddhist ideas and their supporters were allowed to enter the congress of scholars. For example, toward the end of King Tri-song De-tsen's reign—a period when Sino-Tibetan doctrinal cross-currents were active—a Chinese monk, who was a follower of the Hoshang (Hva-shang) Mahāyāna, arrived in Tibet. Claiming that his doctrine was superior to the King's, the Hoshang began converting a number of monks over to a doctrine of 'instantaneous enlightenment'—a breakthrough which occurs as a person envisions the experience of 'goal-completion'. The King, curious about the Hoshang's doctrinal approach, invited the Indian Paṇḍita Kamalaśīla[61] to engage in debate with the Chinese monk. After a long controversy that lasted two years (between 792 and 794), Kamalaśīla was finally declared the winner.[62]

One day, the King said to Padmasambhava, "You are a great master, and without your assistance establishment of the Buddhadharma in Tibet would have been most difficult. There is no way we can repay you for all you have accomplished. You have bestowed many wonderful blessings on our country. Many ministers have become successful scholars and monks, and the lay people are materially rich. The rains are plentiful, the harvests healthy, and there is little disease. The people enjoy a stability never before experienced." Indeed, Guru Rinpoche's gifts of compassion never ended. With miraculous energy, he transformed the dismal into dazzling effulgence. Wherever he journeyed, he bathed the soil with the inviolate light of truth. One day, while journeying to the valley of Yar-lung,[63] he approached an embankment and struck it with his staff. Suddenly as if by magic, water began to spring forth from a crack at the base of a large rock. Eventually there appeared a crystalline lake and a beautiful oasis-like garden containing flowers in full bloom and trees bearing fruit. This magnificent transformation attracted many invisible ogres, but the Guru, invested

Padmasambhava

with transcending awareness of a particularly pure nature, transmuted these demons into guardian deities.

At that time, all Tibet prospered under the protective parasol of the King. The territories bordering the four frontiers–China to the west, Urdum-kashgar ('Odon-Kas-dkar) of the Turks to the north, Baltistan (sBal-ti) and Gilgit ('Bru-sha) to the west, and India to the south–were all held under the sway of Tri-song De-tsen. Having proven himself a very powerful King in the eyes of the Tibetans, Tri-song De-tsen was also an exemplary King of the Doctrine (*dharma-rāja*). To signify this, Śāntarakṣita announced that a special ceremony would be performed and proclaimed, "In a small lake north of Mount Sumeru (Ri-rab), there is water that possesses very special qualities, 'The Nectar of Long Life'. With this water, the King shall wash his hair. Now, who is present that can seek out this water and bring it here?" Padmasambhava then replied, "I can perform the task!" So, taking out a large silverpiece and attaching it to a long silk rope, he hurled it into the air. After nearly a half-hour, the rope was drawn in and at the end was a small silver urn containing the life-giving water. Pouring the urn over the King's head, Padmasambhava said, "Wash your hair with this life-giving water, for it has many beneficial qualities, and from this point onwards you will be a very successful Dharma King!"

From time to time, Padmasambhava performed ritual Sādhanas which not only directed the minds of all those present to the quintessence of the Holy Dharma, but also enabled many to experience the vitality of a liberated mind. In the presence of the King and his worthy ministers, he uttered many helpful prophecies regarding the future of Tibet and of Buddhism and, together with his disciples, prepared and concealed numerous secret teachings of the Mantrayāna. He predicted by what succession great and learned teachers would emerge in future times, and the method by which these hidden teachings (*gter-ma*) would be uncovered. The Terma were held in secret because they were incomprehensible to those of mediocre intellect, and never divulged to those who were emotionally or cognitively unprepared. Because they were written in a highly abbreviated language indecipherable to all except the Tertons (masters of the *gter-ma*), these teachings would remain safe until conditions arose suitable to their revelation.

Many spiritual lineages[64] emerged through Padmasambhava's twenty-five disciples. With generous support from the King, they were instrumental in establishing numerous secluded retreat centers, where the esoteric Mantrayāna practices were performed. At that time there were two divisions in the Saṅgha. The lay practitioners, sometimes called the 'long-haired ones', were not celibates and led the life of laymen. This sort of life suited the person of a generally superior intelligence who knew the necessity of self-discipline without a need for the strict regulatory codes of the monastic community. These practitioners were often accomplished yogins who wore white cotton loincloths, ate a diet of lentils and barley, and practiced Tumo.[65] The second division was that of the monks, or 'short-haired ones', who followed the letter of the monastic Vinaya code and wore red or brown robes, resembling the ways of the Hīnayāna Saṅgha in India. Out of the continuous efforts of these selfless monks, the sacred literature and practices of the Hīnayāna and Mahāyāna were carefully transplanted and preserved in Tibet.

According to several historical narratives, it is believed that Padmasambhava stayed in Tibet for 111 months. However, the Great Guru is more than human—he is the incarnation of Śākyamuni Buddha and an emanation of Ārya Maitreya (the coming Buddha), and so the beingness of his existence is beyond the matrix of temporality and spatiality. The power of his mind is beyond the limited domain of origination and dissolution, and thus far exceeds the concretizing tendencies of the human intellect. Consequently, we as humans find it most difficult to apprehend the magnificent abilities of this great Master. It would not be an error to say that he simultaneously dwelled in caves, jungles, gardens and groves, near rivers and lakes, and on mountains. At these various locations he performed initiations and Sādhanas with his disciples and other followers. According to Indian reckoning, it is said that the Lotus-born Guru lived for 3,000 years, which in sidereal time, would be 1,500 years. During this period he journeyed to Persia, Afghanistan, South India, Ceylon, Indonesia, Burma, China, Russia, and many other distant lands—and even to other worlds.

Successors and Suppression: Ral-pa-can and Lang Dar-ma

During his reign (755–797 A.D.), Tri-song De-tsen married a total of five wives, for polygamy was not uncommon in these early times. One of his wives, Tshe-pong-za, bore three sons. When Tri-song De-tsen retired from his duties as King and journeyed to Zung-Kar,[66] his eldest son, Mu-ne Tsen-po acceded to the throne and faithfully continued the projects initiated by his father. He saw to it that the Tripiṭaka translations[67] were carefully completed and presented to the great monastery at Samye for safekeeping, and also initiated the observance of four large religious Sādhanas which were performed at Samye Monastery. However, when he tried to set up a system of taxation, he was troubled because all the people could not give equal amounts. Consequently, he made three attempts to equalize the wealth of the rich and poor through redistribution, but each attempt failed. Those who were formerly rich worked industriously and so quickly regained their wealthy status. Likewise, those who were formerly poor demonstrated their inherent laziness, and so fell again into the abyss of poverty. Troubled by failure at economic reform, he consulted Padmasambhava who explained to him that the gap between the rich and the poor, or one's condition in life, is a consequence of meritorious or unmeritorious actions in previous lives, and that these consequences must be faced as a learning experience.

King Mu-ne Tsen-po showed great compassion for his people and ruled with patience and understanding. He demonstrated his support to Samye Monastery by providing the monks with food, clothing, and many generous gifts. Less than two years had passed when, at the age of seventeen, he was poisoned by his mother who, because he had married a younger wife of his father, perpetrated this callous act out of revenge. The second son, Mu-rug Tsen-po[68] was banished to the frontier for three years for killing a son of the chief minister during a squabble in the inner-court. Thus, the youngest son, Mu-tig Tsen-po, who was just a lad of four, received the crown.[69] Although he was a rather insignificant ruler and a mere instrument in the hands of his ambitious family, he was responsible for a further flourishing of the Doctrine and showed his respect for the Dharma by building the Kar-chung-gya-de[70] temple. His sons were Tsang-ma, Ral-pa-can, and Lang Dar-ma by his first wife, and Lha-je and Lhun-du by a queen of lower rank.[71] The first son, Tsang-ma, out of a desire to increase the popularity and status of the Saṅgha, enjoined many to the monastic way of life. He also wrote an important Śāstra. As Lang Dar-ma loved to transgress the moral codes of the layman, he was unfit to mount the throne. This decision was further supported by the advice of the court astrologers. So, Ral-pa-can (815–841 A.D.), 'the Long-haired One', was next in line for the royal throne.

Ral-pa-can wished to follow the example set by Tri-song De-tsen and began by erecting the temple of Gya-phib-gyu-ngon-can.[72] Seeing that the earlier translators had created a technical language that was precise but difficult, and finding discrepancies in comparison to translations from the Chinese and Sanskrit, King Ral-pa-can issued an order that a community of scholars and lotsāvas be formed to revise the sacred texts of the Hīnayāna and Mahāyāna. He decreed that this work was to be done systematically—every technical term was to be indexed,[73] the rules of grammar and syntax followed carefully, and most important, the intended meaning of the original text preserved in such a way that all intelligent men could understand. So, this new series of translations began, and the earlier texts were carefully revised and edited. The Tantras which had been composed or translated by Padmasambhava and his disciples had been written carefully so as to elucidate the symbolic and intentional meanings, and so these were preserved in their original form, unedited. He also decreed that each monk or lama was to be supported by seven households. Out of his deep respect for monks, during public assemblies the King would tie white silken streamers to his long locks and extend them over the dais to the right and to the left of his throne. The pillows of each respective member of the two head-communities would then be placed over these two cords.

On the frontiers as well as in the central district (*dbUs*), King Ral-pa-can erected 108 temples so weary travelers, herdsmen, and noblemen alike could stop to perform religious observances. He provided a protective umbrella for those Indian Paṇḍitas wishing to settle in his dominion and showered flowers of hospitality on visiting scholars and translators. He also saw to it that the arcana of Mantrayāna teachings and Tantric texts were properly transmitted to those with mature minds and who were sufficiently prepared to receive them. Ral-pa-can is thus esteemed by the Tibetans as one of the three most important Dharma kings in the history of the Dynasty.

Among King Ral-pa-can's many translators and academic deans, Vairocana is particularly noteworthy. This noble Ācārya mastered over three hundred dialects and extensively studied the works of the mystic philosopher Śri Siṃha, a learned scholar of the Chinese and Indian Tantras. The teaching lineage which arose from Śri Siṃha provided a significant contribution towards the evolution of the Nyingma teachings—for Padmasambhava himself received many of the highest teachings from him. Under the guidance of many accomplished Siddhas, Vairocana attained many psychic powers, but always used them sparingly and in private. One of the most important saints in the history of the Nyingmapa, Vairocana recognized the essential practicality of the Vajrayāna tradition and the urgent necessity to preserve these teachings for the last centuries of the Kāli Yuga when it would be most difficult for men to live a truly spiritual life. As one of the twenty-five disciples of Padmasambhava, he also recognized that this deeply inspired tradition would link the future of Buddhism to the rest of the world.

During King Ral-pa-can's reign, there were four insidious ministers who, from the very beginning, remained corrupt and plotted to abolish Buddhism in Tibet. They could no longer tolerate either the King's laws, the many Paṇḍitas who repeatedly demonstrated to them their superior knowledge, or the proliferation of the Buddhadharma throughout the dominion. Thus they performed shamanistic practices, a carry-over from the indigenous Bön religion, so that when they died, they would be reborn into the bodies of four demon-possessed rulers who would bring ruin to all those who continued to uphold the teachings of the Buddha. At the instigation of Ral-pa-can's evil older brother, Lang Dar-ma, these evil ministers had Ral-pa-can assassinated by twisting his neck.[74] Shortly afterwards, they committed suicide and were reborn as rulers possessed by powerful demons. Together, their siege of terror dethroned the monks appointed by the late Ral-pa-can, and afterwards they attempted to throw the precious image of Śākyamuni into the water; but it was too heavy to lift, so they merely covered it with sand.[75] After this, many bad omens appeared, and corruption began to spread like a plague.

Meanwhile, the diabolical Lang Dar-ma ascended the throne. As demons had already taken possession of his mind, he ordered all the Saṅgha to surrender their distinctive marks of monkhood or be executed. He had many monasteries sacked or burned, and the doors of Samye and Phrul-nang ('Phrul-snang) monasteries in Lhasa were boarded up and sealed with plaster. These two precious temples escaped the fiery cauldron of Lang Dar-ma's mind, for he received a threat that, if these temples were damaged or pillaged, the guardian goddesses which Padmasambhava installed would cause great calamities. Nevertheless, an edict was written on the plastered doors ordering the monks to substitute their engagement in religious practices with the indulgence of barley beer (chang), which the insane king freely provided. Many monks fled. Those who stayed were either killed or forced into the forest and fields with hunting drums, bows and arrows, and vicious dogs. Some were forced to be butchers. All the religious customs and observances were thoroughly destroyed. The great river Ma-chu-kyad (rMa-chu-skyad) which runs from Tibet to China, flowed upwards for three consecutive days. Even a mountain by the name of Gya (rGya), situated in an outlying district in the dominion, is said to have collapsed!

After nearly six years of suppressive rule by Lang Dar-ma, Pal-gyi

Dorje[76] who was meditating in a distant cave[77] suddenly had a vision. In this vision it was revealed to him how much suffering was being endured, and so he began to feel great compassion for the now quite insane Lang Dar-ma. Pal-gyi Dorje, realizing that it would be impossible to divert this mad King from performing further acts of terror, reluctantly determined to kill the King. So, disguising himself in a black robe with white lining, and smearing his body and horse with lamp-black, he rode into the capital, dismounted before the King, prostrated, and, as he did, exposed a bow and a single arrow which were concealed in the wide sleeves of his robe. With the last prostration, the arrow, already fitted to the bow, was released and found its mark in the breast of the King. Pal-gyi Dorje then fled on his horse. After bathing in the lake of Mi-nag, he turned his robe inside out, so as to show the white lining. Riding his now white horse, he then met the search party who were at his rear and proclaimed, "I am the white *asura* of the skies, Nam-theo Kar-po." He then continued his flight and successfully escaped his bewildered pursuers, seeking refuge in his beloved snow mountains of eastern Tibet to spend the rest of his days in the solitude of prayer and meditation.

Although the Tantric lineage and formal Saṅgha was forced to flee to the outlying districts, most of the esoteric teachings were preserved by those known as 'Mantra-holders'. Thus the main body of the teachings transmitted orally, or through gestures (*mudrā*), by Padmasambhava, Vimalamitra, Vairocana, and Śāntarakṣita, were safeguarded. And, because Lang Dar-ma feared the guardian goddesses who were watching over the sacred texts at Samye Monastery, the exoteric teachings—the Vinaya, Sūtra, Abhidharma—and the Jewel-like Tantras were also preserved. Out of these priceless seeds, new religious adherents continued all the essential teachings and practices. This lineage, then, from the time of Guru Rinpoche to this present day, remains unbroken, and is aptly called 'The Ancient Ones', the Nyingmapa.

Notes

1. *dam-pa'i-chos-kyi-dbu-brnyes.* Various accounts of this event fluctuate greatly from the date given. However, the date given here seems to correspond more closely with the genealogy of the early Tibetan kings. For a study on the discrepancies in the datings of the early Tibetan Empire, *see* Bunkyo Aoki, *Study on Early Tibetan Chronicles*, Tokyo, 1955.

2. lHa-tho-tho-ri-gnyan-bstan. His birth is probably in the year 254 A.D. (Wood-Dog Year), although his dates range from 154 A.D. to 326 A.D.

3. 'Um-bu-bla-mkhar.

4. Viz., the *Za-ma-tog-bkod-ba'i-mdo* (*Avalokiteśvara-guna-Kāraṇḍa-vyūha-sūtra*), describing the meritorious acts performed by Bodhisattva Avalokiteśvara (Avalokita), the tale of Balahaka, the miraculous cloud-horse, and explanations of the many significations of the Six-syllable Mantra, and also the *sPang-skong-phyag-rkya'i-mdo*, a Sūtra containing epithets of Buddhas, Bodhisattvas, and other higher beings, as well as instructions on methods of conduct and discipline. This work is found in the bKa'-'gyur under the title of the *Ārya-kāraṇḍa-vyūha-nāma-mahāyāna-sūtra* or *Za-ma-tog bKod-pa Zhes-bya-ba theg-pa chen-po'i-mdo*. It is also included in the *Maṇi-bka'-bum*.

5. *gser-gyi-mchod-rten.*

6. *tsin-da-ma-ni gzungs* (*cintāmaṇi dhāraṇī*).

7. *gnyan-po gsang-ba*, 'the secret texts that fell from the sky'. The word 'gnyan' may refer to a certain class of demons (*bdud*) residing in the intermediate space, the *bar-do*. Since the Bön-pos 'adored the sky', these contents were worshipped as mysterious spirits (*gnyan*).

8. Other narratives more acceptable to the Nyingmapa indicate that these articles were brought to the King in a chest by the Indian Paṇḍita bLo-sems-'tsho (Buddhirakṣita) and the translator Li-the-se. When questioned as to the origin of the chest, the Paṇḍita merely pointed his finger to the cerulean sky. This may have been to signify that the chest was carried down from the mountains. However, the Bön-pos, being great sky-worshippers, assumed this to mean that the chest descended from heaven.

9. Samantabhadra may be considered a prototypal Bodhisattva because he is the symbol for 'Universal Goodness and Benevolence' as described in the Gaṇḍavyūha Sūtra. He should be distinguished from the Ādi-Buddha Samantabhadra (Kun-tu bzang-po), "who is the cognitive mode that is for ever in the process of awakening to Buddhahood" (H. V. Guenther, "Indian Buddhist Thought in Tibetan Perspective," *History of Religions*, 3, 1: 88).

10. The genealogy of the Tibetan kings stemming from legendary times up to gLang Dar-ma, according to the *La-dvags-rgyal-rabs* (*Ladakh Chronicles*), the *dPag-bsam-ljon-bsang* (*Lhasa Chronicles*), and other sources is as follows. The first five groupings of Royal Dynastic Kings are a personification of the three principal spheres of the early Tibetan (pre-Buddhist) cosmos and a progressive descent of the kings from the 'divine' to the 'worldly'. For a masterful study of the myth, legend and history of ancient Tibet, *see* Erik Haarh, *The Yar-luṅ Dynasty* (Copenhagen: G. E. C. Gad's Furlag, 1969).

First grouping: They were called the 'seven heavenly thrones' (*khri*) and were said to be connected with sTang-lha, the 'heaven of the gods'.

(1) gNa'-khri-bstan-po. The 'neck-throned mighty-one' who is an ancestor to the line of Ladakh kings. His birthdates vary from 450 to 410 B.C.

(2) Mu-khri-btsan-po.
(3) Ding-khri-btsan-po (Ring-khri-)
(4) So-khri-btsan-po
(5) Mer-khri-btsan-po
(6) gDags-khri-btsan-po
(7) Sribs-khri-btsan-po

Second grouping: These were known as 'the floating ones of the earth' (*Bar-gyi-lding*) and were popularly known as the two *De*.

(8) Gri-gum-btsan-po
(9) bYa-khri-btsan-po. He is the third son of gRi-gum and received the name of sPu-de-gung-rgyal. His reign marked the beginning of the religion of Bön (pron.: purn), whose legendary founder was gShen-rabs of Zhang-zhung (Gu-ge).

Third grouping: These were connected with the realm of the earth (*Bar-btsan*) and were called 'the six excellent ones of the land' (*sai-legs*).

(10) 'O-sho-legs (E-sho-legs)
(11) De-sho-legs
(12) Thi-sho-legs
(13) Gu-ru-legs
(14) 'Brong-zhing-legs
(15) 'I-sho-legs

Fourth grouping: These were also connected with the realm of the earth (*Bar-btsan*) and were called the 'eight commanders (*lde, senā*) of the earth', or the 'commanders of the middle-region' (*Bar-gyi-lde*).

(16) Za-nam-zin-lde
(17) lDe-'phrul-gnam-gzhung-btsan
(18) Se-snol-nam-lde
(19) Se-snol-po-lde
(20) lDe-snol-nam
(21) lDe-snol-po
(22) lDe-rgyal-po
(23) lDe-sprin-btsan

Fifth grouping: These were connected with the realm of the Nāgas (*gYog-klu*) and were called 'the five lower majesties' (*sMad-kyi-btsan-lnga*).

(24) rGyal-to-ri-long-btsan
(25) Khri-snyan-nam
(26) Khri-sgra-dpung-btsan
(27) Khri-thog-rje-btsan
(28) lHa-tho-tho-ri gnyan-btsan (b. 254 A.D.). He is the king who discovered the chest and its marvelous contents in the year 333 A.D.

Sixth grouping: These kings mark the end of legendary times and the gradual emergence of the chronicles.

(29) Khri-snyan-gzung-btsan
(30) 'Bro-gnyan-lde'u
(31) sTag-ri-gnyan-gzigs
(32) gNam-ri-srong-btsan
(33) Srong-btsan-sgam-po (Khri-lde-srong-btsan, 569–650)
(34) Gung-srong gung-btsan
(35) Mang-srong-mang-btsan
(36) 'Du-srong mang-po-rje (Khri-'du-srong-btsan, d. 704)
(37) Khri-lde gtsug-brtan (Mes-ag-tshoms, 705–55)
(38) Khri-srong lde'u-btsan (755–97)
(38a) Mu-khri-btsan-po
(39) Mu-ne btsan-po (797–804)
(39a) Mu-rug-btsan-po
(40) Khri-lde-srong-btsan (804–17)
(40a) lHa-rje
(40b) lHun-grub
(40c) gTsang-na
(41) Ral-pa-can-gtsang-ma (817–36)
(42) gLang Dar-ma (836–42)

11. Srong-bstan-sgam-po (569–650, earth-ox-year). He was born at the palace bYams-pa-mi-'gyur-gling, and was posthumously recognized as an incarnation of the Bodhisattva Avalokiteśvara (Tib.: sPyan-ras-gzigs, pron. 'Chen-re-zig'). His birth name was Khri-lde-srong-btsan, but later he was given the name of Srong-btsan-sgam-po due to his introduction of a moral code.

12. bLon-po mGar-dam-pa-strong-btsam. He was later regarded to be an incarnation of Vajrapaṇi (Phyag-na rDo-rje). Descendants from the famous Gar family (mGar-Khri-'bring), who were ministers under King Tri-song De-tsen (see below), later resided at Samye (bSam-yas) monastery and were instrumental in the formation of the early Nyingmapa.

13. These statues depict Lord Buddha at age eight and age twelve. The metals used (probably gold, silver, copper, and iron) were extremely valuable because it was these very metals that the Buddha is said to have blessed and used to represent the four points of the compass. It is believed that the statue itself was a composite of earlier statues, and so each metal, forming a different aspect of the statue, represented a different style of sculpture. This statue was also very precious because it was blessed by countless Arhants and Bodhisattvas through the ages. The statue representing Śākyamuni Buddha when he was eight was actually an image of Akṣobhya Buddha, constructed by Viśvakarman and brought to Tibet by the Nepalese princess. It was first placed in the 'Phrul-snang Temple, but was later exchanged with the statue representing the Buddha at age twelve (*see also* n. 75).

14. 'Od-zer-go-cha (Aṃśuvarman).

15. Bri-btsun.

16. sGrol-ma.

17. Ong-co, Hla-gcig-'un-sing-kon-jo (Chin.: Wen-ch'eng Kung-chu). She was referred to by the Tibetans as *Gyasa* (rGya-bza'), 'the Chinese consort'.

18. Seng-ge-btsan-po, Emperor T'ai-tsung, 'The Lion King'. He ruled the T'ang Dynasty from 627 to 649 A.D.

19. Thang ka'o-dzung (Chin.: T'ang kao-tsu).

20. T'u-yu-hun or T'u-ku-hun ('A-zha), in the Ko-ko-nor region northeast of A-mdo, which is presently the Ts'ing-hai province of China.

21. dMar-po-ri.

22. Of those invited were the Brāhmaṇa Śaṃkara and Ācārya Kusara (India), Ācārya Śīlamañju (Nepal), Hva-sang Mahādeva-tshe (China), and Tabuta and Ganuta (Kashmir).

23. 'Thon-mi Sambhoṭa.

24. The Brāhmaṇa Li-byin and the Paṇḍita Lha'i rig-pa seng-ge.

25. He wrote eight grammatical Sūtras, including the *'Thon-mi-mdo-rdsi*, and translated a number of Indian works, including the *mDo-sde-de-kon-mchog-sprin* (*Ratnamegha Sūtra*), the *Karaṇḍavyūha Sūtra*, and 100 precepts on ethics, morality, and spiritual worship—the *Pan-gong-phyag-rgya-pa*—which marked the first formal introduction of Buddhist Vinaya and Sūtra texts into Tibet.

26. Not only was Song-tsen Gam-po considered to be an incarnation of the Bodhisattva Avalokiteśvara, but his Chinese and Nepalese wives were recognized as incarnations of Avalokiteśvara's consort (*rig-ma*), Tārā (*sgrol-ma*). The Chinese princess was recognized as the white Tārā, whereas the Nepalese princess was given to be the incarnation of the green Bhṛkuṭi Tārā. The fact that neither wife bore him offspring (the King actually had six wives) verified the divine nature of these two wives in the eyes of the early Tibetans.

27. *mi-chos*. The following is a list of the 'Sixteen Moral Rules of the Saintly Kings of Tibet', as adapted from G. Tucci, *Tibetan Painted Scrolls*, Rome, 1949, p. 692, n. 251:

(1) He who kills deserves to be killed (as the influence of Buddhism increased, capital punishment decreased considerably, and was non-existent in later times). He who steals must return that which was stolen and be fined eight to eighty times its value depending on the circumstances of the theft. The adulterous shall be fined, mutilated (the cutting off of a nose or ear), or banished from the region. He who is accused of speaking falsehoods shall swear in proof of innocence or be punished.

(2) Take refuge in the Three Jewels—the Buddha, Dharma, and Sangha—and practice the Holy Doctrine.

(3) Reciprocate parental care with filial piety.

(4) Respect old age, imitate the gentle and learned, and violate not the righteous and noble, but accept their admonition.

(5) Have a kind and understanding heart towards kinsfolk and friends without annoying them.
(6) Be as helpful to your fellow citizens as you would be to yourself.
(7) Be unassuming and straightforward in your speech.
(8) Model your behavior after the righteous, believe in the causal nature of Karma and its effect, and think upon your future life.
(9) Practice moderation in eating, drinking, and accumulating riches.
(10) Do not use rude language to your friends.
(11) Pay your debts in due time.
(12) Do not counterfeit weights and measures.
(13) Be of an even temper with all and bear no envy.
(14) Do not lend an ear to the words of wicked friends.
(15) Speak kind words.
(16) Be welcoming and generous, but do not interfere with the business of others without being asked for help.

28. This is the reason Tibet was sometimes referred to as the 'Country of the Red-faced' (*dgong-dmar-yul*).

29. The Chinese princess constructed the temple of Ra-mo-che gTsug-lag-khang, 'Temple of the Gods', and the Nepalese princess was responsible for the building of Ra-sa-'phrul-snang-gtsug-lag-khang. The latter temple received its name of the 'Goat-earth-miraculous-appearance-temple' because it was constructed over marshy ground and supported by logs hauled there by goats. The name 'Lhasa' is said to be a modification of 'Ra-sa' and is the first Buddhist temple to be built in Tibet. The temple was built in the year 644, four years after Song-tsen Gam-po's marriage with the Chinese princess, and was modeled after the Indian Temple, Vikramaśīla.

30. *chos-kyi bdag-po*.

31. *chos-sna*.

32. Thugs-rje-chen-po bCu-gcig-zal. This famous statue may not have been of Indian origin, for some accounts indicate that it spontaneously appeared before King Song-tsen Gam-po after he returned from deep meditation. It is said to have emitted two beams of light, each symbolizing the two deities, Amṛtakuṇḍali and Hayagrīva. This statue was placed in the Jo-khang temple, the same location the Jo-bos were located previous to the erection of two temples by the wives of the King (*see* n. 29). Another traditional account indicates that Song-tsen Gam-po died of a fever epidemic and that the Chinese princess died in 680 A.D.

33. The formation of a Buddhist monastic community assumes that there are teachers available for instruction who follow a spiritual lineage extending back to the time of the Buddha himself. Monks generally keep a record of their spiritual genealogy as well as pertinent information concerning their various ordinations. The visiting scholars were perhaps unwilling to come at this early time because there were as yet no monks qualified to give ordinations.

34. Li-lung-chi, fifth emperor of the T'ang Dynasty (618–907 A.D.).

35. Khri-srong-lde'u-btsan (755–797). He was born at the Palace of Brag-dmar in Samye and was recognized by Padmasambhava as an incarnation of Mañjuśrī. He is one of Tibet's three most famous kings, and certainly the most powerful.

36. Ma-zhang-khrum-pa-skyes.

37. gSal-snang.

38. He expounded the 'Ten Great Virtues' (*daśa-kuśalāni*), the eighteen components (*dhātu*) that constitute the individual's perceptual world, the twelve 'causes' (*nidāna, hetu, pratyaya, samudaya,* etc.) of existence which are the basis for the Four Noble Truths, and the Twelve-fold Chain of Interdependent Origination (*pratītyasamutpāda*).

39. Buddhist monks and lamas inherited much from the social and cultural life of the Bön-pos which predominated at the time of the introduction of Buddhism. It has sometimes been remarked that the Nyingmapa appear to be closely linked with the Bön-pos, but throughout the history of the Ancient Ones, there have always been major differences. Culturally, there may be some similarities, but philosophically and spiritually there is actually no comparison between what is Bön and what is Buddhist. The early Nyingmapa, it may be said, adapted themselves to local custom and thereby assimilated the Buddhist religion into the lifestream of the Tibetan people. Rather than reject the world of spirits and mystifying powers, such masters as Śāntarakṣita and Padmasambhava demonstrated that the shaman-like practices of the Bön-pos possessed no ultimate answers and would not lead the individual out of a restricting sense of being.

Prior to the time of Thu-mi Sambhoṭa, there was little in the way of a written language in Tibet. However, as Bön texts have been known to exist at this time, some form of language was present. The style of script used at this period was U-me (*dbu-med*), which has headless characters and is written in a running hand. This script was apparently Bhutanese, although differing sectors of Tibet did vary in their character-style.

As the Bön-pos began to adopt the Buddhist doctrine, it became increasingly difficult for those except monks and lamas to distinguish between a Buddhist and a Bön monastery. In later times, the Bön-pos had their own equivalent of the Nine Yānas, as well as a comprehensive set of Sūtras and Tantras, astrology, medicine and rituals. The Bön monasteries soon became receptacles of a vast repertoire of religious instruction, and a number of Nyingma lamas, not limiting themselves to only one set of orthodox views, studied at the Bön monasteries in order to gain new insights into the nature of human consciousness. Through their studies, the Nyingma lamas discovered that what the Bön-pos had done was to copy the early Buddhist texts, only to replace certain technical terms or symbols with Bön inventions in order to make the texts appear to be of Bön origin. By the late nineteenth century, the Bön sect began to dissolve, and, by 1950, there was scarcely a single monastery in existence which operated under the auspices of the Bön faith.

40. *mi-snag*, 'invisibles'.

41. *mi-ma-yin*, (*amānuṣa*) 'malignant apparitions' (lit.: 'non-humans').

42. Some scholars wish to place Uḍḍiyāna (Oddiyana, 'O-rgyan) in the Swat Valley, however there is no evidence to support this. Moreover, his birthplace must have been a location experiencing rich cultural exchanges, so it is unlikely that such a remote place as Swat is correct. As this was a period of much intellectual activity, Buddhist ideas were assimilated from many places. The ox routes or trade routes that extended from northwestern India to Central Asia are a more likely candidate. As the origins of Bön-po ideas point to the West (i.e. Persia), and as Padmasambhava was evidently well acquainted with Bön 'metaphysics' before his visit to Tibet, it seems likely that both Padmasambhava's place of birth and the spread of Buddhist ideas had extended further West than has previously been assumed.

43. The name of the Nāgā King, Ma-dros, is often an appellation for Lake Manasarovar (Ma-dros-pa), which lies at the base of Mt. Kailāśa. The Nāgas (*klu*) are legendary beings stemming from the Indian legends about guardian beings, whose bodies end in serpents' tails and are said to live in the depths of the waters, guarding such precious articles as the Wish-fulfilling Gem, as well as very sacred treasures of doctrine.

44. bSam-yas, located about thirty-five miles southeast of Lhasa.

45. *Chos-skyong* (Dharmapāla).

46. *bstan-ma-bchu-gnyis*.

47. gThang-lha. For a fuller description of this adventure, see *The Legend of the Great Stupa*, pp. 82–86.

48. It was modeled after the Indian monastery of 'O-tantra-ri (Otantapurī), which is the Indian town located near Nālandā in Magadha (northern India). The original Indian monastery of Otantapurī was destroyed by the Muslims in 1193. The full name of the famous Samye Monastery is bSam-yas-mi-'gyur-lhun-gyis-grub-pa'i-gtsug-log-khang.

49. *The Legend of the Great Stupa*, p. 87.

50. Propitiation (*bsnyen-pa*) is not the appeasement of some deity which is supposed to inhabit some unapproachable realm, but a creative act which requires responsiveness, commitment, and intelligence as both a unified value-pattern and integrative action, and is the basis of all ethical behavior (*spyod-pa, caryā*). The practice of *bsnyen-pa* involves the deeper and more esoteric aspect of Sādhaṇa (*sgren-pa*) practice, wherein the adept requires sufficient training by a gifted master. In Buddhism, the phenomenal is never swallowed up by some (theistic) 'Absolute', but both rest on equal ground. As such, the divine presence of one's own mind is found to be indistinguishable from the presence of the divine itself.

51. Mi-'gyur-lhun-gyis-grub Temple. Construction began in 763.

52. The architecture of the main temple was particularly interesting inasmuch as the top section was constructed in the Chinese style, the middle section in the Indian style, and the lowest section in the Tibetan style.

53. Dharmāloka: Chos-kyi-snang-ba. Ratnasena: sGro Rin-chen-sde. The long list includes such notables as Aryadeva (from Simhala), Kamalaśīla (from Maruca), Bha-sang, Khri-gzir, Śam śi (from China), Mahāsūtra, Prasanna, Śantīdeva, Buddhagupta, Chandrakirti Dharmagīti, Viśuddhasiddha, Dānaśīla, Kalyāṇamitra, Surendrabodhi, Jinamitra, Śīlendrabodhi, Vasudhara, and many others.

54. *sde-snod-gsum.* This Dharmakīrti (Chos-kyi grags-pa) should not be confused with the Dharmakīrti who lived in the seventh century. He was a prominent teacher of the Mantrayāna and wrote a number of significant commentaries, including those on the *Abhisamayālaṅkāra* and the *Hevajra Tantra.*

55. *gsang-sngags-rgyud.*

56. Lit., 'the seven men on probation' (*sad-mi bdun*).

57. *rDzogs-pa-chen-po.*

58. *rNam-gyi-snying-bo.*

59. The lower Tantras generally refer to the Kriyā-, Caryā-, and Yoga-tantras. In the Kriyātantra, an emphasis is placed upon ritual acts in such a manner that one's whole life becomes a ritual of perfection. In the Caryātantra, a higher intellectual acumen on the part of the adept is assumed, and so greater emphasis is placed on the contemplative life. However, in the Yogatantra, ritual activity has less significance and a total effort is placed on the harnessing of one's contemplative energies. These three Tantras stress the outer aspect of one's life, whereas the higher Tantras (viz., Mahā–, Anu–, and Ati-yoga-tantra), as preserved by the Nyingmapa, stress the inner and mystic aspects. As a process that elucidates ways of achieving freedom through a growing realization of being, Tantra is as old as Buddhism itself. For instance, the Kriyātantra was explained by the Buddha at Benares (Vāraṇasī) and the Yogatantra was expounded by him in the Agnijvāta (Jvālāmukha) hills northeast of Punjab (Panjāb).

60. *Man-ngag-lta-ba'i phreng-ba.* Two commentaries were written on this work, one by Rong-zom Chos-kyi-bzang-po, a great intellectual and yogi of the Nyingma sect (eleventh century) which no longer exists, and another by Kong-sprul bLo-gros-mtha'-yas (1813–99), a very prominent Nyingma scholar, in his *gDams-ngag-mdzod.*

61. Kamalaśīla—along with Vimalamitra (a highly exalted figure and a proponent of the Yogācāra-mādhyamika-svātantrika line of thought) and Śāntarakṣita—was instrumental in establishing a firm doctrine for the early history of Tibetan Buddhism. Kamalaśīla's major works were the *Dun-brgya-pa'i bshad-pa*, *'Phyags-pa rdo-rje gcod-pa'i rgya-cher 'grel-pa*, *Chos-thams-cad-ngo-bo-nyid med-par grub-pa*, *Chos-thams-cad-ngo-bo-nyid med-par grub-pa*, *sGom-pa'i rim-pa* (*Bhāvanākrama*), and the *Rigs-pa'i thigs-pa'i phyogs-snga-ma.*

62. The decision on the part of the King to declare Kamalaśīla the victor was possibly based upon political rather than doctrinal considerations. As relations between the Tibetan and Indian Masters of Doctrine could not

have been better, the King wanted to keep it that way. The Hoshang (Hva-shang) Mahāyāna taught the Uccheda-vada theory which promotes the method of 'sudden realization' (*ston-min-pa*), which is known in China as the Ch'an school, and should be distinguished from the Hoshang which is Taoist. The system taught by Kamalaśīla, and reaching its quintessence with Tsong-kha-pa four centuries later, favored the 'gradual method' (*rtsen-min-pa*). Simply stated, the Indians approached Buddhism from a more intellectualist perspective, whereas the Chinese approach emphasized meditation and direct experience, undisturbed by discursive thought. However, to say that the Indian masters tended toward 'intellectualism' does not in any way denigrate those who journeyed to Tibet at the time of Padmasambhava. Buddhism was flourishing in India in the eighth century, and those who approached the matter of enlightenment did so from many perspectives, including the distinctive approach of describing the experience of 'how it is' from the viewpoint of having actually reached the final goal, enlightenment. For further commentary, *see* H. V. Guenther, "Early Forms of Tibetan Buddhism," *Crystal Mirror* (1974) 3: 88–89. Just what, if any, similarities exist between the Nyingmapa and the Chinese Hua-yen school which was founded by Fa-tsang (643–712) is a subject of future study.

63. The Yar-klungs area is marked by a fertile valley, watered by a tributary of the Brahmaputra, to the southeast of Lhasa.

64. A 'spiritual-lineage' is one in which the teachings are passed from teacher to disciple. Two additional types of lineages are the 'clan-lineage', and the 'incarnation-lineage'.

65. *gTum-mo*, 'the yoga of psychic heat'.

66. Zung-mkhar. He is said to have died one year after his arrival.

67. i.e., the Vinaya (*'dul-ba*), Sūtra (*mdo*), and Abhidharma (*mngon-pa*) Piṭakas (*sde-gsum*).

68. Mu-rug-bdzan-po (775–804). He was exiled to Lho-grag mkhar-chu near the border of Bhutan.

69. Mu-tig-btsan-po (804–17). He was also known as Khri-lde-srong-btsan, and later received the surname of mJing-yon Sad-na-legs.

70. sKar-chung-rgya-sde.

71. gTsang-ma; Ral-pa-can; gLang Dar-ma (lit. 'youthful ox'); Lha-rje; and Lhun-grub.

72. rGya-phibs-gyu-sngon-can, lit. 'having a Chinese roof of turquoise color'.

73. Forming the text of the famous *Mahāvyutpatti*.

74. The assassins were sBas-stag sna-can and Cog-ro-lha-lod, and the King was age 36. It is said that the assassination occurred in the garden of the Shampa Palace in Katsel (Ka-tshal) Monastery, about 40 miles east of Lhasa.

75. The statue of Lord Buddha at the age of twelve was called the Jo-bo-chen-po and is the most famous statue in Tibet. Historical narratives say that it was made by Viśvakarman in Magadha out of the precious metals

mentioned earlier (*see* n. 13). It was first placed in the Ra-mo-che Temple, but after Song-tsen Gam-po's death it was transferred to the 'Phrul-snang Temple in Lhasa from where it was stolen and buried in the sand. Later it was discovered by the Chinese wife of Tri-song De-tsen through her paranormal abilities of divination, but it was subsequently moved to sKyid-grong in Mang-yul on the border of Nepal by order of the malevolent Ma-zhang. After peace was again restored under the auspices of the Great Guru, the statue was returned to 'Phrul-snang Temple. Under the reign of the perverse Lang Dar-ma, the statue underwent a second burial, but was once again returned to 'Phrul-snang during the period of restoration which occurred chiefly in the eleventh century. This period marks the beginning of the gSar-ma tradition which originates with Atīśa, the Indian master who came to Tibet in 1038 A.D. He is responsible for the founding of the bKa'-gdams-pa sect, which successfully continued up to the time of the great reformer, Tsong-kha-pa, three and a half centuries later. This sect eventually became known as the dGe-lugs-pa. The bKa'-brgyud-pa sect was founded in Tibet by Marpa in the latter half of the eleventh century, and formally established by sGam-po-pa and others. The Sa-skya sect formed in the final quarter of the eleventh century. These schools, as well as other prominent sects of the gSar-ma tradition will be discussed in the next volume of *Crystal Mirror*.

76. dPal-gyi-rdo-rje. He was one of the twenty-five disciples of Guru Rinpoche.

77. Located in the Yer-pa'i-lha'i-snying-po mountains.

PART TWO

TEACHINGS

Long-chen-pa

The Natural Freedom of Mind

Long-chen-pa
translated by Herbert V. Guenther

Since your mind has been since the very beginning a deity,
Its body is a maṇḍala and speech a mantra—
A reach and range of pristine cognitions
In which everything is spontaneously perfect.

LONG-CHEN-PA, Sems-nyid ngal-gso

The spiritual followers of Guru Rinpoche, such as the twenty-five disciples and others who accepted and practiced the early Tantric texts and Sādhanas, later came to be known as the 'adherents of the Old Tantras'—those translations, texts and oral instructions which were spread throughout Tibet during the eighth and ninth centuries. During the brief suppression of Buddhism by Lang Dar-ma (d. 842), the disciples were forced to go 'underground', but they continued to foster an intricate interweaving of teacher-student relationships which were vital to the early preservation of the Nyingmapa.

Two features, among others, distinguish those recognized as the Nyingmapa: first, their reliance on the 'continuous' transmission of personal instructions from teacher to student (*bka'-ma*), that is, the validity of quick, powerful and effective practices to achieve a heightened state of awareness; and second, their reliance on a 'continuing transmission', represented, for example, by the discovery of Terma (*gter-ma*) or 'buried treasures' which were concealed by Padmasambhava and his disciples for revelation at a later time. This 'continuous' and 'continuing' transmission of symbolic, oral and textual instruction thus serves as the source and fountainhead for all the lineages which subsequently developed from the original esoteric teachings.

By the fourteenth century, the six principal lineages of the So, Zur, Nub, Nyag, Ma and Rong had already undergone an extensive development, encompassing an enormous terrain of teachings designed for rapid progress along the spiritual path. At this time, the widely divergent trends within the Nyingma reached a point of synthesis in the life and work of one of the most renowned masters of the Nyingma lineage, Kun-mkhyen Klong-chen-rab-'byams-pa (1308–63).

Long-chen-pa studied with many of the most exemplary Masters of his time, and, in his writings, he ordered the philosophical truths and psychological applications of the rDzogs-chen into a cohesive system. Although he was abbot of Samye monastery early in his life, he later declined his responsibilities in order to live more simply in the mountains of Tibet. There he practiced meditation in caves and hermitages and prepared his most profound and enduring treatises, composing many lucid and systematic commentaries on Mahāyoga, Anuyoga and Atiyoga. Despite the depth and complexity of these subjects, Long-chen-pa's works are exceptionally clear and are considered to be the most brilliant and original treatises in the whole of Tibetan literature. All of his writings are inspired by the Dzog-chen teachings as revealed in his exhaustive *mDzong-bdun* ("Seven Treasures") and the *sNying-thig ya-bzhi*, which describe the outer, inner and secret meanings of Sādhana practice, oral teaching and initiation. All together, he wrote well over two hundred works, of which twenty-five survive today.

Revered as an incarnation of Mañjuśrī and a manifestation of the Indian master Vimalamitra, Long-chen-pa was honored by the distinguished title of 'Kun-khyen', which means 'omniscient'. He spent his last years repairing the Stūpas near Samye and meditating in the cave at Chim-phu which was formerly used by Padmasambhava, and there, through visionary experiences, received personal instructions from Guru Rinpoche who revealed to him some of the Terma which had been concealed for dissemination in his time. When Long-chen-pa was fifty-six years old, he gave his students their final instructions and passed away. At that time, according to his biography, it was winter in Tibet and ice and snow covered the entire country, but at the place where Long-chen-pa died, seven earthquakes shook the ground, the air was filled with music, the snows melted and flowers blossomed.

Four centuries later, another Nyingma lama, 'Jigs-med-gling-pa (1728–98), received meditative visions (*dag-snang*) of Long-chen-pa who inspired him to compile the Nying-thig teachings into a collection of thirty-four volumes which are now known as the *rNying-ma'i rgyud-'bum*. The Nying-thig is the simplest yet most sophisticated and potent of all Buddhist teachings. While they surely elucidate the subtle movements within one's meditative practice and lead to a freedom that is the ultimate expression of enlightenment, they are, at the same time, traditionally considered to be inaccessible to those who might approach them with insufficient preliminary training.

Soon, with Dr. Guenther's assistance, we are also planning to publish a translation of Long-chen-pa's *Sems-yid ngal-gso*, a work in the *lam-rim* style, which charts one's quest for 'absolute fullness of life' through a poetic and systematic presentation of Nyingma thought. We hope this work will greatly assist those who sincerely wish to prepare themselves to receive the Nying-thig teachings.

TARTHANG TULKU

Translator's Introduction

The Natural Freedom of Mind by Klong-chen rab-'byams-pa is the first work in a trilogy [*skor-gsum*] that has as one of its major themes the problem of Freedom. Although in its English translation the title appears to be very simple and straightforward, the original Tibetan version [*sems-nyid rang-grol*] points to a profound philosophical insight.

'Freedom' [*rang-grol*] is not an evanescent sentiment, but an 'existential' reality and as such not so much a final state or achievement, but rather a beginning and a continual presence, only to be lost the moment it is interfered with. Similarly 'Mind' [*sems-nyid*] is not conceived of in the manner of an individual mind as a subject or self which perceives, feels, imagines, and reasons, or as a metaphysical substance which is contrasted with matter or material substance. Rather, to borrow a term from science, it is the 'Energy' that suffuses the whole of what we term reality. Thus again, it is 'existential' in a primary sense and, consequently, 'Mind' or, more precisely, 'Mind-as-such' [*sems-nyid*] is antecedent, while 'mind' [*sems*] is derivative.

Therefore, Mind-as-such is not merely an attribute of something else. To speak of it as self-existent and naturally free does not mean that in its Being it is dependent on its apprehension by a mind. Any apprehensive awareness implies Being, but the implication is neither of an antecedent nor of a consequent. 'Awareness' and 'Being' are like the two sides of a coin, to which a third consideration can be added, namely, that Being remains constant or 'invariant' despite the fact that it may *appear* at certain times as this or that which in its *apparent* or seeming existence is variable and relative to everything else. Its invariableness remains unaffected by its changing modes, 'self-same' [*mnyam-nyid*] and naturally free.

From this follows the logical order of Klong-chen rab-'byams-pa's trilogy: while every cognition is a mode of consciousness or a mind [*sems*] as ordinarily understood, the awareness in knowing or Mind-as-such [*sems-nyid*] is not identical with mind whose existence is a mode of *seeming*. Hence the first work is specifically entitled 'The Natural Freedom of Mind-as-such' [*sems-nyid rang-grol*]. The awareness in knowing or Mind-as-such is also an awareness of the reality of Being [*chos-nyid*], not merely a cognition of this or that particular existent [*chos*] which exists only in dependence upon its *being conceived*. Hence the second work is entitled 'The Natural Freedom of the Absolutely Real' [*chos-nyid rang-grol*]. Inasmuch as Mind-as-such and the awareness of the reality of Being constitute the 'invariant' in the flux of phenomena, the third work, 'The Natural Freedom of the Self-sameness of Being' [*mnyam-nyid rang-grol*] is the logical conclusion.

This work, 'The Natural Freedom of Mind', is divided into three sections: the foundation, the progress, and the climax. In the first section Klong-chen rab-'byams-pa elucidates the existential reality of Mind-as-such, ever present, but never caught. The second section deals with 'meditation' which is understood as a free performance, not as a mechanical fixation of the mind on some object, which, as a matter of fact, is the abolition of freedom. The last section climaxes in a vision of reality vibrant with life.

HERBERT V. GUENTHER

PRAISE TO MIND unlimited and unbiased in its pure subject-object function constituting the multiplicity of conscious experience as the absolutely specific characteristic [*mtshan-nyid*] of a mind which presents itself as an essential creativity constituting its spontaneity as its actuality [*rang-bzhin*], which, in turn, derives from that which defies being turned into an object of concretizing thought and hence is the purity of absolute fact [*ngo-bo*].

Listen to my explanation of how I have understood the freedom of Mind-as-such [*sems-nyid*], this marvelous ruler holding sway over appearance and mind without subjective tendencies and in primeval freedom, from its vantage-point of self-sameness, the unoriginatedness of all that is.

The Foundation

Pure vision has neither limiting periphery nor fixed center. It cannot be shown as this or that; it is neither wide nor narrow, neither high nor low; it is beyond eternalism and nihilism, and free from the taint of the four extremes of judgments. If one searches for it one does not find it and when one looks for it one does not see it. Free from opposites and restrictions, and beyond all objects of thought, it has nothing to do with philosophical systems, with void or non-void, and has nothing before it that could be calculated by understanding or non-understanding.

Since all that is has been from all beginning in a state of absoluteness [*byang-chub*],[1] it has never come into existence nor has it ceased to exist and so defies articulation in word and thought. Since this absolute perfection in self-sameness [*mnyam-rdzogs*]—in which there is no reference whatsoever to something termed impure, pure-impure, and naturally pure—has never been in a state of bondage and in a state of having been freed, there is no coming or going or staying to it.

In this state that feels like an apparition of a subject-object division with its postulates of appearance and openness of being, Saṃsāra and Nirvāṇa, happiness and suffering are like pleasant and unpleasant dreams. From the time of their appearance onwards, they have been in themselves without propositions about them. It is from that state that the mutual conditioning of origination and cessation stems which is like a dream, an apparition, an illusion, a phantasma, an echo, a reflection—with no substance to it.

Since all that is, and about which one speaks of, origination and so on, has never originated, it never ceases to exist. And throughout the three aspects of time it does not step out of itself into something other nor does it change into something other than itself. Not coming from somewhere, not going somewhere, and not staying somewhere, it is like a dream or an apparition.

The belief in an ego or Self as something abiding in this flux of appearance which ignorant people desire to be real, breaks in the same way as the spell of an apparition, were one to touch the young girl in the apparition. Although unreal in view of its deceptiveness, appearance is causally effective as long as it appears.

The worlds of the six kinds of beings as well as the Buddha-fields are not an agglomeration of atoms, but the mere self-manifestations of Mind in the minds of sentient beings. Just as in a dream Buddhas and ordinary beings seem to be real and immeasurable, when one wakes up they are but a momentary thought. Know Saṃsāra and Nirvāṇa to be like this.

There is no openness of Being apart from the appearance of Being; they are one like fire and its nature, heat. The claim that they are different is made by the intellect. The water and the moon's reflection in it are indivisibly one in the well; so also appearance and openness are one in the absolutely real.

This appearance which has never come into existence as something other than itself, i.e., Being, is like a reflection of flawless, naturally pure absoluteness of Being [*chos-kyi sku*].[2] Since the postulates of the intellect about its existence or non-existence are deviations from reality, do not concretize what appears into something ultimately real.

Samantabhadra, the primordial Buddha

The apparent object is an image of the mind, like the reflection of the face in a mirror. The appearance as duality, although not being a duality, is the habituation of tendencies since beginningless time. Although mind and appearance do not constitute a duality, their working is like the appearance of a dream to a person fallen asleep. Know mind and appearance, dream and sleep as not different in substance.

When a small child sees himself in a mirror, he will either assert or deny an external world, while the mother looking into the mirror will wipe it and create an artificial external world through the relationship that holds between cause and effect. A beautiful woman looking into a mirror will rub her face. Similarly a person who knows this-ness will look at Mind-as-such within. This is the unconcretized and essential pursuit of reality.

The multiplicity of the world before a mind that has no substance to it has arisen within, through the condition of objectivation. It is like the appearance of a reflection in a mirror or in the water of the ocean.

The play of appearance, whose multiplicity is its specific characteristic in the unceasing actuality of its fact of Being which is an open dimension, is the bursting forth of the one Mind-as-such in the duality of Saṃsāra and Nirvāṇa. It is like a crystal assuming different colors dependent upon whether there is a white or black cloth.

Although the ground for the emergence of the multiple world, unchanging in its fact of Being, seems to change with the emergence of the conditions for multiplicity when the multiple appearances emerge, actually it does not change, just like a pure crystal. Mind-as-such, open since time without beginning and independent of a foundation, is not affected by the appearance of what constitutes Saṃsāra and Nirvāṇa.

The fact of Being–perfect as the ground of all that is, not stepping out of itself into something other than itself and not changing into something other than itself, a state of thorough positiveness in which the three aspects of time are timeless–is not affected by the appearance of the six kinds of objects, but is like the moon reflected in the water. Do not accept or reject, deny or affirm, hope for or be afraid of Saṃsāra and Nirvāṇa which are like a phantom that appears and yet is not.

To be free through knowing what a phantom is, means that even if one is taken in by seeing an army of phantasmata, by knowing them as what they are, one is neither terrified nor scared. There is no need to discard the apparent objects.

Since the very fact of mind in its actuality of Saṃsāra has never come into existence and is in a state of Nirvāṇa, one becomes free by seeing Mind-as-such in its actuality of becoming.

At that time no other peace is to be realized. It is as if one were afraid of one's own army by taking it to be another hostile one, but then by realizing that it is one's own, one feels happy again.

As soon as by the grace of the glorious Guru the fictions of a possible world [*srid-pa*] are understood as Dharmakāya, a self-sufficient bliss arises from within. There being no need to accept or to reject, appearance and its possibility have arisen as the Guru. There being no end to instruction, everything becomes an aid to the realization of the absoluteness of Being [*byang-chub*]. In this peace and happiness the mind is continuously happy.

The ceaseless play of the multiple realities [*chos-can*] deriving from the absolutely real instant [*chos-nyid*] in which everything is happiness, manifests itself as Dharmakāya and Rūpakāya, as appearance and openness, as the two accumulations of merits and knowledge. Responsible action and discriminative awareness, composure and the post-composure state are spontaneously present. Uncreated and self-sufficient, the five value-patterns [*sku*] and the five original awarenesses [*ye-shes*][3] are perfect in the state of intrinsic awareness in which appearance and mind are without subjective taint. It is the levels and paths, mantras and concentrations—a genuine state of the absolutely real—in which the qualities associated with Buddhahood are spontaneously perfect. This free-rising, absolute, intrinsic awareness, devoid of all contraries, is not deceived by objectivity nor is it fettered by subjectivity.

What is the use of pursuing a concentration that can be formulated in thought and words concerning the pure and non-dual which is of the nature of an apparition?

In it there is neither a developing nor a fulfillment stage, neither duality nor singularity, neither philosophical systems nor divisions into spiritual pursuits. These are mere postulates, paintings of the intellect. Freedom in itself is merely a key to this free-rising state.

Do not grasp as this or that the intrinsic awareness that has no tag of 'this or that'. Do not vitiate by artificial means Mind-as-such, surpassing the intellect, uncreated and perfect in its spontaneity. Let it be as it is.

When the absolutely real, which remains what it is whether understood or not understood, is not spoiled by the snare of meditation, there is neither being nor non-being, neither appearance nor nothingness pertaining to the presence of reality [*gnas-lugs*]; it cannot be characterized by such attributes as one or many; it is beyond the confines of vision and attention to the vision; it cannot be affirmed nor negated, it does not come nor does it go. Such words as 'without limits', 'non-dual', 'apparition-like', 'dream', are used to abolish the desire to believe in the two truths as real entities. The absolutely real has nothing to do with 'absolute' or 'relative' truths.

However one may analyze it, it is not present as this or that. The belief in 'this is it' is to ensnare it. However much one may want it, when once one has fallen into the clutches of desire, Saṃsāra does not stop by efforts to make it stop. Due to good and evil actions one roams in this world. Happiness and misery, high and low ranks, are like a water-pail going up and down in a well.

Throughout the three aspects of time the beings of the three realms roam in Saṃsāra on an erroneous course. They are afflicted by the disease of chasing after the postulates brought about by unknowing. How pitiable are these beings for whom there is no beginning or end in time.

Ah! all this is merely a dream, an apparition. The absolutely certain has nothing to do with this going in circles and someone going in circles. Everything is originally free and in a state of utter positiveness. Be happy since there is no concrete ground.

Mind-as-such, uncreated and pure from all beginning, is not

affected by whatever may appear. As with a reflection, there is no apprehendible entity in the apparent object and in the free-rising intellect there is no apprehending entity. In this, non-dual original awareness appears as a duality in the wake of appearing. Therefore 'object' and 'mind' are its unending ornaments.

The elephant of non-subjectivism, roaming freely over the plains, is adorned with the garlands of non-duality, moving in intrinsic freedom. Having crossed the swamp of acceptance and rejection, expectation and anxiety, it enters the lake of non-duality holding the power of intrinsic understanding.

Without fettering with the rope of addiction to what aids renunciation, the free and unrestrained procession of what is free in its rising, vision, perfect as a great surge, is preserved in its wide openness, and the world of appearance, perfect in its great creativity, rises as Dharmakāya.

When Mind-as-such—unlimited, the creator of the incessant appearances of the six kinds of objects, himself devoid of any essence—has become free with nothing to rest on, intrinsic perception, in which Saṃsāra and Nirvāṇa are not two, has reached its source and real being. This is the 'attainment of the highest realization'. Since one has reached the ultimate of completion as sufficient in itself and ever ready for others, one awakens enlightened in the Akaniṣṭha realm.

Alas! those people professing to meditate but suppressing all thought, and conceited about a conceptless state which they call a 'presence', and for this reason being as stupid as cattle, turn themselves into animals by habituating themselves to this state. And if they do not, they nevertheless have no chance of becoming free from Saṃsāra, even if they 'meditate' on the sphere where no forms obtain. Therefore, the more conceited they grow, the more they are possessed by the demon of their own systems. Running after the fictions set up by their minds, they do not see the absolutely real because of the pollution created by their postulates.

Even if they deal with the two truths, they fall into the extremes of eternalism and nihilism, and even if they come face to face with that which has no limits they profess a view which is merely the peak of a worldly experience. Whatever they do, they remain fettered by their systems and never have a glimpse of the genuine pristine awareness.

The Real is dimmed by objectifications that can be thought and talked about, and since it is not recognized that the latter is the former in disguise, that which is sought is missed by the seeker.

Mind and pristine awareness are like the water and its moisture. That which throughout time is such that nothing can be added to nor subtracted from it, is falsified by a mind that by rejecting and accepting introduces a division.

Whatever appears, be this an object or a mind, is as such the pure fact of genuineness, but by taking a partial view of it, its open dimension is restricted.

If you now want Dharmakāya that is non-objectifiable, stop the desire to make an object of the King who has manifested himself, by not excitedly seeking for the Real as an object. That which cannot be circumscribed or limited cannot be taken as this or that, and not being found as it has manifested itself, it is not such as it appears. The wide-openness and absolute freedom of the common mind with its appearance is the vision of the natural completeness.

Although one refers to the actuality of the entities of reality by the analogy of space, space itself is not objectively seen as something. Even if one says that Mind-as-such is unborn and that the entities of reality are like space, one has merely put a label on them; that which is independent of such predication as 'it is this' or 'it is not this', and which is beyond discursive thought, cannot be shown as 'this is it'; it is the originally perfect and overarching unity.

Ah! since the world of appearance is pure in itself, it arises purely and incidentally in a non-subjectivistic awareness. It stays nowhere when it has appeared, and is seen as absolute completeness free in itself.

Since Mind-as-such – pure from the beginning and with no root to hold to something other than itself – has nothing to do with an agent or something to be done, one's mind may well be happy. Since intrinsic awareness with no objective reference whatsoever, has no intention as to this or that, one may well be full of love toward all. Since vision and attention to the vision are not disrupted nor falling into contraries, having nothing to do with acceptance or fear, high or low, one may well be joyous. Since enactment and goal, having nothing to do with acceptance and rejection, expectation and anxiety, are not seen as something to be obtained or missed, one may well feel an inner warmth. Since everything is but an apparition perfect in being what it is, having nothing to do with good or bad, acceptance or rejection, one may well burst out in laughter.

Appearance and subjective mind are darkish, evanescent, unclear, dim and discontinuous, but that which is wide-open and genuine is unconcerned with whatever appears, be it this or that or may it seem as this or that: it is Dharmakāya independent of an intellect which is moving in the confines of a 'this is it' and 'this it is not'. That which has nothing to show for itself is but a random appearance.

When the noetic capacity that is not a subjective phenomenon is free in non-duality, all that appears as the world of appearances and the mind perceiving it, is the greatness of the creative playfulness of mind. In Mind-as-such which is not an entity and has no other ground or root than itself, all qualities are complete in uncreatedness and spontaneity. Since negation and affirmation are free in Dharmakāya, the individual mind finds happiness.

All intentional objectifications are artificial. When there are no intentional objectifications there is pristine awareness. Since acceptance and rejection have lost their coerciveness in freedom, the mind finds happiness; since acceptance and rejection have lost their coerciveness in freedom, one has passed beyond the object of thought.

The whole of Buddhahood, naturally pure, is not to be found anywhere else than in one's mind as Mind-as-such. That which is sought is not found apart from the seeker. It is similar to an apparition or the water in a mirage.

The belief in the duality of Saṃsāra and Nirvāṇa, which are not two, ceases in genuine, self-existing intrinsic perception. He who has seen the existential identity of all that is and has understood that Mind-as-such is like the unborn sky, goes to the realm of the identity of spontaneity and perfection, which is unborn and is the field where appearance and its possibility, the world and the beings therein, are pure in themselves.

Since the mere fact of a world of appearance and a mind perceiving it is an open dimension, it is what is meant by Dharmakāya, and since its actual presence is unceasing and thus the manifestation of Sambhogakāya, by knowing its distinct features in their multiplicity as Nirmāṇakāya, everything turns out to be the pure field of the three kāyas and their pristine cognitions. Since there is no more tendency to reject what is artificially contrived, the individual mind is happy.

Ah! friends, as long as they reside in Saṃsāra which is like a dream or an error, the beings are caught in the net of cause and effect in Saṃsāra by the belief in duality. By conditioning themselves to the conceptless substratum awareness, they err into the world of formlessness; by conditioning themselves to the radiant awareness as an open substratum, into the world of forms; and by conditioning themselves to the six sense-patterns, into the world of desires.

Those who desire liberation on the stairs of the world fashioned by the mind, must enter the peace where mind is inactive, the real and uncreated peace.

The common noetic capacity, original and not stained, is free in itself as it is not vitiated by the belief in the duality of Saṃsāra and Nirvāṇa. Since it is free in itself, the moment it settles itself, then, in the sphere of Dharmakāya which has no conceptual division in its presence, there is Sambhogakāya as a radiant and open, unceasing starting-ground. If there issue manifestations and one is certain about them as Nirmāṇakāya free in its rising, one is certain about the idea of Saṃsāra becoming Nirvāṇa.

Ah, while the world of appearances and the mind perceiving it may change, look into the mirror of Dharmakāya having nothing to show for itself. When there is no longer a belief in the absolutely real that has nothing to show for it as something, there is the mystery of mind. Nothing else can be shown; the very essence of what has risen as spontaneous intrinsic perception, has settled in itself–do not vitiate it.

When all that is has no substance, mind, no longer grasping, like the sky, has neither circumference nor center. Although this peace that cannot be grasped by negations or affirmations, rises in an uncreated and unceasing way, know it as never stepping out of itself or turning into something other than itself throughout time.

The genuine pristine awareness in which the object and the mind are not two, is revealed in understanding, but not as some thing. The real Mind-as-such is beautiful in itself. Steady concentration, scrutinizing discrimination, instructions and teachings are mere objects of understanding. They can never reach the naked pristine awareness.

Although one may point to the sky with one's finger and say 'this is it', one's lived space like the sky is not an object one sees, but merely a differentiation. When by the grace of the Guru this experience rises as one's intrinsic understanding, the event is like the sun dispelling darkness. Simultaneously with the vision of reality as Dharmakāya in an instantaneous intrinsic perception, unknowing and the emotions become pristine awareness. Blessed by not being swayed by concrete things, one attains in this life the ordinary and supreme accomplishments.

Fools hate the world and seek Nirvāṇa, but never reach it. Having cast away the real jewel, they take up some substance that has to be cleaned, and when they have removed the dirt, they have merely found a glass trinket.

When one knows the precious jewel of Mind-as-such, free in itself, as what it is, the dirt of error disappears by itself. In this knowledge one possesses the treasure of precious qualities, which is the essence of fulfilling one's own and others' aim.

When there comes the understanding of what Mind-as-such means, it is like the water and the waves; wherever they move they remain the water, and so whatever there is remains Dharmakāya; in whatever form they arise, there is no need to affirm or deny them. Therefore there is no need ever to affirm or to deny.

This yoga where mind is happy at all times, is the great yoga which is like a flowing stream. The sphere of the actuality of everything remaining what it is in utter perfection is a brilliant light that comes in a flash, and in whatever fashion it may shine forth, it remains the absolutely real.

Since emotions and their counterpart are not two entities when the radiant light, as an intrinsic perception that has no limits or a center, is present, rejection and what tends towards it, detachment and attainment, expectation and fear become free by themselves. By not knowing the figure of speech of calling a jewel a lamp, one hankers after the light of the lamp rather than looking for the jewel. If one does not differentiate between the sentiment of freedom and the intellectual concentration on it, one fetters oneself by hankering after what is in itself free-rising.

If one does not distinguish between a sentiment and real understanding, one mistakes the habitual sentiment for understanding. After a real understanding there is no longer any good or evil movement or change. From habituation to this there comes the feeling of value. Just as in space the four elements evolve, yet space is never disturbed but stays like the blue sky, so also in the understanding of Mind-as-such there is no good or evil understanding even if one has the feeling of increase or decrease. If there is good or evil then there is sentimentality, not understanding. Search for the real understanding and stay with what is not disturbed.

Attention to this is the real vision and the person of highest intellectual acumen is freed in seeing it. Independent of habitual sentiments the all-encompassing understanding arises. Since there is nothing to be rejected there is nothing to assist a person in rejecting something, just as a healthy person has no need for any medicine. Know that a vision unaffected by contraries has nothing to do with subjectivism.

Chapter one of 'The Natural Freedom of Mind' in the rDzogs-chen philosophy, dealing with freedom through understanding the Foundation of Being.

The Progress

Meditation left to itself remains absolute freedom and, there being no need for artifacts, whatever presents itself in it remains absolutely perfect. In this primordial sphere where nothing is to be accepted or rejected, the without and the within, Saṃsāra and Nirvāṇa, retain their unitary character.

Intrinsic perception[4] of whatever comes before it operates without stress through the six sense-patterns and intrinsic perception in its genuineness should be left to itself like a little child. When in the sphere that has no foundation other than itself the mind has passed beyond a state of non-interference by the intellect, the inconceivable king Mind-as-such rules unchangingly and spontaneously.

The common noetic capacity operates without stress in its naturalness and the noetic capacity left to itself should be like water poured into water. The non-dual noetic capacity should be left in a state where no artifacts occur and the uncreated noetic capacity should stay with the absolutely real.

A mind that rises from the depth of its peace is happy in itself and, left to itself and imposing by its power, should be left to itself like an old man. In its sphere of self-manifestation that defies all calculation, intrinsic perception, absolutely free, should remain with its absolute vastness of scope.

Intrinsic perception with nothing before it to limit it is far-reaching in its scope, and intrinsic perception not holding to anything subjectively should be left to itself like a drunkard. In its sphere of impartiality when intrinsic perception is concerned with ritual performances, the various detrimental conditions arise in the form of a play of the absolutely real.

One's own mind with its various contents is the magic show of intrinsic perception and should be left to itself like a fearless lion. In its sphere of pristine awareness overcoming the delusive appearances, intrinsic perception coming in the wake of the pristine awareness arises in absolute freedom.

Until true understanding becomes the creative center, let your mind be like a jackal's eye, not distinguishing between day and night. When through habitualness and acceptance your realization is like the meeting between a mother and her child, everything will arise in unitary vastness.

Intrinsic perception without partiality has neither a periphery nor a center and should be left to itself like the celestial space that cannot be pointed out as 'this is it'. Intrinsic perception with nothing to meditate upon has as its content that which is not artificial. Intrinsic perception that arises by itself rises from its own depth.

That which is free from pollution by the emotions is an absolute self-luster, and intrinsic perception which is this luminosity should be left to itself like the ocean. Intrinsic perception that is free in its rising is like the waves of the ocean; it comes like the reflection of the face in a mirror.

Mind-as-such, unmoving, neither steps out of itself nor changes into something other than itself, and the absolutely real, unmoving, should be left to itself like a mountain. Intrinsic perception, perfect in its self-sameness, is perfect in its spontaneity and uncontrived. When effort and purpose do not obtain, equanimity is spontaneously present.

Mind-as-such in its genuineness is absolutely free in its self-manifestation and in its uninterruptedness should be left to itself like a river. Whatever thought-constructions there may be, they are one with Dharmakāya and, there being no need to accept or reject the one or the other, there is the over-arching unity beyond suffering.

In brief, whatever arises is the play of the absolutely real, and composure free in itself with no objective reference is spontaneously present. In this sphere of continuous meditation when no alteration of states of consciousness is observed, diligently exercise the creative power to true understanding.

Since there is nothing to accept or reject in dealing with all that is as an apparition, even detrimental conditions as part of the path leading to the spiritual gain of true understanding become the path; and in order to fuse the concentrative and post-concentrative states, dance and sing and indulge in all sorts of thoughts when you have come to places where the mind is agitated by objects such as mountain-peaks, cremation grounds, islands, trade-fairs and so on; and, each moment free in itself, vision and attention to it fuse. Afterwards everything has become the way. But in the meantime the world of appearances, the devotion to the Guru, the accumulation of merits, the removal of intellectual and emotional obscurations, the meditation on impermanence and death—all the realities of the world of appearances are like a dream, an apparition, an echo, a mirage, a reflection, a magic show. Since it is but a mirage or the moon's reflection in water, while nothing as such, do not for a moment concretize whatever appears in this darkness of untruth,

When one exercises the fusion of the concentrative and post-concentrative states, undisturbed by day or night, there comes a state of happiness, translucence and undividedness, present as such and free in its emergence. When the meditation present by itself is not interrupted, the delusive dream that constitutes our world with no truth to it turns into a radiant light and in the fusion of day and night, Saṃsāra and Nirvāṇa lose their coercive hold in freedom.

While vision involves duration, meditation-restlessness, enactment-conditions, and fruition-fallacy, true understanding stays in undivided pristine awareness, never stepping out of itself nor changing into something other than itself.

At that time there is only one reality and one has firmly seated oneself in what is not something to be meditated upon in its primordial state. Thereafter the goal, absolute happiness, need not be looked for. Intrinsic perception with whatever comes before it is the spontaneity of the three patterns of Being, and being-for-oneself as well as being-for-others comes without effort, and intrinsic perception in all its richness without limitations rules supreme.

The yogi who in his lifetime has won this freedom, will have the experience of the dissolution of the constituting elements of solidity, coherence, temperature, movement and consciousness in a radiant light, and when pristine awareness as the subjective pole has thus fused with the aesthetic continuum as the objective pole,[5] he has seated himself firmly in his primordial place.

The two existential patterns[6] that are there for others are formulations of pristine awareness, and their appearance before the beings like a dream is their necessary value. This is the actuality of intrinsic awareness and the mystery of mind; in a moment it is there as the peak of utter freedom.

Its increasing value is like the waxing of the moon from its first day to its fifteenth day. Although there may seem such an increase in this world, actually there is neither increase nor decrease. Similarly, although one may exercise oneself in habitually seeing true understanding, true understanding itself does not move, and this absence of movement is the value of habituating oneself to it.

The brighter the moon the smaller the shadow or, as others say, the smaller the shadow the brighter the moon; so also true understanding increases by the waning of the belief in duality or, by the increase in true understanding, the emotions grow less disturbing. Even if one says that the values of renunciation and of true understanding reach their climax, the fact is that the pure fact of Being remains unchanged, its actual presence never stops, and the absolutely real remains pure in its freedom of conditions assuming many forms.

In brief, until the emotions become true understanding there is no other way but to give up these five poisons. If one does not know this mystery of our existence free in itself, one is deceived by the belief in the duality of the emotions and their counterparts.

When in the end the subject-object duality does not lose its coercive hold in freedom, however loudly one may speak, it is but the voice of Māra; however positive one's concentration may be, it is but the result of a former pleasant feeling; however much one may exert oneself, one merely moves within the confines of cause and effect belonging to Saṃsāra. Better it is to broaden the vision, to attend to it in all details and to enact it without coercion and purposiveness.

When, in this wide sphere where there is no duality between what arises and its freedom in rising, things are allowed to rise in such a way that they have nothing to show for themselves, this becomes the sign that the yogi has crossed the ocean of worldliness.

He is not fettered by the object and he has no attachment to the subject. Everything, perfect in its self-sameness, becomes the blissful center of creativeness as Dharmakāya. He has no fear in crossing a mountain pass, in traversing a valley or passing over an abyss, and having reached his destination—he has left all expectations and apprehensions behind.

In such a practice there are four experiences which come with the intensity of warmth felt in pursuing the path that has nothing to do with subjectivism:

a) When all the preconditions for this practice are present due to one's merits acquired through previous positive actions and the Guru's compassion and one's knowledge about the appropriate time and the means, then there comes the visionary experience of the immediately intuited absolutely real [*chos-nyid mngon-sum*] at the moment when one truly understands the self-existing intrinsic perception unlimited in its scope to be without trends in its free rising.

b) When one has found, by the investigation of what appears as the without and the within, that everything is Dharmakāya, there are no longer such contrivances as acceptance or rejection with respect to whatever may manifest itself, and when this unique creativeness of truly understanding everything is present and becomes ever more intense, such detrimental conditions as the without and the within, negation and affirmation become the path. There is freedom in its rising and happiness in its presence, and when through its practice various values inherent in intrinsic perception such as the divine eye, the higher cognitions and mystical powers are manifest, one will know this as the visionary experience of intensification of the experience [*nyams-snang gong-'phel*].

c) When this practice growing ever more intensive has become the central force, intrinsic perception—luminous and open and a bare pristine awareness—is ever like a stream, there being neither elation nor depression, neither agitatedness nor non-agitatedness, neither a concentrative nor a post-concentrative state. When its value, the feeling of warmth has reached its highest degree, one has the visionary experience of intrinsic perception having reached its limits [*rig-pa tshad-'phebs*].

d) When one no longer moves from this state and does not find anything determinate to cling to, one is beyond the object of one's desire that falls within the range of renunciation and of what leads to it. Everything is perfect in its self-sameness and has nothing about it conducive to purposeful clinging. When preoccupation with the things of the without and the within has subsided, one has the visionary experience of what is meant by the end of the absolutely real [*chos-nyid zad-pa*].

Thereafter intrinsic perception has reached its culmination in the ground [of Being], and the form-patterns of beings pass into Dharmakāya. In this freedom that is beyond appearance and nothingness one has seated oneself firmly in one's primordial place.

When one has become accustomed to these experiences, the path of one's spiritual progress will not fail and can be illustrated by three features of dreaming:

1) When a bad dream is turned into a good one by one's having become accustomed to the free rising of the world of appearances and the mind perceiving it, there is as its sign the unique flavor of positiveness since the evil karma has been wiped out. This is like smoke rising from a fire or a sprout coming from a seed.

2) As for the simultaneity of the grasping of the dream image and the momentary feeling of freedom, which comes through further habituating oneself to this experience, there is as its sign the freedom

resulting from the counteragent to dreaming having lost its coercive hold.

3) Lastly, when one is fully accustomed to the experience having become the center of the spiritual life, dreaming is stopped and day and night there is present the experience of a radiant light and its sign is the fact that all concepts of Saṃsāra have completely disappeared.

Since there is a unitary feeling in what is by itself beyond frustration, one is now close to seating oneself firmly in one's primordial place. As the three gates to the three world-spheres have found their freedom in the three existential patterns, one passes into a peace that is not restricted to a realm of quietness.

In Mind-as-such which from the very beginning has had nothing to do with proof or disproof, its genuine realm, which is not in need of counteragents against artificiality, presents itself spontaneously without there being anything to meditate upon or anyone meditating, when it has been freed from all bias.

Thus the noetic capacity in its ordinary self-existing freedom has passed beyond the confines of subject and object, no without or within being discernible. In itself free of negation and affirmation, it presents itself as genuineness and is free in having nothing to show for itself in such a way as to make it possible to say that whatever it may be it will be this or that.

This all-encompassing pristine awareness in which there is no need for acceptance or rejection, is spontaneous, unlimited bliss that is nowhere found as something. Absolute freedom resting in its primal freedom cannot be concretized into all and everything or into being and non-being, having nothing to show for itself and not grasping subjectively.

Ah! since intrinsic perception, operating effortlessly, is thoroughly free from any one-sidedness since its very beginning, it remains free in its sphere of self-sameness. Since as the ruler, perfect in spontaneity, it has never been born nor will ever cease, it stays nowhere, cannot be objectified, and is in itself ineffable, so everything is this sphere of uncontrived genuineness.

Ah! intrinsic perception comes laughing at the miracle of appearance that has since its beginning been pure in itself. Since the agent of appearance in whom neither object nor mind exist, is devoid of any essence, he cannot be pointed out as 'this he is' and so he remains the freedom that has nothing to show for itself.

In this unique state where appropriate means [*thabs*] and appreciative awareness [*shes-rab*][7] are perfect in their self-sameness, everything is motionless and remains in the self-sameness of reality. In this state no planets and stars are observed, no minutes counted; it is beyond time and the connections with it; the four continents are absent; there is no world-mountain nor are there sun and moon; there are no maṇḍalas nor is there a recitation of mantras nor a practice of austerities; there are no objects and there is nothing of mystical channels [*rtsa*], predispositions [*khams*] and focal points [*'khor-lo*]. Since the external world is not objectified into something in its appearance, the five objects in the sphere of the world are essentially nothing as such.

Nothing has ever come into existence, but all that is is a self-existing divine mansion; its creator is not objectively observed, but he is the real divine force [*lha*]. The coming and going of thoughts is the great play of pristine awareness; the objects before the mind are the clouds of offering; pristine awareness is divine worship; the assembly of divine forces is perfect in spontaneity, words are mantras, the emotions become forms of pristine awareness; the state of fulfillment [*rdzogs-rim*] being self-existent, need not be reached but is in itself spontaneously present.

The state of transcendence [*pha-rol-phyin-pa*] in which the spiritual levels and the spiritual paths are perfect in themselves is a state of pure unity that does not reside in a 'middle' [*dbu-ma*]. Since not the slightest trace of renunciation, of what aids it, of failure or of obscurations is found, whatever presents itself is meditation, uncreated, spontaneous.

Since that which can be analyzed and that which cannot, black and white, good and evil, actions and their effects are all relative to each other, they are ultimately nothing as such, and without rejecting these images know them to be utter freedom that passes beyond everything.

Through good and evil actions the heights and depths of Saṃsāra are established; when one has gone beyond karma one has naturally passed beyond suffering. When one neither accepts nor rejects, one certainly becomes free from evil influences, but even if good should be realized, one should not fetter oneself by hankering after it.

Then, instead of searching for the real that has nothing to do with acceptance or rejection, to attempt to establish logical proofs is to engage in meaningless, delusive, foolish things. Rather should one always listen to and think about the teaching by competent persons, and should attend to what is the unfailing preparation for true understanding.

In lonely places and mountain solitudes one should control the mind and be concerned with the ultimately real. Instilling the ideas of impermanence and of disgust with the world in one's mind, one should strive and realize the Dharma deep within one's heart.

If now in this life one does not travel the path towards liberty, it may be difficult in the future to find again the favorable condition for becoming a human being. Having hoisted the banner of victory in solitude, what else is there to attain if you should die now?

And while your bodily existence that is but an apparition may fade when day and night you thus strive for the ultimate, Mind-as-such, without birth and death, remains seated on the throne of unchanging Dharmakāya. This is the highest realization and the real meaning of life. Persons of mediocre and low intelligence may find freedom in the Bardo state or later reach the path leading to freedom from Saṃsāra when each action has its result, and when Mind-as-such remains firmly seated in great bliss; this is the quintessence of certainty.

Having set out on a path that leads to error one will never find the essentially and absolutely real because of the many pitfalls on this path. If one succumbs to this life, the future has no meaning. Therefore seek a vision that is unfailing and attend to it unceasingly.

When there is neither love nor compassion nor an enlightened attitude there is certainly something other than the Mahāyāna path. When one meditates on what is given in the ordinary way and then gives up, there is certainly the differentiation into entities of reality other than a self and an individual self. When one busies oneself with a meditation on the without, on concrete entities and on what is in between, there is certainly no chance for a true understanding of non-duality. When one does not bother about renunciation, disgust with the world, and mortality, one is certainly fooled by the demon of desires for this life. When, in spite of meditation, the values lying within us are not brought out, there certainly come the feelings of elation and depression reflecting the depth and thickness of pitfalls and obscurations.

If insight [*lhag-mthong*] is not watered by tranquillity [*zhi-gnas*] it is a mere picture of understanding, but not insight. Although one may talk about non-duality as if it were an intellectual object, one merely associates with the five poisons, unable to deal with unfavorable conditions. And if tranquillity is not tempered with the creativeness of insight there is but a state of mental darkness, but not tranquillity.

A concentration in which there is attachment, even if it is of a positive nature, remains a meditation resulting in animal states because the precondition for higher states is saturated with feelings of elation and depression. But when there is never any attachment there is the creativeness of pristine awareness operating through insight. Since this has been pointed out by competent persons, every form of meditation becomes an aid to enlightenment when there is the true understanding of the immaculate. An uncontrived happiness, translucence and undividedness rise from the depth of one's being. Anything that is not this is not the absolutely real and certain.

If one does not understand this mystery of intrinsic perception one is fettered by chains of acceptance and rejection that hold one away from real meditation.

When desires are few, non-desires can descend like rain; when expectations are not fulfilled, fear is continuously harmful. Although there may be fleeting feelings of happiness, translucence and non-dividedness in body, speech and mind, they are of no use, but are like a jar that breaks in the hands of a child. It is better to look for true understanding, genuine and settled in itself, which is the very place from which the values of one's being, uncreated and unfading, rise.

Even if one brandishes the spear of a glittering and brilliant perception in which all concepts have been suppressed when the posture of the body has been straightened, speech restrained and mind brought under control, simply by having suppressed ideas and feelings in the subjective sphere, this perception moves within the area of the four concentrations, the formless worlds and Saṃsāra.

Where the apparent object before the senses, the luminous appearance without interfering concepts and the five emotional poisons, is naturally free, there is the sphere of absolute pristine awareness.

In this preoccupation with what has to be renounced in the subtle aspect of their perception subject to elation and depression and an intermediate phenomenon, these asses are eager to make renunciation by referring to what is to be renounced as subtle, coarse and crude.

They inspect a former cognitive situation by a subsequent one and, counting the number of these situations as they come and go, in mere sentimentality declare this to be the vision of the genuine. Such meditation which considers the prolongation of the passage of concepts as the real non-duality, is plain error. However much they may exert themselves, the fact is that when out of this network of concepts a later one emerges, a previous one has faded and the claim to natural freedom remains in the before and after, but is not natural freedom.

Indulgence in the pleasures of the senses in following the path of action [*thabs-lam*] is usually the cause for going into evil forms of life because of the attachment to sensuality. Even if one obtains a happy form of life one is born in a lowly status. To say that yoga is the only possible way, is a mark of having gone astray and of being engulfed in obscurations. It is then difficult to see the meaning of true understanding.

Those who alternate between the two accumulations of merits and knowledge, the developing stage and the fulfillment stages, being and non-being, have little success, however hard they try to find what is called certainty. Heaven cannot put an end to Saṃsāra.

In brief, pitiable are those who travel the lowly path of error because they lack opportunities coming from a previous life. If only all would attain the unerring path and find freedom accordingly!

The path that is unerring is the greatness of the openness of Being and compassion united; freedom at every moment, present in itself, is the path of Dharmakāya. The self-sameness of tranquility which is just being present is the 'means' [*thabs*], and of pure insight which in constantly arising is appreciative discrimination [*shes-rab*], is, in the unity of the two, self-settled, free from all artifacts. What is disturbing through change is overcome by steadiness.

In what way this state, in which there is neither elation nor depression and in which the emotions have been uprooted, may manifest itself, it is Dharmakāya, naturally free; in what way it may be present, this state of self-sameness, where no duality obtains, is the peacefulness of Mind-as-such, when there is no need to accept or to reject.

Let this practice through which one accustoms oneself to the pristine awareness dealing with the absolutely real, the genuine fact of Being, proceed uninterruptedly. This is the natural freedom of genuine Being; it is the highest form of meditation, the most profound and unsurpassable experience. In it the very essence of Being is gathered in ever-growing intensity, the quintessence of all peak experiences of the indestructible reality.

Chapter two of 'The Natural Freedom of Mind' in the rDzogs-chen philosophy, dealing with the realization of freedom on the path as travelled by persons of mediocre and low intelligence.

The Climax

Goal realization coming spontaneously is of two kinds: incidental and final.

A. In the incidental realization values are achieved through attention to the vision: the emotions and the subject-object division lose their coercive power in freedom; firmness is achieved as regards the without and within; the divine eye, higher forms of awareness and mystical powers are gained; true understanding deepens and compassion for others grows.

At that time there are present in this pristine awareness with its intrinsic perception, every moment, the following values:

Appearance [*snang-ba*] is the appropriate means [*thabs*], the developing state, the accumulation of merits; the emotions and concepts that come with the idea of an objective world have been left behind. Openness [*stong-pa*] is the appreciative discrimination [*shes-rab*], the fulfillment state, the accumulation of knowledge; the obscurations by the knowable that come simultaneously with the idea of a subject have lost their hold in freedom.

Miserliness, hypocrisy, anger, laziness, restlessness, fickleness of mind, stupidity, faintheartedness, lack of interest, and infatuation—these ten facets of Being become perfect as the ten transcending functions [*pha-rol-phyin*] of generosity, good manners, patience, energy, concentration, appreciation, appropriate means, power, interest, and pristine awareness.

When through the Guru's grace true understanding arises, the superb joy and pleasure that is born in us is the first spiritual level called 'The Joyful One' [*rab-dga'*]; when the emotions have lost their hold in freedom there is the second level 'The Stainless One' [*dri-ma-med-pa*]; when there is happiness, lucidity, and non-dividedness there is the third level 'The Illumining One' [*'od-byed-pa*]; when the concepts that rush forward have lost their hold in freedom there is the fourth level 'The Flaming One' [*'od 'phro-can*]; when actions have no longer an objective reference there is the fifth level 'The One Difficult to Conquer' [*sbyang dka'-ba*]; when true understanding is distinctly present there is the sixth level 'The One which is Present' [*mngon-du gyur-pa*]; when there is freedom from Saṃsāra there is the seventh level 'The One which goes Far' [*ring-du song-ba*]; when true understanding is unshakable like Mount Sumeru there is the eighth level 'The Unshakable One' [*mi g'yo-ba*]; when everything is in its best state there is the ninth level 'The One Lasting Good Discrimination' [*legs-pa'i blo-gros*]; when the individual mind is as all-encompassing as the sky there is the tenth level 'Cloud of Dharma' [*chos-kyi sprin*]. When in the combination of the accumulation of merits and of knowledge one becomes accustomed to seeing what is meant by true understanding, this state is called the 'level of goal of freedom' [*grol-ba'i 'bras-bu'i sa*].

Freedom throughout the three aspects of time is the completeness of the Tripiṭaka; purity of the three gates of action in body, speech and mind is the purity of the three trainings in self-discipline, mind-control, and appreciative discrimination; all-liberation is the enactment of reality, and true Understanding taking charge of our life is the supreme yoga.

The fourfold classification of Tantra distributed over nine gradations: Śrāvakas and Pratyekabuddhas are concerned with their own problems, followers of the Mahāyāna with those of others (as well); true understanding belongs to the Kriyā, familiarization with it to the Upa; enactment to Yoga; appropriate means and appreciative discrimination are distributed over the Mahā and Anu; and perfection in itself belongs to the Ati, and they have mantras and contemplations sustained by pristine awareness.

When natural freedom, detailed into moments, is present, it is the one topic for what is understood as the spiritual levels, the paths and Buddhahood. Genuine pristine awareness, in which the ordinary operations of a mind have ceased, is Mahāmudrā; perfection in self-sameness, coming in absolute spontaneity, is the one and overarching reality.

B. The final realization is the primordial state that cannot be located anywhere; it is the ultimate realm of Dharmakāya, inconceivable and ineffable.

When the aesthetically felt continuum and its pristine awareness have fused in uniqueness of flavor, the three existential patterns of Being that are revealed in the process of enlightenment, are spontaneously present. In the fusion of such subtle awareness and its field which is vast like the sky, all-comprehensiveness is present in a continuous coming to life. The absolutely real is there, perfect in its spontaneity, since it has nothing to do with proof or disproof, and it is like the sky, not having come into existence as some thing or other and not passing out of it.

Out of it comes the pure sTug-po bkod-pa realm and from its maṇḍala, perfect in its spontaneity, shining in a luster that glows by itself, there issue rays which are the perfect marks of the teachers of the five Buddha life-worlds. From each cluster of five pristine awarenesses —the pristine awareness of the aesthetically felt continuum of reality, the pristine awareness receptive and revealing like a mirror, the pristine awareness of the self-sameness of all that is, the pristine awareness of the individual features of all that is, and the pristine awareness of the fact that all is as it should be—there come the circles of those to be led to enlightenment, self-manifesting in the ten regions and over the four aspects of time, each circle having five worlds arranged like a heap of sesame grains, and filling all space, above, below, and in between. The gates and architraves, the raised platforms and railings are ornamented as befits the various life-worlds.

This state of being as a single maṇḍala in which everything is perfect in its spontaneity, is pervaded by its perfection in self-sameness in such a way that no circumference or center can be found. It is the three aspects of time, and yet has no time and still is Kun-tu bzang-po time.[8] It is the state of the foundation, perfect, not stepping out of itself nor turning into something other than itself.

Out of it come the five life-worlds of real Nirmāṇakāya;[9] 'Og-min, mNgon-dga', Rin-chen yongs-gang, Padma-brtsegs, and Las-rab-grub. In each of them, throughout time, the teacher holds up the mirror of beauty to the assembly in the ten spiritual levels in the five life-worlds. Through clusters of rays he purifies the observations of the ten spiritual levels and performs the charismatic act of setting the beings on the path of the all-light. This field appears to the assembly of the superior Buddha-sons.

From the rays that issue from the face of the Sambhogakāya there come the Buddha manifestations in the form of brGya-byin, Thags-bzang, Śākya-thub-pa, Seng-ge rab-brtan, Kha-'bar de-ba, and Ava-glang-mgo who in the world of the gods, demons, men, animals, spirits, and denizens of hell lead the evil-doers to the realm of peace.

Through their various manifestations as artisans, or ordinary beings, through ponds, bridges, flowers, trees, medicines, jewels, lamps and many other things they provide pleasure to the beings and perform ultimately positive actions.

When there is no one to be guided, the guiding agency subsides. This can be known in three ways:

a) The disappearance of the various manifestations and of the guiding of the beings is like the disappearance of the reflection of the moon in the water when there is no large vessel with water.

b) When the mere play of rays coming and going ceases, on the level where those that are to be guided live, the five life-worlds of the natural manifestations of the guiding agency fade into the self-manifested Sambhogakāya. This is like the moon setting in the sky.

c) When the self-manifested Sambhogakāya dissolves in Dharmakāya, the great maṇḍala of reality resides in itself, not shining outwardly, there being no before or after, no increase or decrease, no going forth or change. This is like the moon, remaining the same, despite the fact that it seems to wax and wane.

But when there is someone to be guided, then everything will appear as before.[10] This is the final goal of freedom.

Chapter three of 'The Natural Freedom of Mind' in the rDzogs-chen philosophy, dealing with spontaneity of the goal.

Thus, this sun of elegant sayings has been made to shine by the appearance of its stainless rays. In order to clear up this present time of strife, shrouded in the darkness of evil views, the sure path to certainty has been prepared. May, through this good, all beings sharing the same plight as I, without exception, find freedom in primal, overarching reality and realize the values that come through renunciation and understanding. May they become Dharmarājas spontaneously working for the benefit of others.

This 'Natural Freedom of Mind' has been composed for the benefit of future generations by the yogi Dri-med 'od-zer (Klong-chen rab-'byams-pa), having been blessed by the sublime teacher from Uḍḍiyāna, Padmasambhava, at O-rgyan-rdzong, an ornament of Gangs-ri thod-dkar.

Notes

1. *Byang-chub*, short for *byang-chub-kyi sems*, is, as Klong-chen rab-'byams-pa points out in his autocommentary on his *Chos-dbyings rin-po-che-'i mdzod*, fol. 173a, not an ordinary thought (even if it be termed 'enlightenment thought' [*bodhicitta*], in which way this technical term is often translated), but rather that which makes every thought or mind possible; that which is the creativeness of the absolute rather than the mere play of its creation: "The term *byang* means that, since the pure fact of intrinsic awareness has never been polluted by categorical postulates, Saṃsāra has never been experienced as existing in itself; the term *chub* means that the value of this fact is spontaneously present and hence it may appear in any form whatsoever; and the term *sems* means that, since response to pure and present fact is all-encompassing, it is a luminosity that engulfs both Saṃsāra and Nirvāṇa and is coming to life in each of us as an individual awareness. Since the ordinary mind with its mental events and host of categorical thoughts makes its appearance out of the playful creativeness of the absolute in 'impure' (i.e., postulational) forms, it is not the *byang-chub sems*, and since it contradicts the latter in view of the fact that it belongs to Saṃsāra, there is a great difference between creativeness as such and the play that stems from creativeness." The division into impure, pure-impure and naturally pure is a reference to the Uttaratantraśāstra I 47.

2. *Chos-kyi sku*, Dharmakāya, is used in the sense of the absoluteness of Being and in the sense of the whole of reality experienced in its absoluteness.

3. *Sku* and *ye-shes* refer to 'existential' experiences that are felt and known to be of tremendous value. The symbols such as Vairocana, Ratnasambhava, Amitābha, Amoghasiddhi, and Akṣobhya, used for *sku* point to patterns, not to persons, and the various kinds of 'pristine awarenesses' [*ye-shes*] associated with them, point to functional states of being aware.

4. *Rig-pa.* This term, apart from corresponding to what we understand by 'intrinsic perception', indicates also a state of being at its optimal level.

5. *Dbyings-rig: dbyings* is basically the open dimension of Being and *rig-(pa)* its immediate awareness. Similes for the intimate relationship between the two are the sun and its rays and a house and its occupant. See *sNying-thig ya-bzhi*, vol. 8, p. 35 and vol. 5, p. 399.

6. Sambhogakāya and Nirmāṇakāya, the former representing the empathetic awareness of Being, the latter the apprehendible meaning of Being.

7. *Thabs* and *shes-rab* are key functions on the 'way'. In particular *thabs* is the appropriate way of dealing with a situation, deriving its appropriateness

from the assessment of the situation that is both appreciative and discriminating [*shes-rab*].

8. Kun-tu bzang-po, Samantabhadra, is in rDzogs-chen philosophy a symbol for the absoluteness of Being experienced as wholly positive. As 'time' Kun-tu bzang-po is not merely an event in time, but time-as-such. This rDzogs-chen symbol must not be confused with the Bodhisattva Samantabhadra.

9. A distinction is here made between the 'real' Nirmāṇakāya [*rang-bzhin sprul-pa'i sku*] and its realms of operation, and the 'impure' [*ma-dag*] manifestation to ordinary persons who concretize a vision into a dead and deadening 'world'. This theme is elaborated in the third work of Klong-chen rab-'byams-pa's trilogy.

10. Klong-chen rab-'byams-pa discusses this theme in his *Brub-mtha' rin-po-che'i mdzod*, p. 237.

Bringing the Teachings Alive

Tarthang Tulku

Through generosity enjoyment is attained,
And through discipline, happiness,
Through patience, beauty,
And through diligence, splendor,
Through concentration, peace of mind,
And through intelligence, you reach freedom.

LONG-CHEN-PA, Sems-nyid ngal-gso

As long as we have a mind and body, our own natural being is meditation. This is one of the most important truths we can discover. In the beginning we can only point this out with words. But once we remove all our fixed patterns of perceiving and behaving, our own natural being is already present. When bees extract the nectar from flowers they do not destroy the flower. The flower is there and they leave it there. Similarly, we leave behind our concepts, emotions and ideas—and particularly our ego and self-image—and just use their energy to become meditation.

We might think, "I can concentrate, practice visualization, and develop my awareness. I may stop thoughts or watch thoughts, or transcend all my emotions." But when we are in the meditative state, techniques are not very important. Just remain in that calmness state. Let your body, breath and mind completely relax—without trying, without expecting anything. Whatever activity is going on, simply recognize it and then be still. Once you are within meditation, do not try to find some better experience, or try to be more 'aware'. This only creates fixations about what meditation is and what it should be.

When you are trying to understand conceptual instructions, at that time, yes, listen and try to be aware. But once you enter into this process, accept everything as fine and beautiful, just as it is. You are not trying to improve anything. Nothing is to be made more perfect. Imaginations, fantasies, confusions, experiences of darkness and dullness, and so-called 'problems' arise because we are not in the meditative state. Once we learn to meditate properly, we do not need to worry. Doubts and questions drop away.

There are many different ways I can say 'this is meditation' or 'this is not meditation', but this will not necessarily help you. When our body is calm, our senses become quieter. The breath is quiet, the muscles loosen, and our mind naturally becomes meditation. But if we create many inner dialogues, interpretations and qualifications, we only disturb our inner stillness. When you meditate, you do not need to grasp, interpret, or judge anything. Once you properly accept yourself and your situation, you can meditate any place, any time. This is what I am trying to point out to you.

Whatever situation you are in, try to learn from it rather than escaping or refusing to deal with it. There is really no way we can ultimately escape facing ourselves and taking responsibility for our actions and the quality of our everyday awareness. More important than 'happiness' is balance—balance between your body and mind, and between you and your world.

Certain kinds of intellectual knowledge may require books and extensive preparation before mastery. But meditation does not necessarily depend on anything other than our own understanding. The person who is very intelligent, very clear and intuitive, may directly penetrate the meditative state. However, to practice sincerely and devotedly, deep study of the Buddha's teachings will provide much useful knowledge. The more you study, the more you practice, the more you inwardly understand what 'natural being' means without any further preparation.

The following short talks were given at the Nyingma Institute during classes and seminars, and after ceremonies at the Tibetan Nyingma Meditation Center. These talks are not necessarily sophisticated or intended to present specific philosophical viewpoints, but just what I feel is necessary to say at this time in America. Once you have a preliminary understanding and direct experience of the basic teachings, then you can increase your knowledge by studying the Abhidharma, the Yogācāra, Vijñānavāda, Mādhyamika and Prajñāpāramitā.

Traditionally, certain teachings are presented privately to insure full comprehension, but first it is necessary to learn how to practice meditation properly and to extend the meditation into everything you do. These talks, then, are some of the basic instructions passed on to me by my gurus. What my teachers have said to me, I have tried to share with you.

Meditation

Meditation is absolutely natural, but still we need some explanation or instruction with which to begin. Otherwise we may become fixed in habitual patterns—frustrated, bored or depressed. If we have some idea of where we are traveling, then the terrain seems more familiar.

How does one start to meditate? Someone who is not accustomed to meditation often feels it is something foreign, unusual, unnatural. He may feel that meditation is something outside, an experience to be achieved . . . that meditation is somehow separate from the person, another facet of Eastern psychology or philosophy to study and explore. Meditation, though, is not necessarily something foreign, separate or external. Meditation is within your own mind . . . your whole mind's nature can be your meditation.

Most human knowledge is expressed in dualistic terms—subject and object. We always need to experience 'out there' conceptually. We want to find out something and internally report it back to ourselves. We need to explain our world. But look at it this way . . . to *whom* do we need to explain it? The explanation immediately separates us from the experience. The more we try to interpret the experience, the more we move away from it. We are left with a fixation, some idea concerning the nature of our world, so that our responses and reactions to daily situations do not flow from a natural state of mind. We are always walking outside the wall, just touching the surface, so we do not discover this natural mind. We may spend a long time, years and years, explaining, thinking, analyzing and feeling, but never reach that natural state. By properly meditating, we can find it, because meditation *is* the natural state of mind.

Starting to meditate is very simple . . . just let the body and mind become very relaxed. As much as possible, physically relax your muscles and thoughts . . . not a tight relaxation, but completely loose. The same with your breath—breathe openly and quietly. Actually, there are many techniques, different ways to breathe or visualize or sit. But sometimes, in the beginning, too many instructions may distract and almost hypnotize you. So just very naturally, experience your body, your breath and your mind.

'Natural' means 'unfixed' . . . no expectations, no compulsions, no interpretations, no predetermined plans. When meditation deepens, there is no need to fix it or improve it or perfect it. There is no impatience to go forward or somehow progress, yet everything moves on naturally. This has nothing to do with this or that philosophy, belief or condition, but is the natural state of reality for all of us.

This meditation can deeply affect our whole being. Later on, an 'enlightenment-quality', or a spontaneous inner awareness, will arise without any creator or manipulator. But we need to take the first step by simply and quietly meditating. Since mind, in its true nature, is without duality, not separate from the unity of all things, our whole life may become meditation. Once we understand this, we won't need to fight or push or struggle. Ego and the emotions, discriminations of good or bad, positive or negative, spiritual path or Samsara—they all dissolve. Once we have the experience, spontaneous awareness arises by itself, without effort.

So meditation begins by making everything tranquil . . . by allowing our body and mind to relax deeply and completely, by giving ourselves warmth and nourishment. If you can be very calm and still, and listen to the silence within your mind . . . this becomes your meditation. Even if you are not formally meditating, but just dealing with everyday situations, try to remain loose and relaxed. Each day we reinforce a variety of muscular and mental tensions . . . we feel unhappy and dissatisfied, trapped and walled in by our problems. As the mind builds up the specific world in which we live, habits, desires and judgments become very solid and real to us. Soon we may find we cannot let go of this solid world: we cannot go back to a natural state of awareness or to simple direct experience. During meditation, we can simply focus on the present moment in itself and keep our attention there. By just being there our awareness becomes sharper, looser and more calm.

Giving ourselves warmth and nourishment is much more than just being relaxed. It is a feeling that we can heal all our difficulties by simply letting go, letting everything be just as it is. At first we may feel very calm and peaceful, but then a voice inside us—a speaker, a judge—rises to the surface and creates disturbances, and we lose our inner silence. Let go of that judge in the back of your mind who is constantly making decisions and thinking thoughts. Within your meditation, don't think, don't act: just be open. You are not even trying to

Tarthang Tulku, Rinpoche

meditate. Thoughts come and feelings come . . . but don't follow these bubbles. Just let all your ideas and concepts disappear by themselves without becoming involved or trapped in these fluctuating dramas.

We often find ourselves hearing something, saying something, reading something, thinking something. Then our ego interprets, and all of a sudden we are no longer really listening . . . our inner dialogue has completely spoiled the immediacy of the experience, and real meditation doesn't come. We are always interpreting and adjusting our inner feelings, separating ourselves from the immediate moment and holding on to temporary sensations which seem to make things better. Instead of allowing our understanding of meditation to deepen, we continuously interrupt our inner silence and balance through a variety of conceptual biases and emotional distractions. But if we simply remain silent within the moment—without grasping for some security, without trying to figure out our problems, without trying to do anything—all that remains is awareness. Within this all-pervasive awareness, emotional conflicts and problems begin to lose their holding power and become very cloudlike. Once you stop feeding the problems, they just disappear within awareness itself.

There is another type of meditation in which you visualize or fix some image before the mind. Then you simply watch the image with complete attention. By staying within the immediate moment, it is possible to enter the space between thoughts. But this practice is, in a way, very difficult because thoughts, emotions and fixed concepts always attempt to define, change or control the natural process. Then meditation becomes a struggle. We say, "I should stay with this one image," yet at the same time, we lose ourselves in endless distractions. Then I have another idea of what I *should* be doing . . . so one thought stands on another thought, and the cycle keeps repeating itself, back and forth, until there is no meditation . . . just thoughts. In the end, we have only acted out an elaborate internal game, without ever having begun to meditate. We can play these games within our own minds all our lives, but you should know that nothing meaningful will result.

First we need to observe and identify the deceptions created by our self-image. Until we can see through the mind's posturings and pretenses—all our explanations and excuses—we are only playing . . . we are only trying to satisfy the demands of our self-image without any feeling of real fulfillment. We may often 'talk' about our intrinsic self-nature, but still we cannot see it clearly. We are always playing some game of identifying, separating, acting or posturing. Ideas and explanations generate new ideas and explanations. Our minds go this way and that way . . . is this a game or not? Until you can look *backwardly* at your thoughts, you will not be able to tell. But when you look directly at the patterns of your thoughts and concepts, you may be able to observe the game-player playing the game. From moment to moment—is this our true nature or is this just another game we are playing?

This process of observation is very important because as long as thought vibrations continue to play, our consciousness remains frozen in fixed views. For example, as soon as I hit a gong, sound comes . . . as soon as I hear a word, an image is immediately projected and conceptualized. But *behind* the word or the image is an experience with very precise and exact feeling-tones. By staying within the immediate moment, it is possible to enter the space between thoughts. Once you go 'behind' or 'within' this experience, without involving words, images or concepts, you may discover a certain type of inner atmosphere or environment which has no shape, no form, no specific characteristic, no specific structure. In other words, you do not need to defend or belong to any position. If there is any position—a holding position, an examining position, or any kind of ideal or 'beyond' position . . . or even a 'lostness' position—"Oh, I am lost, my mind is lost, there is nothing but emptiness"—you are still referring to something which is ultimately related to 'me'. If you think about it, you will find that any position belongs to ego.

The famous 19th-century Nyingma master, Pal-trul Rinpoche, once said, "Completely break, cut up, throw away meditation." In other words, as long as you have any concepts of meditation, *throw them away*. If any kind of 'experience' comes, throw it away, don't hold on . . . and that is the best way to meditate. Many yogis love deep meditative states, but they can easily become addicted to them: "I have a powerful meditation," or, "I have many beautiful, dream-like experiences" . . . they are really only stuck there. On the other hand, Pal-trul said, "The best water is rocky water." Why is rocky water the best?—because when water falls from a great height, it is completely agitated and purified. Moving water takes no positions. So the best meditation is one which is flowing and free: there is nothing to hold on to. Once you have a position, you become fixated, you possess something, you focus on something. When another Nyingma master was asked, "You are concentrating, but where is your concentration?" he answered that he has "no position, no specific fixed place," because natural mind has no fixed ideas, no structure, no limitations. Whoever knows meditation well has no fixed position—no goals, no focusing, no subject.

We often see and experience the world and other people with rigid viewpoints, and so we set arbitrary limits and restrictions on ourselves. If we can't describe or label our experience with words or ideas, we feel lost or empty. We think, because this experience is not related to my senses, concepts, or projections, then it has no value. But according to the Madhyamika dialectic, if we transcend dualism, go beyond objectifying concepts, beyond space and time, what is there to lose? If there is anything to lose, it may only be our fear, our fixed ideas, or a tense clinging to an imagined security. Since there is no position, the natural state of mind has nothing *originally* to lose.

Even good meditators may spend twelve years in a cave—completely quiet, with all the windows and doors shut—but still, their thoughts are just going back and forth and running on for a long, long period of time. If you don't learn to meditate properly or accurately, you can waste a lot of valuable time. But if you receive precise instructions, you can transmute many kalpas of negative karma in a very short time. For example, if you don't know how to produce atomic power, you might work for hundreds of years with no result—no explosion. But if you have accurate knowledge, in a certain limited time you may produce a nuclear reaction. The simplest way to discover this secret 'formula' or 'path' that leads to successful, higher meditation is by not identifying, not taking a position, not holding on to anything within the meditation. If you think, "I won't think anything," this too may cause blockages so that your muscles, nervous system or inner organs become tight and constricted. But someone who knows how to enter meditation directly can transcend ordinary labels and concepts very quickly.

This 'secret' knowledge of proper meditation becomes a self-sustaining source of inspiration which is not dependent on words, concepts or specific viewpoints . . . there is no 'center'. Many English words, such as 'center' or 'position' or 'clarity' or 'awareness', are useful but they are too vague to describe the internal process of meditation. For example, if I am 'centered', it means I have a position, I belong to some 'one'. Just forget about trying to identify or judge this 'one'. Become center*less* . . . with no subject, no object, nothing in between.

There is nothing between you and meditation . . . the experience is always very new, very fresh, very clear, beautiful and natural . . . beyond time . . . but at the same time, there is continuity. Everything is just 'as it is'. No 'one' is adding or subtracting anything. If you think about these qualities, then while practicing meditation you may understand: not fixed, not projecting, no position, no center . . . clarity, newness, naturalness. But as long as words and explanations or doubts and anxiety continue to filter into your meditation, meditation is lost in that very moment.

One of my teachers once explained that great fighters, such as the samurai, practice and examine every move very carefully before they engage in battle. They sharpen their swords and perfect every gesture beforehand. As soon as they encounter the enemy, they no longer need to practice . . . they are completely prepared. There's no doubt how to cut or how to maneuver . . . each movement has been perfected and no questions remain. They no longer think about it, they just do it . . . and every move is automatically perfect and flawless. But in meditation you like to think about this and that, you doubt and worry, and then real meditation disappears. When you study, or when you are just walking or sitting, stay in the spontaneous, present moment. Everything becomes practice and preparation until you have complete confidence and there are no questions left. There is no need to ask, how is it? what is it? who is it? . . . no need to report back to yourself elaborate and lengthy descriptions of your progress. Just meditate completely and directly without any restrictions or 'second thoughts'.

Without this kind of inner attitude or character, enlightenment can be a very long process. Each day, moment to moment, expand your inner openness, and awareness will grow freely, naturally. There is no further preparation required. You may meditate back and forth for twenty years, or, in a very short moment of time, completely and accurately meditate with much quality and value. When you meditate with this openness, and when you leave all doubts and hesitation behind, you automatically begin to discover the teachings within through your own spontaneous inner guidance. On the other hand, you might ask, "Why do we need the six perfections, why preliminary practice, why visualization?" All these questions arise because we cannot directly penetrate the secret path of inner meditation. But once you understand meditation, once you have the key, you can intuitively remain in that state of awareness no matter what you do.

Meditation is not just a technique or a way to escape this world. Meditation is like our parent, the original source of our being. We always live within this consciousness, for it is our intrinsic nature . . . our own home and not a separate place. But usually we feel separate and don't realize this. If we learn to use meditation properly, we can touch our innermost being with no walls dividing . . . we can come into contact with our own wholeness.

So whatever happens, make friends with meditation. Most of the time we create so many problems—we don't like our body or our mind or our personality. In the view arising from meditation, everything is fine and beautiful. However we work, however we think, however we talk—everything has beauty . . . each situation naturally has its own intrinsic value. If we can bring the light of this meditation into our lives, everything will become happier and more positive—not fixed or solid, but flexible and spontaneous. When any situation or condition can be accepted, life becomes easy and light.

These are very simple instructions, but they are important. In a way, meditation is not so difficult to achieve because it is part of you already. But proper meditation requires great intelligence and diligence, otherwise you will only create more concepts, inner dialogues and speculations. When you have no thoughts left, no problems and no extremes, then your whole mind's nature can be your meditation.

Watching the Watcher

Rinpoche: Now tell me, who is watching the watcher?
Student: When I was watching my thoughts, I would have the watcher watch my thoughts, and then I would watch the watcher. . . .
Rinpoche: I would like to listen carefully to what you are saying. . . . Please, one word at a time.
Student: Okay, when I had thoughts, I would watch the thoughts. . . .
Rinpoche: When you have thoughts, then. . . .
Student: . . . then I would remove myself from the thoughts and just watch them. . . .
Rinpoche: When you have thoughts, what do you do?
Student: I would watch them.
Rinpoche: Wait a minute. Again . . . when you have thoughts . . . you recognize there is a thought. Now, which one is the watcher?
Student: Well, what I was trying to do was to watch the watcher watching the thoughts.
Rinpoche: Okay, now what do you understand that to mean? . . . Okay, now I am you. I have become you. There is a thought. I watch that. Now what do I do? Which one is the watcher? Let's use very simple language. This is my thought, and I'm watching there [points out a wooden object in front of him]. I am watching this thought. Now what do I do?
Student 2: Okay, I'll guess!
Rinpoche: Okay, you guess, good! Here is my thought, I see it here. Now, what am I supposed to do next?
Student 2: So, the next thing I do is say, "*That's* not me, and *this* is me."
Rinpoche: That's another thought!
Student 2: That's the problem. . . .
Student 3: Just look at the person that's watching.
Student 1: Yes, that was what I was trying to say, but when I did that, it would feel like I would go out of my body into a very more spacious way of being which felt strange to me.

Rinpoche: All right . . . but still, whenever you have feelings, it may be possible that your thoughts are sort of vibrating. If thoughts and concepts do not even exist, how can you have feelings? In other words, as soon as you recognize a feeling, you are already involved with a thought. If there is a recognition, then someone must be having that recognition. Do you understand what that means? Tell me.
Student 1: It is the one who is watching the thoughts, or the one who perceives what is happening to oneself.
Rinpoche: Right. You need to jump there, chase the *face* of the watcher. That's all. Do you understand? Directly chase *there*, not somewhere else . . . in the very first moment . . . like chasing a tiger. When you are chasing his face, there is no second thought. When you chase completely, you become the experience. Both the chaser and the chased meet together and immediately become the experience. No other thought is involved. You are meeting face to face. If you do this with all thoughts, you will not miss anything.

More intellectually we may say, "My awareness recognizes." In this sense, your awareness has shape. It's like a shell, a specific form or a characteristic pattern with which you receive that thought. You need to chase that thought into this totality. The looker, seer, receiver, perceiver, recognizer . . . just catch it! This immediately becomes the experience. There is no going 'this way' or 'that way'. Nothing is left behind. Every thought is received into this totality. No other thought exists. At that time—at that very moment—your awareness instantly becomes illuminated. There is no division between anything. There is no introducer and no introduced. That very first moment becomes the experience itself.

Normally, you think thoughts as if they were coming from somewhere else. Thoughts do not come from some other place. For example, the recognizer catches a thought. But while he is chasing this thought, he is saying "I am not the one who is chasing you, someone else is chasing you!" This is very tricky. But actually, the first thought is already gone, and the experiencer is creating another thought. The experiencer himself *is* the thought. But the experiencer insists, "I am not the one, I am not the one. You should ask someone else." But actually, the one who is giving answers—that's the one you need to catch. That's the one you need to chase and keep face-to-face. When you finally catch the thought, there is no longer any hunter. There is no longer any recognizer. The recognizer, the watcher, has become the experience.

Student 2: If I give up trying to catch the thoughts that the recognizer is creating, is that the same thing as catching a thought? I mean, suppose I give up meditating entirely and forget all this. Will I be at the same place if I did this and succeeded?
Rinpoche: No. I don't think you understand which thought you need to catch. I am trying to illustrate to you which one you need to bite into with your awareness. If you bite into the right thought, it has meaning and value. What you are saying is that whether you bite into the right thought or the wrong thought, your meditation is the same. It is not the same.

Let's say, "I'm trying to watch any thought . . . oh, there's a thought. I can see it. There it is. I need to catch it." Meanwhile, another thought comes . . . because in order to catch it *your* way, there must be another thought. Otherwise you do not think you have caught it. That is your problem. You must create one thought in order to catch another thought. If there is no hand, how can you grasp? Another thought is there–who catches it? Then another thought–who catches that one? In this way, your thoughts are split every which way. This can go on endlessly and your meditation will never begin.

I will try to explain this a little differently. I say I see my thought. But actually, you are not seeing the thought. There isn't any thought *there*. This is because the seer is self-manifesting. The seer is *projecting* the thought. The awareness is the awareness of a seer, not a thought. There isn't any thought. The way I see it and the way it is are two different things.

Within that moment I can interpret: there is a thought I can feel it, see it, project it and experience it happening. But the thought itself is actually a projection of the seer. The thought is not separate from the seer. Between the thought and the seer, there are no gaps, no words or concepts, no second thoughts. When you directly face the seer, your awareness and the seer become one. The shell which divides the subject from the object completely breaks open. All that is left is the experience itself, or, you might say, pure energy.

Now how do you break that shell? We must think about this very intelligently–who sees? who is experiencing? Just sit very quietly, gently go inside, and watch the thought. When you totally become the seer, the seer no longer exists as a separate entity. Your awareness and the watcher become united. There is no separation or division, no subject or object. When this occurs, you naturally feel a surge of energy. No separate forms exist. You feel a kind of shock . . . like a bubble that expands and expands until it pops. When you watch the watcher, there is no longer any thought form. All that is left is meditation . . . there is no subject, no object, no dual mind. *The thought disappears and the watcher disappears*. The mind is totally silent. Literally we are saying, watch the thought, but eventually you will understand that the thought and the watcher are the same.

Watching the watcher immediately and directly leads to the experience itself. When you meditate or sit there, there is a kind of light, or energy, or awareness. Just stay there. That is your meditation. If you try to go beyond that, you will create another thought.

When I'm talking, do you hear something? Then meditate on the hearer. Do you feel something? Then meditate on the feeler. Do you see something? Then meditate on the seer. As your awareness develops naturally, you will begin to understand there is really no watching and no watcher.

When you have pain or unhappiness, or any problems, just stay within the thought. Whatever thoughts come–good thoughts, bad thoughts, angry thoughts, confused thoughts, or desires–become the anger, become the confusion, become the attachment. Within the very first thought-moment, keep it alive, feel it. When you are emotionally upset, stay within the emotion. Try to do this. It is not very difficult. You do not need to escape or deny or hide from your feelings. At this time, do not try to research, analyze or figure out the pattern of your thoughts or problems, or try to create new thoughts. Just go into the center of the thought without trying to evaluate it. Just be the thought and completely accept it without grasping or holding on to it. Gradually a new awareness will develop inside this experience.

Mostly we have the concept that meditation should be a certain way . . . something calm, relaxed or beautiful. We fail to realize that meditation involves every mental event. When you are working or when you have strong emotions–as long as there is mind–still you can meditate. There is no specific time or place which necessarily excludes your meditation.

As your meditation deepens, the qualities of openness and clarity extend to whatever you do. Any activity becomes transformed to meditation naturally. So you do not need to say, "This part is meditation and this part is not." Whatever comes up becomes your meditation. Emotions become the fuel of meditation, but the emotions themselves are not meditation–this is samsaric mind. The more 'heated' we become, the more energy we have. But if we go directly into the center of the emotion, there's nothing there! We can transmute this samsaric mind because the mind itself is emptiness–not a conceptual emptiness or loneliness, but an experience that becomes total openness, total honesty with each situation . . . direct seeing, total freedom from obscurations, complete receptivity.

Therefore, whether you are 'officially' meditating or not does not matter. Actually, we are already meditating naturally. Our mind reality, which is like Buddha-mind–uncreated mind–exists totally awakened in the present moment. Since we are always within that true nature, we can always rely on it completely. Our basic 'not-knowing' is due to our conceptual mind, but conceptual mind cannot judge this intrinsic reality.

For example, I am dreaming: I have a child and he is dying. I'm crying and screaming. But there is a man over there saying, "Don't worry, you never had a child, the child has never died, don't be so upset!" And still I say, "That's not true, I still have a child. . . ." Even if someone from another realm talks to me in the dream state, until I wake up, my suffering is still there–even if it is not true! I never had a child, but it doesn't matter. I am still suffering! Even if you are suffering, you don't have a child!

You could say, "If I am already enlightened, why do I need these things?" But . . . you are still suffering. Until you become free, you need to do these things. Until you wake up from that dream, or that illusion, meditation is necessary to rediscover your original mind nature.

The Enlightenment-mind

We are trying to understand our mind. What is the best way to develop a positive mind? We can philosophize and try to relate our theories to our direct experience, but basically this involves understanding our own mind.

At first, mind seems so familiar, simple, easy. But the more you investigate, the more mysterious mind becomes. Mind is like a painter or an artist: mind creates Samsara, mind creates Karma, mind creates confusion, delusion, misery and suffering. Mind encompasses everything that is happening. Mind is the parent and Samsara and Nirvana are its children.

If I enjoy, it is through mind. If I suffer, it too is through mind. If I hate, my mind hates. If I resent, it is my mind that resents. If I am enlightened, it is my mind that is enlightened. Everything is based on mind. So it is essential that we understand this mind.

Our minds are, in a sense, already completely illumined, capable of seeing truth directly, nakedly, but we fail to see this. Instead of seeing our mind for what it is intrinsically, we always have to relate it to something else that we can grasp or hold on to. To describe mind, we often use words which are descriptions for something else: mind is like this or mind is like that. We try to trap the mind through a series of projections or concepts. Rather than experiencing directly, we dissect the experience with our interpretations. We must always figure out what is happening or have some fanciful idea of what we are doing. But as soon as we try to interpret our reality so that it becomes more digestible our immediate experience is no longer nourishing.

We all have to have things our way, otherwise we fear we will be lost. If we think we are lost, then we are really in trouble. No one is allowed to be lost these days. Everyone is supposed to know where it is that he or she is going. Still, many people seem very dissatisfied and inwardly disturbed.

To understand who we are and what we are doing, we must understand the meaning of silence. Within silence there is balance.

When everything becomes simplified through silence, all the tangles of our inner knots and problems gradually dissolve. Silence is not simply the absence of speech. Silence comes from within. It is absolutely calm, without fixation, without preparation. Just pure naturalness. Nothing is required except, simply, to be. If this *means* something to you, then it is not silence. Silence does not hold on to any *thing*. But often, if we cannot hold on to some idea, or some fascination, or some stimulation, we suddenly feel lost. We seem to have no identity, and this threatens us very deeply.

Within silence we can discover who we really are . . . our mind and body becomes transparent. There is no need to guess when we investigate this directly. But often we seek stimulation and excitement. We must always be doing something. If we have a few moments alone, we may become anxious and nervous because we really don't want to face ourselves.

In that moment we may ask, '*Who* is behind what is going on? My eyes move, I hear sound, I discriminate this and that . . . but who is doing all of this?' You have to identify this person. On the common physical level, we think happiness is just pleasing the body. We become confident and relaxed on the outside, but internally we are still deeply worried. The body is still feeling unpleasant with certain nervous tensions that disturb our awareness. We do not even fully appreciate pleasant sensations. We are always looking forward to the next moment, the next enjoyment. Or perhaps we are complaining that we never seem to get what we really want.

Someone more intellectual is not fooled by the deceptions of emotional attachments. They question and investigate what is the nature of their mind. But still, they are merely doing research because there is no certainty–no one has a specific idea of what mind is or how to go about discovering it. Instead they may project a series of imaginations–that's mind or that's mind–but they only point somewhere else. They only point at the mind that thinks, the 'maybe-mind', which is really just a projection of the self-image.

As long as our self-image is present, we seem to belong to someone else. 'Me' and my 'self-image-mind' are like a married couple who are constantly fighting: there are constant disagreements, readjustments, and clinging. Or, just as a married person might say, "I have a pretty wife," or, "I have a handsome husband," the self-image places labels on our meditation experience and judges it in terms of goodness or badness. But do not narrow down your meditation to some sort of statement as to how it is . . . good experience, bad experience. Just forget about these dualistic judgments. There is no one *owning* meditation. There is no your, no possession, no possessor. This experience has no belonging-to. Neither one exists.

Within the mind is a powerful energy that is capable of allowing us to penetrate with insight into the nature of our minds . . . or of completely exploding through our confusion. Just as electricity and atomic energy are capable of producing much power in the material world, the mind is potentially very powerful in the psychic sphere. When we encounter 'impossible situations', such as depression, anxiety, suffering and all sorts of so-called 'problems', this energy becomes too compressed. Mind-problems are a way of compressing this energy, of limiting our field of vision, of squeezing ourselves into an inescapable mental corner. No matter what our situation in life, our problems are constantly going on at deeper, more subtle levels. The ways in which they choose to surface are through our daily inadequacies and frustrations. But these temporary situations are not the real problem. The real problem is more pervasive, deep within the nervous system. If we constantly try to deal with the problem, then as soon as we think we have it solved, another one takes its place. It's like digging in sand on the beach. As soon as we remove a handful of water, more water seeps in.

Trying to control our thoughts, or to think or analyze our way to the root of the deeper problem will not necessarily help. We only get stuck focusing on a bucket of water and do not recognize the ocean. As soon as we think we have just solved one problem or dissatisfaction, another frustration arises. So we just continue to get stuck in an endless progression of projections, solutions and problems. Even screaming and crying only removes the surface tension. At that time our whole body tightens, our muscles compress and almost squeeze out the tears. After the session is over we feel more relaxed or clear. But this is more like shifting weight. Until we wake up, the same problems or patterns continue to arise.

For just one hour we can count our thoughts and see how hundreds of thoughts arise. If our minds are especially tight or tense with the forcefulness of some narrow concentration which is trying to control our thoughts, we become heavy and exhausted. But if we can gently reduce the number of events in our mind, we can reduce the degree of tightness that occurs. If we can just relax, go into the center of the first thought that arises within the mind, then we can open up to our immediate experience in new and positive ways. The past and future, our memories and our projections, will no longer have such a strong hold on our attention. In the immediate moment of meditation, awareness is allowed to arise naturally.

We always seek a good guide. But the best guide is ourselves. We want to find self-fulfillment and nourishment within our experience, *right now*, not some other time in the vague future. It is *now* that we are alive and living. We have a physical body which is very precious. We have many possibilities to find deep satisfaction within all our experiences and situations. First, however, we must develop full confidence in ourselves. The answers, the really important answers, are already within our consciousness, ready to be discovered.

You need to take refuge in nothing else but your own mind. Once you have found yourself completely, you will discover that this inner knowledge, or certainty, has no particular ownership or territory. If a 'problem' arises, you do not necessarily have to identify yourself with that problem. Once you are free, even for a moment, you will find that there is nothing to protect, nothing to hide from. There is no need to go somewhere else. When everything is seen as complete in itself, confidence is spontaneous. You become totally balanced. Anxiety, insecurity, wandering here and there, trying to feed fascinations: these things fade away on their own once you are no longer fixed in a specific problem.

So first we must decide what is really important to us, and then let go of all our attachments to past patterns. Awareness moves freely within the moment, within the present situation, whether we are meditating, talking to someone, or just quietly walking. If we can experience this openness and freedom from the patterns which constantly create problems, these patterns begin to shift. Everything we do becomes more positive and open, more balanced and satisfying.

Experience does not necessarily occur only on the sensational or physical level, nor is experience strictly mental. Experience does not need to be so tightly defined. Interpretation, inner dialogue and conceptual speculation are all forms of grasping, of trying to identify ourselves with a particular state of being, or with a particular view we have of ourselves, or who we think we should be. Such talk can continue on and on, yet Nirvana or enlightenment is not necessarily some *place* that we are supposed to arrive at. Whenever we talk about enlightenment, we are talking through our conceptual mind. Until the time when the enlightenment-mind becomes part of our inner experience, we need to keep developing our mind. When that time comes, there will be no need for any further descriptions or explanations.

What exactly is this enlightenment-mind? Enlightenment is not really something mysterious or other-worldly, but rather the result of an unrestricted and subtle awareness within the activity of our body, speech and mind. It is a subtle energy that is not easily detected because of our own internal blockages. The current is stopped, dammed up within us. Though we speak of these energies on a physical level, they are not necessarily dependent on the laws governing physical substances. This Enlightenment quality is not a 'thing': it has no fixed position, no substance we can point to . . . its nature is more like 'open space'. It is never an awareness of some 'thing', which could just be another projection of our self-image—it is neither a subject- nor object-oriented 'looking'. This experience cannot even be interpreted conceptually, but is a natural openness that takes place when awareness is left to function freely, on its own, without hindrances, interruptions or distractions.

In everyday language, awareness generally means to be 'aware of some thing' . . . to look at objects, to recognize, identify, try to understand, and to re-experience. This is commonsense awareness. But as a living experience, natural awareness is not like that. Awareness is simple and direct, open and responsive, without concepts, words, images or interpretations. Awareness takes place within the very first moment, not before and not after. It is immediate and spontaneous. There is no other 'thing' to obscure the moment—neither a subject nor an object, neither time nor space. All that remains is within this open space, which neither words nor concepts can adequately describe. There is complete freedom from our restless attempts to hold on to something, to be secure in some distraction or some other trance-like fixation. There is no fear and no guilt—no desire to escape or be any other way. This awareness becomes complete self-acceptance and generates a fresh new outlook all of its own.

The experience of our own inner awareness is definitely not a *re*-experience. It is not a memory or a projection. It is not like 'this' and not like 'that'. It is not associated with any 'thing', but a perfect, beautiful, immediate and spontaneous presence. This natural awareness becomes its own experience, but without a tight clinging to the past moment and without trying to project the next moment—without, we might say, any experience or any experiencer. It is totally free of fear, guilt, worry, expectations, projections, fixations, ideas, concepts, judg-

ments, images or taking positions. When we experience or become involved with this open nature, nothing is lacking, for this 'lacking' is simply the projection of our unawakened ignorance. There is nothing to defend and nothing to do, yet at the same time the natural movement of this awareness eliminates all obstacles to seeing things just as they are, and the natural expression of this awareness provides the perspective which makes all positive action possible.

At first we may be rigid, unwilling to let go of security, afraid of falling into just one more answerless confusion. But the more we persevere, open up and loosely relax our tensions, we begin to discover a new space, a new openness and freedom. In the process of this new exploration, old constrictions gradually evaporate and a fearless commitment to our own self-health and growth begins to mature.

But *how* we do this is very important, for we can easily lose our initial insight. Studying the Dharma can help us focus our experience, like a magnifying glass which reveals the intricate weave of small dots in a photograph. The teachings can illuminate the subtle details involved in discovering and distinguishing the various movements of our mind. Common or ordinary knowledge is mostly just an arrangement of interpretations. In the West, for example, it seems that when anyone talks about mind, it is only 'mind-sensing' that is meant. The physical world is projected within the mind so that images, interpretations, and concepts form, but these all maintain the inner quality of subjective, subtle feeling-tones—positive, negative or indifferent, according to the specific situation—in which all our senses and operations of mind (*skandhas*) are involved. This 'feeling-tone' quality of our perceptions and thought processes still retains various residues dependent on sensations. Commonly, such occurrences as thinking, feeling happy or sad, believing, wishing, doubting, and such experiences as seeing, hearing, smelling, tasting and perceiving, represent particular states of mind. But this is not what Buddhism means by 'mind', for mind itself is not limited by any conceptions we might have about it.

Mind itself has no substance. It has no color and no shape. It has no form, no position, no characteristics, no beginning. It is neither within nor without; it cannot be discovered as this or that thing; it is not mixed together with other things, yet is not apart from them. This mind cannot be discovered, invented, destroyed, rejected or accepted. It is beyond reasoning and so-called logical processes. Discriminating awareness and intuition can lead us to the door of this unoriginated awareness, but through the door is a vastness beyond all that can be expressed, and can only be entered nakedly, for it is without beginning and without end, beyond time and beyond all existence—natural, spontaneous openness.

This mind, in the absence of conditions, is without memory and association, and is like muddy water which becomes pure by itself when it is not interfered with. When there is no mind, no minding, no intellect, no sensation, no perception, no memory and no association, what then is the mind of a sentient being? Sentient being can only be spoken of as long as these function-events are operating.

Normally our ideas depend almost entirely on images, on habitual ways of seeing, hearing, sensing and responding. So we merely carry on the same patterns of inadequacy or confusion and continue to experience these patterns according to an inner network of interpretation. This type of functional knowledge, while helpful when we wish to accumulate information, is useless if it merely reinforces premises which fall apart under investigation. This knowledge is like a stream that eventually dries up if it is not supplied by a fresh undercurrent or natural spring of spontaneous awareness. Discriminating, judging and categorizing our experiences and perceptions into subject and object, seer and seen, only solidifies feelings of separateness, and results in a lifeless trickle of actions that perpetuate frustration.

Inner clarity develops once we stop trying to cover over, hide from, or escape dealing honestly with our daily experiences. We begin to accept things as they are, without trying to reconstruct them to fit some idealized or conceptualized pattern, or force things and people to satisfy our self-image. Suddenly, there is no 'one' to defend and no 'thing' to hide.

Throughout this inner development, one of the most important things to remember is not to support or maintain a center. A bird can fly almost forever. As long as there is space, the bird can fly on and on. Similarly, as much as you are able, as long as there is free space, keep going on. Keep yourself open. Do not step back or retrace your steps. If you say, "How's my meditation?", the meditation experience disappears.

In Tibet, people who mine for gold are constantly looking back at what they have just dug up. They continually want to check, "How much did we get? How good is it?" . . . constantly evaluating. Similarly, we continually want to evaluate our meditation. We want to know whether meditation is good or bad. If it's a good meditation, you say, "Oh, how wonderful my meditation was" . . . or, "Oh, I'm having all sorts of problems." Instead, just keep going on. All sorts of openings are there in the space between the thoughts. And once you open up, you won't be able to find any center, nothing to hold on to, nothing to point to and say, "That's it!"

Pretend for a moment that all the planets, stars, meteorites, black holes, gaseous nebula—all objects in the heavens—completely disappear. What we have left is empty space. No inside, no outside: there is nothing that can be stood upon or pointed at. There is no gravity, no direction . . . no position and no judgment. You cannot find any center.

Dual-mind constantly finds its support in identifying with external objects. When the mind loses its hold on any concept, idea, good thought, bad thought, right way, wrong way, true gold, fool's gold, there is no judgment, no loss, no gain . . . because there is no longer any identity. 'Identity' means some 'one' related to some 'thing'. But when you begin to look at the world without these separations or divisions, that which labels experience as 'my', which refers to all perceptions and possessions as 'mine', which prevents us from seeing the world as it is—personal identity—falls away.

Once we completely transcend our subjective viewpoint, our recognizable identity or self-image disappears . . . as though we were stepping away from a mirror. When self-reflecting identity vanishes, there is no projector and no projection . . . there is no one left to project or to receive it. Our initial reaction to losing our sense of identity is to feel deeply threatened. That fear is really a manifestation of the ego's residues: fear is the ego's greatest protector. But at the same time that we lose everything–we completely surrender and give up–still we are completely and totally functioning. We are 'reborn'. We have a *new* awareness. But this sustaining awareness is not on the samsaric level. It is without predispositions, without taking a position, without identifying anything, without making things solid or fixed. Within this completely open and awakened awareness, everything functions in a new, fresh, open and positive way.

It is possible some day that all our perceptions will become transmuted into the nature of Buddha-mind. It is also possible for Mind-itself to disappear. At present, it is only our fixations or beliefs, or need for something solid that tricks us into thinking that mind exists. What we believe to be mind is not really mind, for whenever we say 'mind is this' or 'mind is that', we are immediately lost in some fantasy, conceptualization or description of mind. But if we experience meditation properly, we will eventually understand that Mind-itself is totally empty, without content. Therefore, there is nothing we can point to and call 'mind'. To say that mind is nothing is still an attempt to describe or define mind according to some conception. But as soon as speech begins, meditation is interrupted. This is why silence is so important. Words and concepts can only point to interpreted fragments of our experience, but in silence awareness comes alive.

Still there is no way we can directly talk about or illustrate the nature of Mind-itself. Mind is not the product of some summation. Mind is not an abstraction. Mind is absolutely structureless. A big rope cannot go through the eye of a needle, but a very fine thread passes through easily. When we go into the thought, into the gap between the thoughts, there is an infinite and vast space . . . an openness with no identity.

Shunyata

The teaching of Shunyata originally comes from the Buddha. After the Buddha was enlightened under the Bodhi tree, he thought to himself, "No one will be able to understand this supreme knowledge, therefore I will not be able to teach it to anyone. This is the nature of Shunyata." So he silently decided to live in the forest . . . until all the Rajas in the heaven realms begged him to turn the Wheel of the Dharma so that suffering sentient beings could hear this precious teaching. Then they presented the Buddha with many auspicious offerings—a beautiful golden wheel, an umbrella, a conch shell, cymbals and so on—saying, "Please turn the wheel of the Dharma. You cannot be silent." So at that time, before the first Dharmachakra, the Buddha privately taught a few disciples the teaching of Shunyata.

Shunyata has four or five general qualities: *zab-pa* means 'great depth', *zhi-ba* means 'great peace', *'od-gsal-ba* means 'great clarity' or 'lucency', *sprol-pral*—which is generally translated as 'voidness'—means 'a freedom which has nothing to do with conceptual ideas, symbols or gestures', and *'dus-ma-byas* means 'unconditioned'. These five qualities of Shunyata are like nectar, but, as the Buddha himself said, "I found this vast knowledge, but if I reveal these teachings, no one will be able to understand them either verbally or symbolically." This was the basic problem: Shunyata has no characteristics and no essence, so he could not point it out anywhere. Shunyata cannot be described or explained—it cannot even be experienced, either physically through the senses, or conceptually through images and thoughts. So how can we contact this deep teaching?

First, there is no way we can interpret Shunyata—we can't do it this way, and we can't do it that way. All our ideas, concepts, mental activity and intuitions cannot explain it. We can't say anything. All we can do is chop down, completely destroy, throw away everything . . . unmask everything . . . and let our minds become totally silent, peaceful, empty and clear—*become* the experience, become Shunyata. If we truly and completely forget everything, our whole being becomes the nature of open space. Within this open awareness or lucidity, between the thoughts, before the next concept forms, there is no subject and no object, no experience and no experiencer.

When I say, chop down or completely eliminate all preconceptions and judgments, it seems like a negative experience—everything is destroyed. Yes, but from the viewpoint of Shunyata there is nothing to destroy, nothing to tear down, nothing to clean up. So the philosophers questioned Nagarjuna:

"Why is this?" And he responded: Because everything is already totally and perfectly the nature of Shunyata.

"When does this occur?" There is no beginning.

"When does it end?" There's no end in time, because there is no time.

"Where is it?" There is no location, and yet, at the same time, Shunyata is every part of everything, but is itself not standing *on* anything.

"Then *who* can realize this Shunyata?" *No one.* There is no 'you' to experience, and there is no experiencer. You are still making 'realization' the goal of a subject-object relationship. This so-called 'realization' is only your interpretation . . . there isn't anything to realize . . . there is nothing to point to in the subject, nothing to point to in the object . . . nothing inside the subject, and nothing inside the object.

"Well, then, I am completely lost—there is nothing inside and nothing outside." Yes, that's true. You are no longer here and no longer there. There's nothing in between . . . there's no space, no time, no matter . . . there is no *thing* . . . there's not even any mind.

"Then how and when and where are all these things functioning? Do you have to guess these things?" No, everything is already perfectly existing within Shunyata.

"But then, you are really contradicting yourself. You are seeing, you are touching, you are talking. How can you say that nothing exists?" That's only the way you interpret my words. Actually, on the level of absolute reality, you are not talking, you are not hearing, you are not understanding, you are not even realizing. You only *think* you are realizing something. As long as you 'think' in the subject-object way, you will continue to think there is something to realize. There is really no such activity.

In this way, Nagarjuna continues and finally says, If there is any*thing* left there, point it out. Verbally, conceptually, intellectually, there is nothing to reject and nothing to accept. Neither reject it nor accept it . . . . *as it is* is perfect Shunyata.

Nagarjuna and Candrakirti were the most important Mahayana Buddhist teachers of the Shunyavadin or Madhyamika doctrine. They were most concerned with what Reality *is*, what Being *is*. Other philosophers would say 'this is' or 'that is' and provide many definitions. But *is*-ness, they simply said, is 'to be'. But to be what? A person is sitting: to be like that? That kind of being? Or is this some special relationship to space? What kind of being is it? But Nagarjuna and Candrakirti do not give any descriptions or characterizations or categorizations or qualifications. The inner nature of every 'thing' is beyond description. As soon as you give descriptions, or interpretations, you are outside looking *at* it, standing *on* it . . . you are not *inside* that state. From the outside you can only make interpretations. Once you make comments, once you predict something, you are only intellectualizing from a subjective point of view. Even the most precise analysis and explanation still reflects the human mind's conditioning and obscures its own depth and clarity.

In Tibetan, Shunyata is *stong-pa-nyid*. Stong-pa means 'empty' in the sense of 'clear', or 'absolute openness'. It has nothing to stand on, either inside or outside: it is completely non-dual, without taking any positions. Therefore, everything past, present or future becomes united. Space, time and matter become inseparable. When we say 'empty-ness', the *ness*-ness implies some quality or some description: it is distinguished from something else or implies some negation. But this negation is only verbal. Shunya, or total openness, has nothing to do with positive or negative connotations. These are only our human interpretations. Shunya means: I cannot grasp it, I cannot see it, I cannot touch it, I cannot smell, interpret or experience it. There is no 'me' grasping, seeing, smelling or experiencing. Shunyata has nothing to do with form or formlessness. It does not deny or accept the physicality of material substance, nor does it describe things comparatively as existent or non-existent. It's not that kind of emptiness. Every*thing* is emptiness. Empti*ness* is everything.

So Nagarjuna explains this by saying: This Emptiness cannot be added to or subtracted from, because it has no essence—no-'thing'-ness. If you look, you will not find it. Still, there is never any contradiction whatsoever between distinctions such as existence or non-existence. Everything exists according to certain natural or karmic laws, but at the same time, all form exists within space, within the Shunya realm. Mind itself has no particular form. Mind in its emptiness is like a crystal in which all 'existing' things reflect, but of itself has no substance, and cannot be said to exist in any place. The crystal and the forms of the objects it reflects are inseparably united.

"But it seems like nothing is there, I feel sort of lost, I cannot touch it, I cannot grasp anything . . . I have nothing to do. . . ." Yes, Shunya says, because you do not realize you do not exist apart from these things. You *think* you need to touch somewhere else . . . but the toucher is already touching, the seer is already seeing. As soon as we postulate something as being separate, or isolate something in order to try and understand it, we lose sight of the fact of Shunyata.

The term 'Buddha' means the 'Enlightened One'. In Tibetan, 'Buddha' is *sangs-rgyas*, which means 'one who is cleansed', 'one who recovers from not-knowing'. When a person eliminates, burns up and throws away all obstructions, that person is historically called the Buddha, and is symbolically represented, according to the more esoteric teachings, as Nirmanakaya, Sambhogakaya and Dharmakaya—on the practical level, the symbolic level and the absolute reality level. But even these three Kayas—the outer, the inner and the secret—are only symbolic explanations to communicate non-verbal understandings to human beings who can only touch, or see, or feel. Symbols only bridge the human being's understanding with the outer, inner and secret levels of reality.

In the beginning, we use symbols to point to something, as though Shunyata were some 'form' of experience. My meditation becomes higher and lighter, and finally everything disappears, so then I become enlightened . . . there is no longer anything left. No. This is only another commentary. But actually, *whatever we are involved in* is already within Shunyata. We can never get in and we can never get out from Shunyata. What, then, is Enlightenment, or Absolute Reality? That is Buddha. That is Shunyata.

"Then why are we not enlightened?" From the viewpoint of absolute reality, all distinctions vanish. We *are* already enlightened . . . but there is no 'we', no individual characteristics, no possessor or experiencer . . . yet everything is already completely enlightened. 'Already' means there is no beginning in time.

"That doesn't make any sense to me. I am still in the samsaric realm. I'm still deluded, I still have suffering and pain. What then is the difference between enlightened ones and sentient beings?" In the absolute way of speaking, there is very little difference. The only difference is whether we realize it or not. The subtlety between realization or non-realization is so small, so difficult to distinguish, that we always miss it. If you cut up one single thought a hundred billion times, one portion is realizing and another portion is not realizing. Cut it up one hundred billion times, and the quantity is almost nothing! One side is Samsara, the other is Enlightenment. Yet if I distinguish this way or that way, then I'm lost. In the absolute sense, there is no difference; in the relative sense, there is a tremendous difference. On one hand, Nirvana, or the enlightened state, has great richness, openness, fullness of being–all positive qualities–and the samsaric state has tremendous pain, suffering, ignorance, stupidity, delusion and confusion. At the same time, both are simultaneously coexisting because Shunyata is the root of both Samsara and Nirvana.

So then, how do we see the world and yet fail to see it? For example, a person is in deep sleep. As he gradually awakens, his awareness of his own situation increases–"It is morning, I am in bed." He selectively senses his surroundings, has his characteristic feelings toward them, remembers his immediate situation concerning the past and his present hopes or plans for the future. And there he is. This is one description of awakening to the world. But what really goes on in our minds? In this first state of deep sleep, we are very open, but very dull and heavy–there is no awareness, no sharpness, no clarity. Then we gradually awaken, and vague feelings gather around a vague center. Then we have definite feeling-tones–we recognize objects through our senses, and we selectively emphasize certain aspects of this field . . . we have a body, we see, we hear, something's uncomfortable . . . and then we associate all of this with our customary way of thinking and relating, to our remembered past and to our anticipated future.

In a fraction of a second, we construct 'my world' or 'my self' according to habitual patterns and reactions. Our senses distinguish the objectifiable world and our mind interprets what is received as perceptions, thoughts, words, images, judgments, feelings, concepts and so on. We define our 'self' only after we have recognized, categorized, and catalogued these various fragments. But these individual aspects are subject to many changing conditions which obscure our original awareness or clarity. So we see the world through a series of filters. Although these fragments or appearances seem to be real, they do not have any separate existence of their own. So the final image or picture is not to be obsessively clung to. If we examine all of these 'reflections', or fragments, we may find a broader, more light-hearted and comprehensive way of appreciating them. This is the point of 'Shunyata'.

"But now, why do you say Shunya? Why not choose some other word?" The reason is that Shunya, or *stong-pa*, is only a symbolic description. Actually, there is nothing to say, nothing to symbolize, no words to describe or explain it, nothing to intellectualize, nothing to interpret or contact. All concepts, every possibility on the relative level, dissolves, melts away . . . and becomes silent, beyond all description.

Now you may say, "If there isn't any description, why do I need to investigate or talk about Shunyata? If there is nothing to explain, what value is there?" Well, as long as my mind exists, as long as there are suffering human beings, I need to examine and investigate my situation as sharply and clearly as possible. You may say, "This feeling seems very negative, like a vacuum, a huge, empty tunnel." But the Shunyavadin says, Even *this* you are creating and projecting. You make it like this or like that. Your description is merely your own relative interpretation which creates separation. It has nothing to do with Shunyata itself. From the viewpoint of the highest realization, everything is already perfect. Not one single imperfect thing exists. No 'thing' needs cleaning or perfecting. Each form, each specific quality is already perfect in being whatever it is . . . just as it is.

From the very beginning, the very first, everything is part of a total perfect condition which is Shunya. 'Perfect', you may say, implies a description of some quality. But this intrinsic perfection is beyond all relative interpretations. One might say, on the absolute level, 'behind' or 'beyond' all Reality (Enlightenment) is Shunyata. But according to the Shunyavadin doctrine, there is really no fictional beyond. 'Beyond' is already within you. Before you begin, everything exists perfectly within Shunyata. Even when something relatively imperfect is said to exist, its Shunya nature is absolutely perfect. There is nothing else other than Shunyata.

Many commentators have written endless volumes trying to explain the meaning of Shunyata. On the absolute level, all appearances and forms—pure or impure, Nirvana or Samsara—are manifestations of perfect being. Practically speaking, Shunyata simply means accepting the world as it is rather than how we would like to make it. This is not mere passivity or just some balance between the extremes of eternalism or nihilism, but seeing the whole of Reality honestly and directly—without playing games and without distortion. At that time, there is nothing to gain, nothing to lose, nothing to realize, nothing to perfect.

We begin to understand this, first, by cutting out all preconceptions. If you believe Shunyata explains tremendous vastness, cut it out. If you believe nothing, then cut that out. If you believe in 'mind', or that everything is mind-created, or that there is some foundation or substance, throw it away. You might say, "How can you talk like that? Don't you believe in Karma?" Yes, but now I know Shunyata and that in itself is enough. There is nothing left outside. Everything is completely open. Everything 'fits' perfectly, because all conditions and relationships are within Shunyata.

So look carefully: Where is your mind coming from? Where does your mind go? Who are the parents of consciousness? Where is your original life coming from? Where is all existence created from? Shunyata includes every possibility, every philosophical interpretation, every argument. It alone makes itself completely clear. Until you understand the meaning of Shunyata, you will continue to take a position and contradict yourself. After you have completely exhausted every logical explanation, everything is still absolutely perfect.

So therefore, finally, Nagarjuna says, I do not accept anything, I do not reject anything . . . I am silent. This doesn't mean I have no answer. My answer is 'silent' in the sense that everything is already speaking it—there's nothing more to say. The perfect answer is silence. There is no other word: the perfect condition, the perfect realization is totally silent, and that's my answer. That's my meditation.

Dream Practice

Buddhist philosophy involves both theory and practice. Generally, most Buddhist countries practice the Theravada or the Mahayana. Within the Mahayana are the esoteric teachings of the Vajrayana. Dream Yoga is one of the practices or techniques of Vajrayana Buddhism and seems very closely linked to the Vijnanavadin or Yogacara school of the Mahayana.

We usually think of human beings and the world as two separate things. Actually, you cannot separate yourself from your world. Samsara is based on this duality of 'my world' and 'my self'. Each supports the other: the object supports the subject and the subject depends on the object. Dream Yoga stems from their ultimate inseparability.

In early times philosophers asked, "What is this universe? What is reality? What is this experience? In the fourth century, Asanga and Vasubandhu explained that the world *is* mind-projection. Our mind projects the universe. They did not use this word 'mind' in the ordinary way. For them, 'mind' is a deeper, more basic foundation from which the conventional world and mind develop. Likewise, our consciousness or awareness is like a mirror which reflects within itself. This type of awareness is not necessarily 'aware of some thing'. The object does not belong separately to anything other than itself. The object is not somewhere else, but within awareness. All the life experiences we have are included or reflected within awareness.

This awareness is not necessarily meditation awareness. Philosophers were merely trying to point out that whatever life experience we may have—mental or physical, conscious or unconscious—the experience is within awareness. Then they said, this intrinsic experience is based on 'light'—without any outside sources or forms or objects or causes . . . self-illuminating. How big, how large, how tall . . . there is no way we can measure experience. On the commonsense level, we may have some ideas about how or what we experience. But experientially, feeling has no form; so therefore, it's difficult to measure. Mind itself, you may say, is formless.

As human beings we assign various categories or qualities to our feelings, perceptions and cognitions, but these things have no form. Various mental events are specifically explained in the Abhidharma literature; later on, more sophisticated, esoteric teachings explain that awareness and mind are identical. Wherever mind is, there is awareness. This is not a grasping awareness, but an illuminating, lightness quality within the mind realm: the sensitized mind is itself 'light', or we may say, self-lucent. Any mental experience–whether happy, joyful, painful, negative or neutral–is within the mind realm and does not extend beyond it.

So now the philosophers ask: "What is this light? What are its signs, where is it located, how do we find it?" And they try to examine this situation closely. But the more they examine it, the more mysterious it becomes. You can almost 'see' it . . . yet at the same time it seems unreal. Whether it is real or unreal is very difficult to determine. We can only describe it by saying, "It seems *like* a dream."

What is real is the dream itself. You can say that our daytime experience is another kind of dream. We are born, we seem to have a long life, we have been working many years–we have the same body, same mind, same interests, same job. Our experience goes on and on. Our lives up to now are like the reflection of past memories. Memory seems to be the only way we can verify our past experience. All we have left is memory. All the images and pictures of past experiences are collected within memory. If you look carefully, these memory patterns are very similar to nighttime dreams.

Commonly we think that the dream is unreal, untrue, not stable, not permanent. But when we are in the dream, it seems permanent. If the person is not awake within the dream, then the experience of night-dreaming or day-dreaming–or passing through imaginative realms–seems to be a 'real' experience . . . the same as now. When you are within the dream, it is very difficult to distinguish whether the dream is real or unreal. The only difference–once you are *in* the experience–is whether or not you *realize* it. We may think there is a wall between the two sides–between 'real' and 'unreal', day-dreaming and night-dreaming–but any kind of experience you can get on one side, you can get on the other. Both have very similar characteristics. Any experience we can humanly have, such as suffering or happiness is equally available as 'reality' and as 'dream'. One reflects the other.

We can only speak about this from the awakened state. Usually we say, "This is a 'daydream'," but the difference lies only in the contrast. When we take away the wall, day-dreaming and night-dreaming, real and unreal, knowing and not-knowing, become one.

But underneath, who is projecting all of this? Again we need to research . . . is there any projector? The more we look, the more we see a very similar pattern. It's difficult to tell . . . whether inwardly is projecting outwardly, or outwardly inwardly. Which is the center? who is inside? who is outside? If you examine this way, you cannot find any center, you cannot find any place.

Daydreams and nightdreams do not seem to have any 'place'. If there is a specific functioning place, there must be some*one*, some*thing*. This, too, we must research, find out. Where is mind located? This is important, because whether something exists or not is determined partly by its location.

If I cannot find any specific place where this experience is happening, then I have to think: where does everything originate? Some philosophers say, "Well, this is all part of Maya, Illusion." Another philosophy says, "Who cares?" or, "There's an Original Mother which is undiscoverable." Still others say, "Whatever . . . it is beyond our ability to measure or grasp it."

Dream philosophers do not comment or explain this way or that way. Simply, they say, this is the same as a dream. From one viewpoint, the dream is real; from another, it is not real. But real or not real only depends on our subjective theories, concepts or labels. If I ask, where do my inner pictures and images come from? Where is mind? Some of you may say, "I have a background in philosophy or theory," and I believe *this* way," or, "I follow *that* system." But theory *alone* is not the experience. Normally we say, 'a rose is a rose'—there is no further analysis. I see it, I identify it and I label it—this is a rose. But if someone takes away the color, and one analyzes the chemistry, and one removes the odor, and another the petals, and this and that . . . where is the rose?

In early times, the yogis would climb up very high mountains, between steep canyons, and they'd sing and talk very loudly . . . and then listen. Immediately, to whatever they'd say, would come the reply, the echo. They'd listen and ask, "*Who* is giving this answer?" Sometimes they would go to a beautiful lake and watch the reflection of their own image, and concentrate on that: where is this really coming from? You can do the same exercise within the dream. Similarly, the dream philosophers examined, "Where does my mind come from? Where do my awareness and consciousness go? Is there any place? Do they end in space? as matter, form or energy? Where do these things originally come *from*?"

Dream philosophers say that mind has no 'to' and no 'from' . . . yet something seems to be happening . . . 'like a dream'. We may dream at night about what we did during the day. We may have a definite experience, but where does it come from? Some philosophers say, "From within your collective unconscious." Or, "Images are symbols for various experiences and projections." Or, "You are re-experiencing today within your dream in order to resolve your conflicts." There are many possibilities, but these explanations still attempt to describe reality according to a point of view which is itself 'within dream'.

Dream Yoga has been practiced for a long time. Why? Because the whole world has problems, and each individual has his or her own particular problems–something is uncomfortable, unbalanced or dissatisfying . . . we have internal conflicts, an unhappy or unhealthy mind . . . maybe often, or all the time. "The main reason," say the dream philosophers, "is because you are so serious, because you *believe* in it and think *this* reality is true. You seriously believe your subjective viewpoint is real and unchangeable." So I take my reality seriously and find that it does not fit my desires and expectations. I have set up my ideas a certain way according to very specific, narrow rules. I have fixed ideas of happiness and so on. If reality does not fit, I struggle and suffer.

Once you understand your experience as part of the dream, and that the dream is not a very solid or final reality, then you no longer have to treat your life as a serious problem. If you understand this completely, even painful experiences or mental conflicts become part of the dream. You may not have to suffer from your own interpretations. You become less tight and more flexible. Once you awaken to this experience, everything seems like a dream . . . your mind is dream, your perception is dream, pleasure or happiness is dream. The dream includes everything.

So once you completely realize this, you may still have pain, but you no longer identify with psychological pain or conceptual fear, because you yourself are included within the dream. I am not only the subject or the projector watching the images, but I am included within the picture. I am the watcher, but the watcher is also watching *me*. Subject and object are both included within the dream.

Yet we still think the dream belongs to someone else or is some particular experience. This is only another duality, another conceptual inner dialogue: this is a dream experience, and that is a reality experience. My inner awareness—the experience or the judgment—is not necessarily in one place. You can't explain whether this experience is coming from here or there or inside or outside. Both the judger and the judgment are part of the dream. My consciousness, my awareness, my ability to intellectualize—everything is included within the dream. When we understand this, then we realize that the external world and the world of ideas and mental images are both the same.

Why do we try to understand dream? When you remove the fear, dualism, attachment, worry, grasping and negativity, you can see that your experience is not as serious as you thought. Your personality changes and your relationships with other people and the world improve. Most of our human difficulties are created by an insecure identity—craving, escaping, fighting. We become so seriously involved in the dualistic situations we build within our minds that we cannot escape. We have lost flexibility, awareness, responsiveness and positivity. But once we surrender the idea that dream is something unreal, untrue, far away and not part of our world, then nighttime and daytime become equalized and unified. The dream state of consciousness is not separate from the waking state. You and others, love and hate, the projector and the projection, you and your world—all are inseparable.

Once we reach this understanding, we cannot lose it. Sometimes we say, 'you can become enlightened'. Enlightenment is also part of the dream state. It has no origin, no beginning, no end: it cannot be lost. Therefore, we do not need to go somewhere else to find it. The reality, the God-nature, the Absolute Truth, or, you may say, a healthy mind is right here.

If you practice seeing everything as equally within the dream, you can cultivate a healthy, balanced mind. You may think, "If I realize that everything's a dream, I might lose my business, or my job and equipment!" But you do not need to hypnotize your mind. Whatever you're *already* doing is part of that dream. You don't have to travel to some other place to live or radically change your life style. Just watch the dream. The dream is anything we are doing! Any expression, any activity or any experience is already within that dream. There's nothing we can hide, nothing we can secretly do that is not part of the dream.

Since everything is part of the dream, my whole world—my mind, my feelings, my consciousness, my cognitions . . . inside, outside, backside, frontside—is also part of the dream. Nagarjuna and other

philosophers explained that illusion itself is part of the enlightened experience. The Bodhisattvas particularly recognized this. Buddhas and Bodhisattvas who are working so hard for all sentient beings have no hardship of any kind, mental or physical. They realize that everything is part of the dream and are working to show us that we are sleeping. Liberation means to wake up to this awareness and realize that everything on both sides of the wall is unified. There's no separation.

From early times, from the stone age until now, the whole civilized world—the ideas, the cultures, the progress—reflects a development of human awareness. So now we have to find out, where is awareness itself coming from? Internally we may try to watch the beginning and formation of observable qualities without losing awareness. Try to watch how the images are reflected to your observing awareness. Then watch how the images become something else. Most of the time we do not observe how this happens—'something just happens'.

Through meditation, you can understand how awareness itself has various densities, various levels, and how images are projected before the awareness. The awareness is self-stimulating, self-feeding, and itself creates images which 'freeze' and become 'real' when we identify with them. As soon as the image becomes solid, the awareness then begins to reflect past actions, or certain past experiences. So past experience is reflected through the awareness which gives rise to various vivid images which then become frozen and form our own particular view of the real world.

In the morning, when we wake up, notice how we lose that image. We don't exactly remember, but between the dream image and the waking reality there is a link. It seems as though something is 'floating' between them. But how this occurs is very illusive. That is why, from ancient times, there are very specific practices to help you to recognize the link and to continue the flow between dreaming and waking. Once you realize that everything is within the dream, do not lose that seeingness quality, or inner awareness. By keeping alive that inner perspective, you can wake up within the dream.

The benefit of dream practice is to balance the mind and provide nutrition for the awareness. Like parents feeding their child, every experience nourishes our awareness. So before you sleep, try not to concentrate too tightly . . . or you may not sleep. Simply, do not lose your awareness. Only the mind can heal itself, but first we need to teach our mind very gently, as though we were teaching a child. The best way to free the mind is to completely relax, breathe very softly, gently and evenly. Make everything comfortable: no worries, no anxiety, no thinking. Let your head, neck and muscles relax. Shut down all past experiences and let everything slow down so that your mind becomes very calm. Then, without making an effort, skillfully watch how the images begin and end. You can enter that dream without losing your 'waking' awareness.

Psychologically, dreams may have many symbolic interpretations . . . it is even possible to discover all your previous lives. But this is not the purpose of Dream Yoga. We are trying to discover what the dream is, what reality really is. Otherwise we can talk endlessly about the symbols behind the images and so on, but these are not very important. Instead we have to understand: what is the difference between *this* reality and *that* reality . . . they may be the same.

From now on, whatever you do, whatever you speak, accept each experience as a dream. Walking, talking, drinking, eating, grasping, craving, thinking, feeling uncomfortable–anything you do–everything is within the dream. I am in dream, you are in dream, we all are in dream. Laughing or crying . . . everything is a dream. There's nothing else other than dream. The daytime waking state and the nighttime sleeping state–both are equally the dream. Do not try to fix anything, just be loose and relaxed. Whatever you feel, just accept it as a dream. Your personality or self-image, your own inner psychological expressions and inner dialogues–whatever is within you–everything is part of the dream. The world, the pictures, the colors, your body, your clothes, your food, your bed–anything belonging to you–everything is part of that dream. Just accept it. Your mind is dream, your body is dream, your feeling is dream, your concept is dream–everything is part of dream. There's nothing you can find other than dream.

Questions and Answers

Question: If we say, dream itself has no foundation, do gods and goddesses have a foundation?

Rinpoche: You are still trying to figure out the dream logically. But dream is like a bubble which pops. The image itself has no seed. First you dream and you have the experience. But where does the experience originally come from? When it's gone, where does it disappear to? Last night's dream, where is it now? Dream is like a bubble. Nothing is separate. Usually we believe that waking reality is 'real' and dreamtime reality is 'unreal'. But the whole conclusion is that daytime and nighttime–both together–are the dream. That means deities–everything–are part of our projection. You can analyze the dreaming and the dreamer separately, but in the absolute sense, they are both part of the same dream.

Question: What techniques would you suggest to facilitate the awareness that we are dreaming?
Rinpoche: One of the most powerful methods is to constantly think: this is a dream. Become completely convinced–the actor himself is a dream. Then awareness develops openly and completely. Once you establish that this is a dream and we are all in it, all your concepts fall away. The dream is not bad or unreal. What happens is that your human relationships become more satisfying. Most human problems are created by our self-identity. We build up a variety of concepts and box ourselves in: this is real, that is not real. There's no way you can escape, and flexibility becomes impossible.

Question: Consciousness apparently doesn't require 'energy', as we understand it in the West.
Rinpoche: I think that our father, our parent, is consciousness, not energy. Energy is related to space and time, but consciousness is not necessarily limited to space and time. This is a very complex subject, but it seems that Western scientific ideas of matter, energy, time and space are very closely related in Buddhism to Nirmanakaya, Sambhogakaya and Dharmakaya. This we need to investigate more.

Question: Is there any ultimate value which is outside the dream to which the dream can be contrasted? The thing that comes to my mind is Shunyata.
Rinpoche: The dream is possible because of Shunyata.
Question: You mean everything that one experiences is a dream, that is, it's insubstantial precisely because the base value is nothingness, beyond all categories?
Rinpoche: We *are* within Shunyata. You can perhaps distinguish this way: Buddhism has the Foundation, the Path, and the Goal or Fruit. If you ask a Buddhist what is existence, or what is the world, first he says: insubstantial, impermanent, transitory. But finally he says: this is Shunyata. So the goal or Enlightenment is *realizing* Shunyata. First we need to make an effort to understand the theory and logic, to

conceptualize and instruct this way and that way—you can't think this way, you can't think that way—until you finally give up all your concepts. Until the dualistic mind becomes totally aware of its artificial nature, you cannot fully realize Shunyata. There are many different methods, but dream is one of the most suitable for realizing Enlightenment, because it's very enjoyable.

For example, if we follow a spiritual path, during the day we still have certain frustrating situations, such as depression, pain, dissatisfaction or emotional negativity. You can change this through your awareness. During the nighttime, you can become aware within the dream and begin to develop fresh insight, confidence and strength that extends into the daytime and influences everything you do. The dream itself can be your teacher.

Question: For some reason, to think that everything is a dream makes me afraid.

Rinpoche: That is because we are very seriously involved in our human problems. We have so many responsibilities, obligations and complicated situations that we have no choice, no freedom. Life includes many painful experiences. But once you realize everything is a dream, these things do not seem so serious, so fixed, so unchanging. To be afraid is to fear openness. Fear is ego's best friend. When ego is threatened, fear keeps the ego alive. If fear is overcome, ego has no protection. But ego only exists in our heads, not in our heart. That the world is a dream need not make you afraid. It's a dream. Just accept it as dream and relax. Let your meditation be very comfortable. Otherwise you may become very rigid.

There are actually eight different similes for dream listed in the Sutras. Dream is like an echo, a mirage, an illusion. Dream practice is also discussed by Candrakirti in some of his Shastras, by Nagarjuna, Naropa, and especially by Long-chen-pa. They say that the world we think we see is only a view, a description of the world. Accepting this is very difficult because we are completely fixed in our own particular view. If you want to understand this dream practice, study the Madhyamika and Yogacara and examine your life logically, philosophically and psychologically. The more you examine and test these things, the more they will contribute to your understanding. But words alone cannot make these ideas clear. Once you understand this, you need to practice and *become* that understanding. Dream is everything you are and everything you are doing. There is nothing else other than dream.

PART THREE

CULTURE

Tibet: The Land, People and Culture

Tarthang Tulku

Imagine leaving the fertile plains of India and toiling for some 200–300 miles over endless mountain ranges, through steaming hot valleys and over cold, cloud-covered passes, fording wild mountain streams, where a slip of the foot means certain death, or crossing the thundering abyss of a torrential river, clinging precariously to a shaky reed rope of uncertain age. . . . Imagine negotiating over hanging cliffs on narrow mountain paths and sharp-edged rock ledges which cut into sore and tired feet. . . . Suddenly the clouds lift and one looks down on the other side into a country of sunshine, where the valleys are lined with fir forests, the ground covered with grass, moss and ferns, flowers and shrubs, and where the vivid colors and chiselled forms of rocks and mountains stand out in brilliant clearness, like the world of the first day of creation.

LAMA GOVINDA, The Way of the White Clouds

TIBET, GEOGRAPHICALLY ISOLATED from the rest of the world, is a land of much natural beauty and grandeur. Immense snow-capped ranges of mountains and chains of glistening glaciers surround vast plateaus, while hailstorms, rain and sunshine, following one another in a matter of minutes, frequently combine to illuminate the landscape with rainbows.

In Tibet–the land of snows, the land of lamas, the land of eternal mystery–the traveler undergoes a strange transformation, where the valleys are as high as the highest peaks of the Sierras, and where mountains soar into space beyond the reach of humans. While strug-

Chortens of the Golden Temple of Tholing (Western Tibet)

gling to cross a gorge over a rope bridge at an altitude of 15,000 feet, the traveler might look up to see the mantra OṂ MAṆI PADME HŪṂ carved on the side of a cliff; or a village of fifty stone dwellings huddled at the end of a verdant, sprawling valley; or an orange sunset reflected in the gilded towers of a mountainside monastery. The Tibetan landscape has all the intensity of color and form that one associates with a vision or prophetic dream where thoughts flow easily and spontaneously without losing their coherence, and where a feeling of elevated joy suggests an even deeper and subtler transformation of consciousness. For centuries, in settings such as these, the Tibetans developed a highly advanced culture—peacefully and quietly, without outside intervention.

Throughout its ancient history, to the middle of the twentieth century, Tibet evolved in peace and freedom, preferring not to interfere in the affairs of others. While Tibetans were engaged in a constant struggle against the hardships of one of the most rugged and inaccessible regions on earth, they simultaneously devoted themselves to a concentrated study of human consciousness—an intense practice of the

Buddha's teachings which influenced every aspect of their lives. Tibet has its roots not only in an historical or cultural past, but within the innermost being of man, and its investigation of the very nature of human consciousness stretches beyond this short life-span, beyond the limitations of a momentary time-conditioned individuality, and beyond the prejudices of so-called cultural differences.

In recent times, a deep echo has resounded from Tibet which has been heard throughout the Western world. This description of the Tibetan people, however, only attempts to provide a general panoramic survey of their customs and lifestyles. In the wisdom of Tibet's ancient traditions are contained the creative seeds that may yet give birth to the vast and deep horizons that are already present within the consciousness of man, but as yet hidden from sight.

The Geography

Tibet is often called the 'Roof of the World', with mountains towering to 25,000 feet, trails winding over treacherous 15,000-foot passes, and many year-round settlements situated at heights well over 10,000 feet. While the tallest mountains are perpetually covered with ice and snow, lower altitudes successively reveal bare rock, vegetation, pine trees, stretches of rolling grassy hills, swift-running icc-cold brooks, and sky-mirroring lakes.

Many people commonly think of Tibet as a series of unapproachable mountains with vast quantities of snow, but the Tibetan climate is far from being cold, wild and inhospitable. In Lhasa, for example, situated at a height of 11,000 feet, summers are a few degrees warmer than our Midwest, and winters last for only three months with little snowfall. Even rain, except for occasional southerly monsoons rising over the Himalayas, is scarce, but plenty of melting snow-water provides abundant irrigation to fields, hillside pastures and woodlands. Yet generalizations about Tibet are impractical because the folds of mountain ranges, the pockets of various valleys and the particular altitude of any given location expose a variety of fluctuating climates amid a vast diversity of local conditions.

Tibet is literally surrounded by mountain ranges which have traditionally formed its rather loosely-defined boundaries. In the north, the Altyn Tagh mountain ranges, overlooking Mongolia and Russia, rear their lofty heads from the tableland, criss-crossing treeless grassy steppes which are liberally scattered with salt lakes. In the east, dividing Tibet from China, several parallel ranges run north and south, while the mighty Himalayas to the south harbor Nepal, Sikkim and Bhutan. To the west, the long, winding Karakoram range separates Tibet from the outlying regions of Kashmir, Baltistan and Persia, and are the source of numerous rivers.

Mt. Kailas in western Tibet forms the spire of the 'Roof of the World', and, like spokes radiating from the hub of a wheel, a number of mighty rivers take their course towards the east, west, northwest and south. These rivers are the Brahmaputra, the Indus, the Sutlej, and the Karnali. In ancient scriptures these rivers are described as outlets from the Manasarovar Lake at the foot of Mount Kailas, which is called Meru or Sumeru, according to the oldest Sanskrit tradition, and which is regarded by the Indians to be not only the physical but the metaphysical center of the universe. The Tibetans call the Brahmaputra, the source of which is in the east of Mt. Kailas, the river 'flowing out of a horse's mouth', which flows across central Tibet (here called the Tsangpo) and then turns sharply southwards and enters Assam and India. The Sutlej, whose source is in the west, is called the river 'flowing out an elephant's mouth'; the Indus in the north, the river 'flowing out of a lion's mouth'; and the Karnali in the south, the river 'flowing out a peacock's mouth'. The river names indicate that they are regarded as parts of a universal *maṇḍala*, with Kailas at the center.

For the most part, Tibet is situated on an elevated plateau–the Northern Plain, Chang Thang–which averages some 15,000 feet above sea level. Since the altitude is too high for farming, herdsmen and wandering nomads, who wear rough sheepskin garments and furry hats and live in thick black tents woven from yaks wool, follow the seasons from pasture to pasture, grazing their yaks, *dru*, goats and sheep, and trading in wool, butter, borax and salt.

In the northeastern plains and mountains, which include Amdo, Golok, Sertal, and Gyarong, pastures slope down into extended valleys where woodsmen raise animals, particularly horses and sheep, and grow grain, vegetables and fruit trees. In the fertile valleys to the east is Kham, including Derge. Here, both farming and grazing are extensive, as well as in the central districts of Ü and Tsang, which include the capital Lhasa, and the larger towns of Shigatse, Gyantse and Hloka. To the southwest and west, known as Ngari Korsum, farming is possible in summer, but in winter the herds are taken to northern pastures. Thus, while the western and northern climates are colder and harsher, the valleys of the eastern and southern regions are warmer and more fertile.

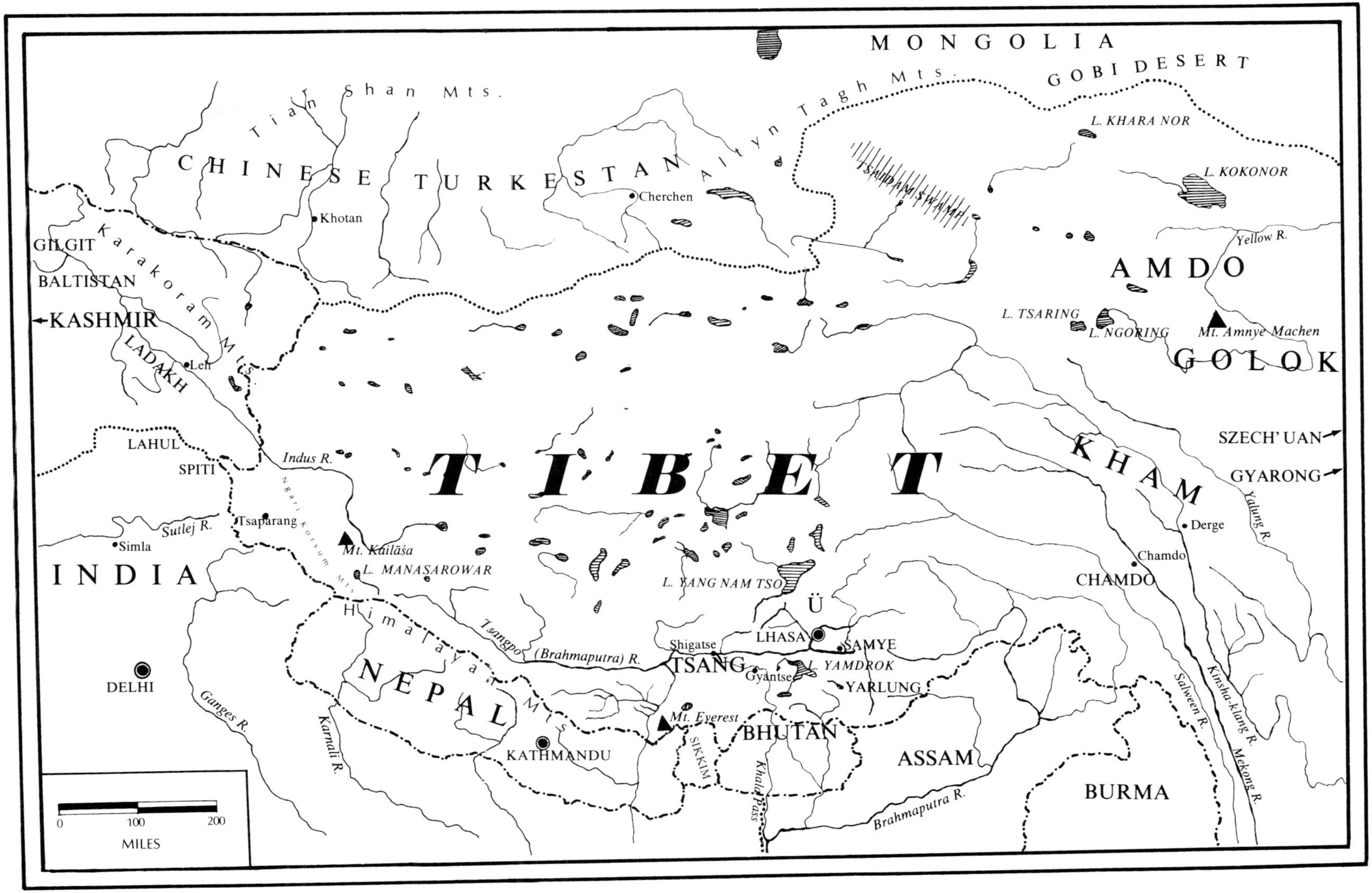

MONGOLIA
GOBI DESERT
Tian Shan Mts.
Altyn Tagh Mts.
CHINESE TURKESTAN
L. KHARA NOR
L. KOKONOR
TSAIDAM SWAMP
Cherchen
Khotan
Yellow R.
AMDO
L. TSARING
L. NGORING
Mt. Amnye Machen
GOLOK
GILGIT
Karakoram Mts.
BALTISTAN
KASHMIR
LADAKH
Leh
LAHUL
SPITI
Indus R.
TIBET
SZECH'UAN
GYARONG
KHAM
Yalung R.
Derge
Chamdo
CHAMDO
Tsaparang
Ngari Korsum Mts.
Sutlej R.
Simla
Mt. Kailāśa
L. MANASAROWAR
INDIA
L. YANG NAM TSO
Ü
LHASA
SAMYE
Shigatse
Tsangpo (Brahmaputra) R.
TSANG
L. YAMDROK
Gyantse
YARLUNG
Himalayan Mts.
NEPAL
DELHI
Ganges R.
Karnali R.
Mt. Everest
SIKKIM
BHUTAN
Khala Pass
KATHMANDU
ASSAM
Brahmaputra R.
BURMA
Salween R.
Kinsha-klang R.
Mekong R.
0
100
200
MILES

Changu Tso (Green Lake)—Sikkim

All of this territory, with its mountains and plains, adds up to a lot of space, nearly one and a half million square miles, a region covering over fifteen times the size of Great Britain, or approximately one-sixth the area of the United States. A journey, for example, from Chamdo in the northeastern region of Kham, across the Chang Thang to Lhasa in central Tibet, is a good 2000 miles by yak, requiring approximately 80 days of travel (from dawn to noon). In northern Tibet, it is possible for people to live in the rugged altitudes of over 16,000 feet, but in the milder regions of southern Tibet, the lowest areas of habitation are at 4,000 feet, while the majority of Tibetans live at elevations between 7,000 and 12,000 feet, which is the upper limit for cultivation.

Under the open skies of Tibet, in the vastness of its solitude, the clarity of its atmosphere, the luminosity of its colors, consciousness is raised to a very sensitive appreciation of nature and its forces. In spite of the feeling of smallness in the vastness and the grandeur of the mountain landscape, in spite of the traveler's dependence on the whims of wind and weather, water and grazing grounds, food, fuel and other material situations, nature itself, and its timeless rhythms, stimulates and heightens a person's capacity to accept with an open mind the unexpected situations of life, good as well as bad, and to adapt to an infinite variety of fluctuating natural conditions.

The Tibetan landscape itself appears like the organic expression of primeval forces. Amidst a wide assortment of natural environments, the Tibetans really only distinguish two types of land: that which is inhabitable, and that which is not (comprising mostly deserts and mountain peaks). According to a ninth-century account, good land–that is, land which is ideal for farming and pasturing–possesses ten virtues: grasslands, with meadows near home and pastures more distant; soil with which to build houses and soil that is fertile; water good to drink and water abundant for cultivation; stones for building and stones for grinding grain; and wood–from trees that turn red in the winter and those that do not–for lumber and fuel. Nowhere, it seems, do these elements combine in the same proportion. Conditions fluctuate with the altitude, the slope of the land, and the natural fertility of the soil–and these determine whether land will be grazed or sown.

Tibet's bare mountains, which are among the earth's youngest ranges, possibly contain more gold and precious gems than the rest of the world combined. The Tibetans, however, have never shown much interest in mining, and an abundance of minerals–such as zinc, copper, lead, iron, and rich deposits of coal and oil–have remained almost completely untapped.

The Tibetans have never faced a food crisis for even the relatively poor have always been able to choose from a great abundance and variety of foods and dairy products. Farmers in the upper valleys generally grow large quantities of barley, wheat, black peas, maize, beans, buckwheat and mustard. In particular, Tibetans enjoy a very small variety of potato, which tastes sweeter than yams, and a red, chili-like bean which is grown in the spring and autumn and which is either ground for flour or boiled and eaten with butter and cheese. In the lower regions, vegetables such as cabbages, cauliflower, tomatoes, onions, garlic, celery, radishes and turnips are common, as well as a variety of fruits (strawberries, grapes, rhubarb) and fruit trees (apricot, peach, pear, apple). In early times, grain was so plentiful that it was customarily used for currency in trade. Because of the favorable climate, surplus barley and wheat can be stored for twenty-five and even fifty years.

Numerous flowers and medicinal plants carpet the entire country, and a great variety of wildlife roams freely. In different parts of Tibet, one finds the tiger, leopard, Himalayan black bear, red bear, monkey, wolf, fox, marmot, hare, wild dog, wild pig, wild goat, deer, musk-deer, antelope, wild yak, horse, lynx, rock snake, otter, and porcupine. Only the elephant, it seems, found the climb through the Himalayas too steep and forbidding, but a large variety of birds, such as the parrot, crow, owl, eagle, duck, partridge, swallow and others, make their homes in the forests of Tibet.

The People: Herdsmen, Farmers, Villagers

Tibetans are a simple, quiet, cheerful people who emulate traditional behavior, if only because tested methods of survival and adaptation have proven most efficient and practical for centuries. Conditions might be rigorous according to contemporary Western standards, but elements of strain and inconvenience affect everyone alike and evoke a deep sense of social unity and spontaneous friendliness among neighbors. Every Tibetan, whether he be a herdsman, village-farmer, trader, soldier, official or monk, is dependent on harmonious communal relations and mutual cooperation. Leaning strongly on their understanding of Buddhism, they realize that nothing ever really happens in an arbitrary way and that there is a reason for everything. One must only be clever enough to stimulate and develop what is beneficial and advantageous, in family, business, society, and religion. A strong moral sense, dictated by honesty and direct negotiation, is coupled with the conviction that one should never expect something for nothing. This is one of the reasons Tibetans are hard-working, industrious, sympathetic, honest, loyal, open, kind, clever and just. Such has been the opinion of foreign travelers who have spent some time in Tibet, and more recently, by those who have encountered refugee Tibetans in Nepal and India.

The common man is herdsman and farmer, carpenter, mason and general craftsman, goldsmith, bootmaker, doctor, trader and businessman. He builds the castles, monasteries, villages, and large tents (*va*), and lives in accord with the natural cycles of weather and land. His wife looks after the children and aging relatives, milks the family animals, churns the butter, weaves the woolen homespun and fashions clothes. Everything is accomplished by the skill of their hands, from delicate embroidery and wood-carving to fashioning a new harness for the ploughing yak.

Although no accurate census has ever been taken in Tibet, in 1956 the Dalai Lama estimated the total population at eight–ten million. Of this number, approximately 48 percent were herdsmen and 32 percent village-dwelling farmers and traders. Monks and nuns, drawn from all classes of society, formed about 20 percent (18 percent monks and 2 percent nuns). Thus, herdsmen and farmers comprise 80 percent of the population and provide Tibet with a broad-based agricultural society self-sufficient in its supply of food. As one occupation supplies and supports the other, herdsmen and village-dwelling farmers interrelate harmoniously for commerce and socializing, while their specific life styles remain usefully different in many ways.

Herdsmen and Traders. Herdsmen form a society all their own. While their physical appearance and way of life may seem ageless, of another world, bound by neither space nor time, beneath their weathered features are concealed the natural virtues of man. Their cheerfulness and strength of character, their generosity and hospitality, are legendary in Tibet.

Most herdsmen live on the Northern Plain, where the four elements of snow, frost, wind and sun, in combination with the undulating desolate plains and the naked rocks and cliffs, create an austere grandeur and subtle beauty unique to Chang Thang. While some provide herding and agricultural services for monasteries, private estates of government officials, and families with an abundance of herds, others spend most of the year traveling to central Tibet on trading missions. But generally they own their herds and travel between summer and winter pastures, erecting large trade *va* (tents) in the center of the plains. Lacking the necessary climate for large-scale agriculture, the herdsman economy depends entirely on breeding herds of yak, sheep, goats and horses in the green but often sparse tableland of the north and northeast. Single families normally graze several hundred sheep and yaks, while wealthier families and clans possess over 10,000, and even up to 50,000 animals which provide abundant wool to support an extensive trading operation with India and other bordering countries.

As the entire northern region is common ground, the herdsmen have no fixed dwellings, but follow available grass and water. However, a particular group of herdsmen and their families normally move to the summer or winter pastoral land where they had pitched their va in the previous season. Thus, even the names of 'villages' refer only to favorite campsites. Ancient fortresses, built on significant junctions, stand unmanned on lofty summits. A few monasteries, nestled into high ridges, overlook gorges and frozen streams, where red and yellow rocks rise like flames against the dark blue curtain of the sky.

A couple of huge black va made of woven yak hair, which are warm, strong and waterproof, and pitched on a level green plot of ground, forms the natural palace of the herdsmen. Some of these va are large enough to accommodate one or two hundred persons and are even divided into separate rooms. From a distance, Tibetan encampments are easily recognized, for many colorful prayer flags can be seen flapping in the breeze while the blue smoke of *sang* (charcoal-incense offerings) rises in front of their va. A few yards from the tent there are always a few gigantic sheepdogs, whose responsible ability to guard the occupants is unquestioned. For fuel, wood of any kind is rare, so herdsmen commonly use small wild azalea bushes, various roots, and yak-droppings which are plentiful and slow-burning. Vegetation, except for grass and medicinal herbs, is scarce in the uplands, and the northerners live on *tsampa* (barley roasted whole and ground into flour), meat, butter and cheese. Abundant milk provides various cheese delicacies such as cottage cheese and cheesecake. Hard cheeses are often strung together and sold in the towns, but the main trading products are usually butter and wool.

To the Tibetans, the yak is probably their most useful animal. Both a pack and riding animal, the yak is sure-footed on the roughest and steepest paths, lives under difficult conditions, and most often finds its own food. Their meat is savory and can be preserved dried for a year or more: and their wool makes warm cloth and durable rope. Tibetans are always highly amused when they hear a Westerner refer to 'yak's milk', for this is the equivalent to saying 'bull's milk'. The *dru* (female yak) and the *dzo-mo* (a cross between a bull and a dru) produce large quantities of milk which is churned for butter in large vats. Villagers often rent yaks and other animals to the herdsmen during the harsh winter months. The herdsmen in turn pasture the animals on the northern plains and make rental payments in butter, usually thirty pounds of butter annually per head of dru. When packed in wet hides, butter becomes well-compressed and can be kept for a year or so. Yak butter, which has a natural, golden color, is an essential ingredient in the Tibetan diet and makes a nourishing drink mixed with tea.

While there are many small towns scattered throughout Tibet, distances between destinations can sometimes require a month or more of travel. For example, northern traders from Amdo, who wish to sell horses and mules in Lhasa, travel nine months of the year. They would leave northern Tibet in April in order to ensure fresh grass for their horses en route, and reach Lhasa in August, arriving back home with supplies in February. Traders and travelers alike either walk or ride the horse or mule, while luggage is carried by horse, yak, mule, dzo, donkey, or sheep. Large bells mounted on their pack animals help to relieve the long silence and strain of a tedious journey, frighten wild animals in jungle regions, and assist travelers in locating their animals during night grazing hours. In western Tibet, sheep are the most common pack animals and each, for instance, carries two ten-pound loads of salt. A dozen traders usually travel together, and each trader has about one hundred sheep. Both the salt and the sheep are then sold when they arrive at the Nepalese or Indian border.

High in mountainous country, the traveler constantly faces the unexpected, where all accepted rules of nature change without notice. Even the contrast between sun and shade is extreme. The air is too rarefied to absorb the sun's heat and thus create a medium shadow temperature. Nor is one protected from the fierceness of the sun and its ultra-violet rays. Even Tibetans, except those who live permanently in the open air, often wear face-masks while travelling to protect themselves from the fierce sun and still fiercer winds, which sweep over the highlands at certain seasons, carrying with them clouds of fine stinging sand that penetrate even the heaviest clothing.

Crossing a river with a thousand animals is not always simple, easy or smooth. Normally, animals and men are carried across by small yak-skin boats which hold about ten people, or by large wooden ferries which hold thirty. In eastern Tibet, known for its swift currents and treacherous cliffs, an ingenious rope bridge connects two sides of a steep hillside at a 60-degree angle. The traveler is strapped onto a small wooden saddle and then slides, feet first, downwards to the opposite side. Even pack animals, lashed upside-down to the ropeway, are sent sliding in this way to the opposite side, sometimes two or three hundred yards above a torrential river.

When herdsmen arrive in villages or towns to trade and purchase supplies, they often arrange for local merchants, who are aware of market prices and experienced in securing a reasonable profit, to sell their loads of butter, cheese, salt, borax, wool and their finely handcrafted leather and woolen goods. In exchange, the traders buy cotton, tea, and large quantities of grain. Some also buy housewares such as religious objects, paintings, books, incense, carpets, silver stands and lids for wooden teacups, ornately embroidered garments, and coral, amber, turquoise, sandalwood and elephant-bone beads with which the women string their popular jewelry. In addition, they might purchase mineral dyes, medicines, spices, herbs, pearls, precious jewels, Kashmiri silk and brocades, Italian wool, and imports from Europe and America.

Such traders from the north are easily recognized in the warmer valleys, for even in the hottest weather they are accustomed to wear their long coats of sheepskin bordered with bright red, blue and green cloth. Their dialect, too, is full of allusions and picturesque metaphors, and they sprinkle many proverbial expressions into their quick and fluent conversation. According to a popular proverb, "Each district has its way of speaking, as each lama his way of teaching."

Village-dwelling farmers. Many non-nomadic Tibetans divide their time between farming in the summer and herding in the winter. These live in the small mountainous towns of the northeast (Amdo) and east (Kham) and cultivate wheat, barley, buckwheat and beans. But most agriculturalists live in settled communities in the southern and central portions of Tibet, and, while mobile, do not range very far except to make occasional pilgrimages or extended trading journeys. Like their northern neighbors, the village-farmers maintain herds of yak and sheep, but often rent them to travelers, traders and herdsmen during the winter. Otherwise, they must feed their animals on grain and barley stalks saved from the harvest.

Daring stone, cement, mud and wood buildings are typical of Tibet, and architecture does not vary significantly for castles, palaces, temples and private houses. For dwellings they often construct high, almost fortress-like, flat-roofed houses which are closed to the outside but open into one or more inner courtyards. Such buildings—whose walls slope inwards prefiguring modern skyscrapers—usually rise three or four stories up the side of a hill, with cattle, goats and donkeys on the ground floor, living rooms in the middle (containing furniture, various utensils of gold, silver, copper and iron), and a small chapel on the top, decorated with elaborate wood-carvings, silk, turquoise-embedded statues and painted scrolls (thankas). As in ancient times, the flat roofs sometimes function as a threshing floor for grain and a storehouse for firewood.

The land is worked by a pair of dzo drawing wooden ploughs, or in some places by a line of men with long-handled, long-bladed spades.

Tibetan village with temple

The dzo's heads are often decorated with red wool and sometimes with little mirrors which reflect the sunlight and can be seen from a far distancc. Seeds are sown in the spring, or as soon as the earth is sufficiently thawed. By June sprouts appear; in July heavy rains sweep in from the south over the Himalayas; and in late September the harvest begins. Crops are then cut with a short reaping hook and taken to the threshing ground on the backs of donkeys. Threshing is done with wooden flails or by driving cattle round and round over the sheaves, and the grain is winnowed by the wind as it drops from basket-work scoops. During harvest, all other work stops and everyone concentrates their energy on preparing their food supply for the next year. The Tibetans always accompany their plowing, sowing, reaping and threshing with a variety of songs, causing the distant canyons to echo with their melodies. After the harvest, their stores brimming, they celebrate a week-long holiday, traveling to visit friends and drinking *chang*, the national beer made from barley which tastes a little like saki.

The tempo of village life, although relatively easy, often requires much patience, for all labor seems to follow the natural timetable of the seasons. Young Tibetan boys learn their work at an early age and are sent off in charge of sheep or yak, living on the high grazing grounds for days at a time with only a sling and a dog to protect themselves and their herds from wolves and leopards. Girls might also tend the animals, but normally they help in the fields if there is work to be done there. The father and brothers might leave for weeks with a team of yaks or donkeys, either trading or portering, while the mother milks the three or four family cows or settles down to her weaving, producing clothes and bright-colored blankets from home-spun and home-dyed wool.

Objects of Tibetan craft reveal the people's main occupations, for their artifacts are generally practical, efficient tools used in work, colorful clothing which adorns the entire population, and ceremonial implements used in rituals of religious devotion. Tibetans show a predilection for bright primary colors, especially the religious colors of yellow and dark red. Hand-woven carpets and canopies depict various silken floral designs and animal imagery, reflecting perhaps, in their use of the dragon and peacock, cultural influences from Persia and China. In more recent times, Nepalese craftsmen brought many skills to Tibet, especially examples of metal work, but the Tibetans were already skilled in manufacturing cooking utensils, weapons, sword-scabbards, horse-saddles and other items, and had developed their own tradition for molding and guilding sacred religious images and ceremonial implements. Work in bronze, silver, copper and gold was done in very early times, and the ancient T'ang annals of China refer to many presents–such as elaborate, hand-sculptured vases and bowls–made of gold, which seems to have been abundant in early Tibet.

Women in Tibet, as in the West, have a reputation for being conscious of fashionable apparel. On special occasions, they wear wide-sleeved blouses under long gowns and multi-colored aprons with their long black hair augmented by plaits of false hair which rest on a velvet-rolled framework ornamented with pearls, coral and turquoise. Long gold earrings, studded with turquoise, are looped over the ears, and amulet charm-boxes, intricately decorated with gold, turquoise, pearls and diamonds, are worn as necklaces.

Amusements in Tibet are few and simple, for work provides plenty of exercise, and, as each day is counted the same, Tibetans do not look forward to the 'weekend'. Everyone generally takes a rest in the afternoons and on certain leisure days after the harvest and during the winter. Visiting travelers carry the local, regional and national news, and during the summer monks and pilgrims pass through the valleys on their way to visit various shrines or monasteries. Singing and dancing, playing the flute or lute-like guitar, and sharing witty compositions of a local, often satiric, nature are favorite communal pastimes. Spontaneous verses on topical affairs are frequently pointed and witty, but seldom crude, for Tibetans have long excelled in orchestrating skillful allusions and concealing implications. For entertainment not of their own making, traveling bards—men of nomadic origin—chant sections of the traditional, ancient epic of *Gesar*, and are accompanied by singers and dancers, while itinerant monks illustrate religious stories from elaborately painted scrolls.

Few villagers can read, and butter lamps provide little light when the day's work is done. But Tibetans in general are a very mobile people and frequently visit resident lamas or a nearby monastery to offer gifts and seek advice on a variety of material, medicinal and religious matters. Their learning is acquired through word of mouth. Buddhist teachings are transmitted in this way from childhood and thus, despite the lack of intellectual attainment normally associated with reading and writing, the Tibetans freely discourse on a number of subjects and draw their information from well-disciplined memories and a vast realm of practical, common sense.

During the year, festivals, often religious by nature, provide the main source of social entertainment. During Tibetan New Year celebrations (Losar), for example, monks sing performances of religious drama and, at other festivals throughout the year, present scenes from the life of Milarepa or historical episodes depicting such well-known events as Padmasambhava's conquering of the evil spirits of Tibet. These dramas thus provide entertainment while teaching the basic doctrines of the Buddhist faith. These popular teaching stories and Dharma-dancing are accompanied by comic relief artists who wear brightly painted, papier-maché animal masks and delight the crowds, while other variously costumed troupes dance to the music of the traditional drum, cymbals and flute.

With the passage of time, these festivals gained commercial and social importance as well. They are like renaissance fairs, where villagers from the nearby valleys and nomads from distant hills could gather together to make new acquaintances and renew old ones. The farmer dresses up in his best clothes—a black or white woolen chuba, a cotton shirt, and new felt boots—while the women decorate themselves more elaborately. Here too, they barter their agricultural and dairy products. But commerce does not overshadow the original purpose of these festivals, and they remain a sincere demonstration of the Tibetans' inborn faith.

Trade. From early times, a barter system prevailed in Tibet, and barley was commonly used to make purchases ranging from clothes to horses. At the turn of the 20th century, a system of paper currency and silver coins was developed. But the Tibetans have never maintained a central bank, controlled foreign exchange or established a credit card time-payment plan. Markets are controlled solely by local supply and demand–and the fluctuations of weather.

The great bulk of trade is drawn southwards to Central Tibet and Lhasa, and from there to Nepal, India, and eastwards to China. The chief Tibetan exports are wool, borax and salt, and minor exports include the skins of various animals, such as the snow leopard and marmot, musk, deer horns, incense, skillfully crafted metalwork, such as gold-leafed swords and scabbards, and a variety of herbs and medicinal goods. Horses, sheep, donkeys, mules and goats are also exported to Nepal, India and China. In return, a variety of imports entered Tibet–cotton cloth, kerosene, hardware, sugar, soap, and even cosmetics. From China came tea and, to a lesser extent, porcelain and silk, along with various medicinal remedies and herbs. Only at the turn of the century have Western products made their way into Tibet, such as cameras, watches, ballpoint pens, glazed windows, steel girders for building, concrete and certain styles of Western and Chinese cuisine and clothing design. In addition, a great variety of vegetables, flowers and fruit trees appeared which were spread by roots, seeds and cuttings all over Lhasa and beyond.

Tibetans do not easily absorb outside customs and influences, but prefer to adopt a few practices in a casual manner and adapt them to their own taste. Culturally, for example, China has influenced Tibet only superficially when compared to the active Indian Buddhist tradition that proliferated in Tibet. Tea was introduced from China as early as the 8th century, but Tibetans brewed it in their own manner, churning it with butter, and serving it as a light but stimulating broth. The only Chinese crafts adopted for general use seem to have been certain stylistic influences in religious painting (e.g. landscapes), the art of papermaking and, especially, printing from carved wooden blocks.

Self-governing People. Throughout most of Tibet, the inner law of man and the physical law of nature were generally the only recognized authorities. But life in Lhasa, in south-central Tibet, was somewhat different. Lhasa had not only been the early site of the Tibetan kingship under Song-tsen Gam-po and later under Tri-song

De-tsen (d. 797), but was fairly accessible to travelers. Situated on an elevated plain just north of the Himalayas, Lhasa thus became the central hub for commercial traffic, linking Tibetan exports and imports with India, Nepal, Turkestan, Russia, China, Japan and, in modern times, Europe and America. When, in the 17th century, the Fifth Dalai Lama built the Potala Palace on a hill overlooking Lhasa, he assumed both civil and spiritual leadership of the central regions, and life in Lhasa accelerated even more.

Tibetans possess a strong sense of self-reliance and a firm conviction of what is traditionally fair; they are strangers to the concept that the end justifies the means. Ever since the 7th century, Tibet's constitution has consisted of only sixteen maxims which were later reduced to thirteen. Unlike the United States, with its governing constitution and vast legal network, Tibetans have never followed any formal codification of laws, but instead based their social interactions on the religious principles of Buddhism. Through the centuries, church and state were always combined, but a clear delineation between the responsibilities of government and religion might have proven helpful in regulating many mundane matters and in formulating policies which were strictly political. Political decisions, however, simultaneously became religious decisions, and many governing laws and policies that might have been introduced were left to the responsibility of the people. Long-held customs and traditions, based on commitments rather than commandments, determined the law of the land.

The cohesion, strength and harmony required by individual groups supplied all the authority that was necessary. If someone committed a crime, or a question of right or wrong arose, the two parties openly discussed their grievances with the headman and people who decided the matter without delay. Some areas of the country maintained a jail, but flogging provided an effective and direct form of punishment. In ancient times, amputations were used as deterrents, but the Tibetans never condoned capital punishment or the taking of life in any way. If someone committed a serious crime, particularly in the northern regions, he might just run away, but by so doing he surrendered forever his traditional and inherited rights in exchange for the life of a wanderer. Tibetans felt this separation or banishment to be the worst possible punishment.

Tibetans have no caste system as in India, but consider all people as equal. Individual differences, seen in the light of Buddhism, derive from the power of each person's self-created Karma. One of the principle features of Buddhism is that each individual is responsible for his present life, which by its very occurrence, determines his future. It is said that one of Tibet's religious kings, Mu-ne Tsen-po (804 A.D.), the son of Tri-song De-tsen, tried to equalize all the people of Tibet by appointing ministers to redistribute land and property. After some time he asked how the reform was proceeding and learned that the rich were becoming richer, and the poor, poorer. He made two more attempts to reform things, but each time the people drifted back to their original occupations and status of wealth. Rather than use the doctrine of Karma as an excuse or an inducement to passivity, the Tibetans understand that a total effort in this life—whether for material gain or the highest awareness—produces beneficial consequences. They work industriously and diligently, practice sympathetic acceptance of themselves and others, and show no limits when helping those in need. Among their social groupings, one person's suffering, misfortune or welfare affects them all.

Family. Because hereditary possession and family rights were so important, Tibetan families tended to be loosely structured, extended by and linked with many other clans in marriage relationships. In any one family or group, no distinction was made between one's own children, those of one's brothers, those of a second wife, or even those adopted, for all rights and responsibilities were traditionally bestowed on the eldest son. Up to three centuries ago, in certain regions of Tibet, polygamy was practiced specifically to keep property in one family, but most people today take only one partner. But just as there are many kinds of human beings, Tibetan marriage relationships, like those of all other peoples, contain elements of unpredictability.

Tibetans regard marriage as an important social function, and Tibetan wedding ceremonies, whether luxurious or simple, vary only according to the particular customs of the different provinces. In Tibetan society, arranged marriages have proven satisfactory for hundreds of years. Normally the son's family makes extensive inquiries among eligible girls. If the couple's astrological charts are found to be in agreement, and the girl's parents consent to the proposal, the engagement date is fixed by an astrologer. In all events, a satisfactory relationship is considered most important, to ensure harmony not only between husband and wife, but also between other members of the family. Both families, though, ordinarily lavish much attention on the prospective bride and groom, and preparations for the ceremony generate in them both a great deal of excitement and positive expectation, and no one marries against their own will. Love relationships have become more common, and the same precautions are taken by the families to arrange a satisfactory marriage. If a marriage should prove to have difficulties, friends and relations consider it an important duty to mediate. Their over-all objective is to maintain the close-knit unity of the family.

Families in Tibet are characterized by their respect for the elderly. Even beggars, or those who have been previously outcast, or those with little knowledge are respected, for age carries the wisdom of its own experience. It is commonly said that parents have children so that they will be taken care of in their old age, and Tibetan families fulfill this responsibility with natural gratitude. Two and three generations often live in the same house: the old look after the young, and the young look after the old. Children spend most of the day playing and receive very little discipline, and controversy among children within the family is usually minimal. They soon discover what is and what is not allowed, and learn rules of behavior, like all children, by imitating the grownups around them. In this way, by ten or twelve, children mature very rapidly through continual association with all members of the family and are gradually given more and more responsibility.

Astronomy and Astrology. Astronomy, astrology (*kar-tsi*), and the mathematical calculations (*tsi-nag*) and casting of horoscopes (*na-tsi*) play important roles in Tibetans' daily activities. In early times, Babylonian astrological influences probably drifted throughout Central Asia and passed into Tibet via traders and travelers. Thereupon the Tibetans conducted elaborate studies of the position, movements, and size of the planets, listing, according to the 19th-century Lama Mi-pham, ten planets and twenty-eight constellations (*kar-ma*). He also made an extensive study of the *Kalācakra Tantra* (Wheel of Time) which was originally introduced in 1027 A.D.

When a child is born, an astrologer-sage prepares a complete astrological chart, indicating the relative positions of the sun, moon and stars, the cosmic influences likely to affect the child's disposition, and a forecast of the child's entire life. Such astrologers are also called upon for advice and predictions in a variety of family situations. A horoscope is cast when a young man or woman chooses a marriage partner, or to determine the auspicious time to depart on a long journey, to build a house, temple or stupa.

The Tibetan calendar system is somewhat variable. Each year certain adjustments are made to adapt the Tibetan lunar calendars to the actual lunar and solar cycles, to omit negative conjunctions and to duplicate positive ones. A new year begins with the rise of the new moon in the Western month of February, and contains twelve months and seven weekdays, which are named, as in the Western system, for the sun, moon, and the five visible planets (Mars, Mercury, Jupiter, Venus and Saturn). Each year in a cycle of twelve is named after one of the following animals: mouse, ox, tiger, hare, dragon, serpent, horse, sheep, ape, bird, dog, and hog. And each of these combine with the five elements—wood, fire, earth, iron and water—to form a cycle of sixty years. The animal cycle also marks the months, while each day of the lunar month and each day of the week are influenced by the distinctive patterns and energies of the constellations, and are associated with specific qualities, colors and natural elements. An astrologer carefully observes the degrees of antagonism and affinity in the combinations to determine which years, months, days and hours are positive or negative. The combination of the tiger and monkey, for example, is inauspicious, just as iron is hostile to the fire which melts it.

Medicine. Though Tibetan medical practice cannot be compared to modern Western techniques, Tibet possesses a fairly advanced medical science of its own. The earliest medical texts came from the Indian Vedic tradition, from China and even Iran, and four lengthy volumes were translated into Tibetan. These translations form the basis of numerous manuals and theses which were later written by Tibetan medical practitioners and lamas, and this knowledge, once assimilated, became uniquely Tibetan. These texts describe the nature of specific illnesses, prescribe medicines, and detail instructions for surgical operations.

Tibetan medicine attempts to cure the patient as a whole rather than cure a particular disease in isolation, for it recognizes the interdependent relationship between mind and body. As such, its techniques include psychotherapy, astrology and herbal medicines. Tibetan doctors immediately investigate the causes of any illness: that is, when did the sickness appear and what symptoms and changes were experienced. Some of the simpler causes for a disorder might be the result of a change in diet, too much or too little sleep, sadness, or any variety of emotional and mental imbalances. Doctors explore the medical history of the patient to determine the presence of hereditary diseases, check the patient's urine and circulation, and examine his eyes, tongue, teeth and skin. Some can even determine a patient's character and predict the general health of the body for the future by feeling the pulse.

Tibetan science actually evolved from a practical investigation into medicine, and a doctor was required to learn basic geology, biology, physics, philosophy and general chemistry. The Tibetans thus possess a scholastic theoretical knowledge of medicine in conjunction with their age-old traditional practices. In early times, medical practitioners developed complete internal maps of the physical system—knowledge gained in part through meditation—which clearly showed the networks of bones, nerves, muscles, arteries and veins, much like the figures of transparent plastic humans seen commonly in the West. They have even created elaborately descriptive 'trees' of health-oriented and disease-oriented symptoms which detailed and compared physical pathways and structures with the movements, harmonies and disjunctions of the planets.

Doctors in Tibet practice a form of pressure-point massage which is similar to the Japanese *shiatsu*. But the practice of surgery is rare, for Tibetans believe that sickness, disease and infection are caused by natural imbalances, and that the body is inseparably united to emotional upsets—anger, impatience, frustration, rejection in love, sorrow in death—and that only a change in mental perspective and outlook will effect a lasting cure. Even such diseases as heart trouble and cancer, common in the West, are caused in large part, the Tibetans feel, by karmically accumulated negative and depressed mental attitudes.

Many remedies, therefore, are similar to Western homeopathy or naturopathy, and doctors employ both living and non-living natural elements in a variety of combinations. Experienced doctors might, for example, prescribe the intake of meat, eggs, natural oils, animal parts, and, in rare cases, elephant's liver, lion's milk, or a special compound of mercury. Lama Mi-pham spent some time as a chemist, perfecting potent vitamin tablets which acted to restore the natural balance of minerals and elements in the body of the patient.

More commonly, however, the Tibetans employ a large variety of herbal medicines—roots, leaves, stems, flowers, fruits, honey, and sixty-four major minerals—which contain concentrated quantities of vitamins and which are combined in over a thousand ways. Herbs might be boiled and the vapors inhaled, drunk as a tea or used as a poultice. Herbal remedies are particularly well-suited for curing delinquent or persistent diseases, but, since they react slowly and steadily, they are less effective in emergencies. One traveler to Tibet describes having received comfort from an itinerant lama who prepared a mixture of herbs and spices (including rosehips) which was boiled for ten minutes, then strained and drunk. Mineral steam baths in natural hot springs are recommended for rheumatism and arthritis, as well as to stimulate the circulation, and fasting is recommended for a variety of other disorders. For repair of broken bones, the Tibetans have acquired much skill while caring for their many animals. One disease which perennially threatened the life of the young is small-pox, but Western medicines, especially vaccines and injected serums such as penicillin, have recently controlled this infectious disease.

Women practice natural childbirth and are assisted by other women in the family or village. Mothers receive plenty of helpful advice before and after birth, the death rate is very low, and children are commonly healthy and normal. In remote parts of Tibet, where few medical practitioners are available, medical knowledge and training is passed down from father to son, and each family has preserved a variety of traditional household remedies. Doctors, motivated by compassion, are known to travel day and night under difficult conditions to effect their cures, and, when certain medicinal remedies fail to take effect after a period of time, Tibetans assume the disease is a natural outflow of the person's Karma. A lama, who is also often the doctor, is called in to perform various ritual ceremonies, *mantras* and blessings, and the power invested in these spiritual aids is frequently successful where medical remedies are ineffective. Similarly, yogis and meditation practitioners often heal themselves through their understanding of natural processes and their use of specific *mantras.*

The Tibetans either bury their dead in the ground, cremate the bodies, or, in a special ritual, dissect the body and feed the pieces as offerings to vultures. The bones of very important lamas are sometimes preserved as relics for stupas and ritual objects, and at times the entire body is dried, gilded and preserved as a sacred image. A deep understanding of the transitory nature of all life is thus deeply imbedded in the Tibetan mentality from the earliest age.

The stable Tibetan life style and the inevitable panoramic perspective that develops through the practice of Buddhism is not conducive to mental illness. Although Tibetans have to face the natural human limitations imposed by illness, old age and death, they experience little mental suffering or intellectual confusion. From childhood they are taught to take responsibility for their problems and to view suffering as a teacher and impermanence as a valuable guide. Their lives are all of one piece, and not disturbed by a variety of sensations and stimulations. Satisfaction comes from an acceptance of their lives as they are, not as they might wish them to be, and so anxiety, resentment and fantasy-filled expectations do not sway their simple, genuine and cheerful natures. Nor do Tibetans suffer from polluted, crowded or noisy conditions. They work steadily during the planting and harvest seasons, and more leisurely during the winter. Clear water and air blend well with their natural, non-artificial diet.

The Dharma

Prior to the occupation of Tibet, anyone could practice the Dharma. As soon as children were old enough to say their mother's name, they were taught the mantra OṂ MAṆI PADME HŪṂ. Even if an individual could not read, every Tibetan–herdsman, villager, trader or official–soon became familiar with the basic teachings: that this life is precious, rare and unique; that life is impermanent and death is inevitable; that the human situation is encircled by frustration and dissatisfaction; and that one reaps the results of past actions in this and previous lives. The implication of these basic Buddhist teachings affect the life of every Tibetan, for a long heritage of faith and devotion has thoroughly permeated their thinking and behavior. Birth, marriage, joy, sorrow, happiness, pain, sickness, old age and death are all seen as intimately interconnected. This insight, which further recognizes that each person has within himself a nature identical to the Buddhas, has become the basis for the Tibetans' widely acknowledged and all-embracing compassion.

According to the law of Karma, each action and thought leaves its imprint on the character. The present situation, thoughts, habits, emotions and all that is perceived–all existence–is seen as the result of the workings of Karma. Past actions thus establish the potential through which the present is determined, and every action subtly prepares the future. As long as a person is conscious of this continuity, the interrelation of all things, all living beings, and all situations, becomes apparent. This unified view informs the activity and purpose of Tibetan life and underlies a deep trust and faith in their understanding of the attitudes inherent in the practice of Buddhism.

There is another reason for this deep spiritual devotion and faith. In Tibet, the great rhythm of nature pervades everything and increases one's capacity for concentration and self-observation, spontaneously and without effort. The vastness, solitude and silence of nature acts like a concave mirror which not only enlarges and reflects the innermost feelings and emotions, but concentrates their intensity into the focal point of consciousness. Mind and nature, thus joined, dispel the constrictions, obstacles and disturbances of daily life to awaken and develop the higher stages of meditation. This heightened sensitivity to the flow and natural rhythm of life seems to emanate a spiritual atmosphere that envelops the whole of Tibet.

Where Buddhist theory and practice are concerned, no effort or cost ever seemed too extravagant. Judging by the thousands of volumes that have been translated into Tibetan from Sanskrit and other languages, and from the enormous libraries of Sūtras, commentaries, biographies, and other teachings, and judging by the Tibetans' skill in mastering complicated techniques of yoga and their profound knowledge of the workings of the human mind, it seems clear that the study and practice of Buddhism became the central occupation of the Tibetan people. Mastering Buddhism in all its varied forms, many teachers were capable of imparting this living tradition to others.

The formal introduction of Buddhism in Tibet began in the 8th century with the arrival of Padmasambhava. By respecting the national feelings and loyalities of the people and without destroying the ancient traditions of the country, he gave a new impetus to Buddhism and succeeded in building the first large monastery in Tibet at Samye. Here the teachings of the Bodhisattva Path (Mahāyāna) and the Tantras (Vajrayāna) were introduced and handed down to Padmasambhava's closest disciples. Later, when Buddhism was suppressed for a brief time, these disciples scattered, transmitting the original teachings of Padmasambhava to their spiritual followers. Some of these yogins married and were known as nag-pa (*sngags-pa*) or lay followers. Others, called the 'silent ones', were solitary wanderers who practiced meditation in caves or remote hermitages. As they traveled, they continued to produce many translations and to spread the Tantric tradition throughout Tibet. These yogins, many of whom were direct disciples of Padmasambhava, believed that the goal of enlightenment, or Buddhahood, could be gained in a single lifetime, and set themselves wholeheartedly on this path.

It is interesting to observe that Indian and Tibetan society have never abandoned those who reject their social norms and conventions.

Since both the yogi and monk traditionally avoid the activity of ordinary human life and its conventional values and devote themselves to the rigorous path of enlightenment, Tibetans recognize and respect all who dedicate themselves to the Buddhadharma without discriminating between members of various schools. Thus if a religious person, on a pilgrimage to seek teachings or visit a shrine, passes through a village, the people greet him warmly and offer him food and lodging in their homes. At times, ten or fifteen lamas might gather together in this way, and perhaps a hundred villagers might participate in the recitation of prayers, meditation and, at certain holy times, ritual ceremonies.

Monastic Life. Buddhism was not introduced into Tibet all at once, but at different times by different teachers. Somewhat later, in the eleventh century, Atīśa founded several monasteries in western Tibet where the study and practice of Buddhism became the recognized central activity of organized groups, the monastic Saṅgha.

Originally, small hermitages were built near the meditation caves of spiritual masters. Not far from Samye, for example, about 500 feet below the summit of a hill, there is a small shrine revered by the Nyingmapas which preserves the site where Padmasambhava practiced meditation. A great number of similar caves served as meditation chambers and as permanent abodes of hermits and monks, so that the entire area became saturated with a fervor of religious devotion and a life of contemplation in an environment of overwhelming solitude and silence. In hermitages such as these, meditators might remain for one, three, five and even ten years or more, practicing visualization techniques and mastering the advanced teachings. Those who lived singly or in small groups often attracted others who were seeking masters qualified and willing to initiate them in spiritual practice. These teachings were often communicated through oral instruction and nonverbal interaction with the teacher and were not given away for the mere asking. To request the teachings required a corresponding commitment on the part of the disciple, and all who came into contact with an authentic master soon realized this.

These small communities, often constructed high in a gorge or far from the normal stream of commerce, possessed little or no land, and they depended for their food and other minimal supplies on nearby residents, the ingenuity of the disciples, or on the families of those who resided there. Monasteries thus developed close relationships with nearby villages, each providing essential mutual services to the other.

Monasteries nurtured the religious, educational and cultural climate of the community, and laymen in turn supported the monks with gifts of food and other necessities.

Tibetan monasteries—except for the large founding monasteries of each of the schools—were relatively small, housing fifty to two hundred monks, and often only ten or twenty. Monks were distinguished from the lay Saṅgha primarily by their observance of a number of disciplinary vows, as well as celibacy. Lamas, on the other hand, might also choose to marry and live as laymen. As many texts became available, and lamas acquired skills in interpretation and commentary, the monasteries evolved into teaching and training colleges and provided formal educational instruction in logic and philosophy as well as the performance of rituals and advanced meditation practices. Within monasteries, the practice of Buddhism embraced an immensely diverse world of scholastic and religious functions. Comparable to modern colleges of arts and letters, they soon became educational centers of encyclopedic knowledge and possessed a rich and subtle philosophy with their own dialectics and metaphysics, an advanced depth psychology which employed meditative techniques to control psycho-physiological functions, and countless ceremonial rituals for the attainment of higher states of consciousness. These monasteries were modeled on the renowned Buddhist universities of a thousand years ago, such as Nālandā and Vikramaśilā, and maintained high standards of scholarship.

Following acceptance, a new student was taught to read, write and memorize the Buddha's discourses, and embarked on an intensive and extensive period of study which normally lasted for fourteen years or more. This included the practice of the Vinaya, or virtues of the monk, and instructions in chanting, mudra, painting and sculpture; an exploration of the Abhidharma literature (e.g. Vasubandhu's *Abhidharmakoṣa* and Asaṅga's *Abhidharmasamuccaya*); the meanings of the Sūtras and their commentaries; the Prajñāpāramitā literature (the study of the doctrine of Śūnyatā); the philosophy of the Madhyamaka as taught by Nāgārjuna, Candrakīrti and their successors, and thereupon, initiation into the Tantras, or esoteric teachings. Upon completion of each area of study, students were granted degrees which correspond, variously, to the number of vows taken, scriptures read, and classes attended—all of which required a demonstration of mastery. Should a student, upon examination, prove to be a master of all studies, he was entitled to a variety of scholastic and monastic degrees, according to his particular school and the function for which he was training, and thus became authorized to train others, academically and spiritually. Progress toward such degrees might take many years, until the candidate's mastery was unquestioned. The teachings of the Hīnayāna and Mahāyāna were available to everyone, but the Tantric teachings, the Vajrayāna, were given only to those who were judged sufficiently prepared to receive and understand them; otherwise these teachings might be misinterpreted or misused, consciously or unconsciously. The practice of the Tantras is likened to atomic energy, which can be used for constructive or destructive purposes. But if these esoteric teachings are pursued diligently, they open up to the practitioner the possibility of attaining Buddhahood in this lifetime.

Some monasteries traditionally emphasized 'learning by heart' to such an extent that writing and notetaking were discouraged. Learning to write and compose Tibetan was not necessarily considered essential to the acquisition of true religious knowledge. Only after a student became a master was he encouraged to write, and these works were often commentaries on the scriptures for one's own self-edification. Lama Mi-pham and others, however, wrote many excellent treatises at an early age. During examinations, which often took the form of conventionalized debates–successful candidates were expected to display a theoretical and experiential knowledge of Buddhist doctrines, quoting liberally and precisely from revered texts. Through years of training, they memorized considerable quantities of sacred literature and became, as it were, great repositories of the Dharma, able to produce from their store any text or quotation which served the immediate argument. It was not unusual for a monk trained in this manner to sit for three or four days and chant the Dharma literature from memory. The success of this concentrated effort to absorb texts for oral reproduction was considered supremely more valuable than possessing a vast library, especially in moments of practice when passages could easily be recalled, deepening awareness and understanding.

Both the academic and business organization of the monastery were under the central control of the Grand Lama who was always a living Buddha (*sprul-sku*, pron. tul-ku). Under his guidance, for example, a variety of regents and administrators presided over religious ceremonies, both within the monastery and in the surrounding villages, managed monastery property and governed its maintenance, conducted affairs of business and trade, oversaw the work of thanka artists, craftsman, carpenters and the cutting of wooden blocks for the

Illustrated manuscript of the Prajñāpāramitā Sutra (Perfection of Wisdom)

printing of Dharma texts, and whatever else was necessary to maintain the monastic city.

Since the time of Padmasambhava, making translations and preserving the handwritten Buddhist texts offered the monks a time-consuming occupation. Books written on palm leaves or other vegetative matter, especially texts brought from India, tended to deteriorate after fifty years, and thus the entire literature required extensive recopying and renewing. One notable craft adopted for general use from China was the art of papermaking and printing from incised wooden blocks called xylographs. To print in this way requires a school of highly trained wood-carvers, for every letter on the page has to be carved with the utmost precision so that it remains standing ready to receive the ink, while the rest of the wood is cut away. A skilled carver might complete an average-sized woodblock (measuring 4″ × 16″ and carrying 300 characters) in seven to ten days. Books were not bound but enclosed between two elaborately carved wooden bookends, or wrapped in silk. From the time of its introduction, this form of printing was a great advance and was taken up eagerly by the Tibetans, for this enabled them to make as many copies of their sacred texts as they pleased. The entire Tibetan Buddhist Canon (*Tripiṭaka*), consisting of 4,681 texts, was first printed in this manner in Peking (1411 A.D.). Thereafter, each large monastery developed its own printing facility, but Derge in eastern and Narthang in central Tibet became two main printing establishments, along with printing centers in Lhasa, and Ragya (Amdo). These monasteries stored thousands upon thousands of carved woodblocks, ready to reprint to order. Even today, however, many Tibetan books, written within the last century by advanced masters, exist only in the original handwritten manuscript. It is a historical fact that when a culture is threatened, the people record their indigenous literature and most important traditions in writing. A few of these texts have been preserved outside of Tibet, and their distribution and translation will certainly become a major task in the years ahead.

Festivals. Rituals performed in monasteries were not open to the public, but religious festivals, celebrated by lamas dressed in elaborate dance costumes, attracted many lay people. These festivals, which were meant to renew the people's faith, also provided a welcome time of leisure.

For example, on New Year's day in Lhasa (or Losar, the first day of the first moon, usually in February), the city's population of 80,000 attended a large prayer meeting which was dedicated to the welfare of all sentient beings. After elaborate preparations, 20,000 monks joined the lay people to swell the city streets where the reading of scriptures, religious debates, feasting and colorful folk dances followed consecutively from dawn until midnight for several days. In the early morning of the last day, the stomping boots of dancers punctuate the clash of cymbals and drums, and the deafening drones of shrill horns announce the beginning of the Sacred Masked Dance (*Cham*). Unlike other festivals which present mime and dance narratives of well-known stories from Tibetan Buddhist history, the Cham is a solemn masked dance performed by trained and agile monk dancers in elaborately designed costumes. Accompanied by music but without words, the dances are masterpieces of choreography and symbolism. Every gesture of the hands and feet is meant to imitate the activity and expression of the deity which is symbolized by each dancer.

In mid-summer, monks and villagers gather on the sloping, green mountain sides for another fire ceremony and enjoy dramatic presentations of Buddhist legends and tales (*a-che lha-mo*). Once, for example, there was a hermit named Milarepa who lived in a cave. One day, a frightened deer, who is being chased vigorously by a wild and savage hound, enters his cave seeking refuge. Seeing the helpless nature of all animated beings, Milarepa explains the all-embracing protection of the Dharma, and saves the deer. When the dog arrives at the cave, he too finds the warmth of compassion and sits down in a friendly fashion next to the deer. Meanwhile, the hunter follows the trail to the cave and is amazed to see the deer and hound sitting together. Aware that he is in the presence of an extraordinary hermit, the hunter questions Milarepa who sings him a song:

> The Buddha, the Dharma and the Saṅgha–
> These three are Mila's refuge.
>
> The View, the Practice and the Action–
> These three Dharmas Mila practices.
>
> The snow, the rocks and the clay mountains–
> These three are where Mila meditates.
>
> The sun, the moon and the stars–
> These three are Mila's expanse.
>
> Bliss, Illumination and Non-thought–
> These three are Mila's companions.
>
> Porridge, roots and nettles–
> These three are Mila's food.
>
> Water from snow, spring and brook–
> These three are Mila's drink.
>
> The Nadīs, Breaths and Bindus–
> These three are Mila's clothing.
>
> [Chang, p. 147]

Upon hearing this, the huntsman experiences a change of heart and requests from Milarepa the teaching of the Dharma and the Path to Liberation.

Literature. While there are many regional dialects in Tibet, one printed script unifies the whole of Tibetan literary culture. Of the students King Song-tsen Gam-po sent to India in the middle of the 7th century, Thu-mi Sam-bho-ta returned to devise a written script for the Tibetan language which he derived from languages similar to Sanskrit. The Tibetan alphabet consists of four vowels and thirty consonants, several of which are said to have been brought to Tibet by

Padmasambhava. In addition, the sounds of at least six Tibetan letters are not reproduced in any other language. *U-me*, the handwritten form of Tibetan, has nine or ten different styles depending on the region, while *U-chen*, the printed script, has remained unchanged from the earliest times.

Just as modern English contains a vast and specific vocabulary of technical terms related to science and industry, the precise nature of the Tibetan language lends itself to the expression of fine shades of meaning and embraces a vast philosophical vocabulary which enables the language to define accurately the nature of mind and consciousness. This is evident from the time of the Golden Age of Padmasambhava in the 8th century when, with the aid of Śāntarakṣita, Vimalamitra and Vairocana, the scriptural canons of the Kangyur (150 volumes) and the Tangyur (240 volumes) were translated from the Sanskrit. These translations were not simply word-for-word equivalents. The Tibetans have always concerned themselves with the 'meaning in usage' of a term, and their translations reflect the interpreted and refined understanding of the translators. In this way written Tibetan acquired a unique ability to express difficult concepts and still preserve the living spirit of Buddhism. Texts which were not translated at that time, but which represent the original works of Padmasambhava and his disciples, or works discovered at a later time (*gter-ma*), were compiled in large collections known as the 'Tantras of the Ancient Ones' (*rNying-ma'i rgyud-'bum*) and the 'Revealed Treasures' (*Rin-chen gter-mdzod*) of the Nyingmapas.

Education in Tibet was primarily the domain and privilege of the monasteries where a strong oral tradition of teaching was faithfully preserved and where indigenous Tibetan literature–epics, biographies, legends and songs–were written down in a permanent form. These lama-authors–unlike scribes of other lands and times who could not understand the language they copied–were prolific scholars of encyclopedic learning and vision. They produced many original works and commentaries on philosophy, logic, religion and ethics; textbooks on grammar, dictionaries and bibliographies; treatises on astrology and medicine; histories, geographies and travelogues; treatises on the art of government and on various skilled crafts such as agriculture, casting, painting and printing; and a vast variety of songs, poems, plays, novella-biographies, collections of tales, and epics.

Not all of this literature, however, originated with the monks. For centuries, Tibetans composed epigrams, rhymes, riddles and metaphorical songs, particularly when entire families and clans—fortified perhaps by a keg of barley-beer—gathered in the fields at plowing or harvest time. Contests featuring clever innuendoes and light mockery, as well as folk songs, dancing and the telling of legendary tales, were favorite pastimes and were spread throughout Tibet by wandering bards, traders and pilgrims. In the 11th century, Milarepa, in his *Hundred Thousand Songs*, popularized Buddhist thought by composing lively lyrical songs containing countless details from real life.

> The lovely flowers of turquoise-blue
> Are destroyed in time by frost—
> This shows the illusory nature of all beings,
> This proves the transient nature of all things.
> First think on these things,
> Then you will practice Dharma.
> [Chang, p. 97]

This practice of using natural imagery, though ancient, reveals a unifying visionary thread which ties folk realism to religious didacticism. In paintings, for example, Milarepa is usually depicted with his right hand up to his ear, a gesture which expresses both poetic and religious inspiration and which characterizes the epic bard who receives revelations from the heavenly muses. At festivals and other times, the bard who chanted portions of the epics—such as the *Wondrous Story of Ling Gesar*—might enter a meditation-induced 'trance', so that through him the epic hero might chant his startling and amazing adventures in the realms of both gods and men. This kind of 'separate world' is traditionally represented as an inexhaustible repository of inspiration and knowledge available to seers and visionaries in the process of meditation.

Other treasures, manuscripts written on rolls of yellow paper and hidden caves, within special rocks and at the bottom of pools, have also been discovered. These texts (Terma), which were originally written down and concealed by Padmasambhava, Ye-shey Tso-gyal, and other disciples to await discovery at a future time, have provided a continuous flow of teachings which have preserved the original spirit of Buddhism. Some of these, most notably the *Padma Thang Yig*, which celebrates Padmasambhava's life and times, and the *Bardo Thodol*, or *Tibetan Book of the Dead*—which comprises a small portion of a larger Nyingma work discovered by Karma Ling-pa—have become well-known treasures of Tibetan literature.

Art. The art of thanka painting plays a major role in this tradition of visionary revelation. Tibetan art does not merely 'hold the mirror up to nature', but reveals, through imagery, color, proportion and symbolic detail, the nature and landscape of the human mind. This the Buddhists term *śūnyatā*, which in the ultimate sense, is void of all earthly and illusory conceptions. This doctrine points out that man's self, his mind, and the objects of his attention are all expressions of a nameless state of consciousness that can be termed 'intrinsic awareness'. The figures of deities and their postures, gestures, colors, ornaments and spatial relationships each carry a message of complex design, and communicate a depth of experience and subtlety of understanding that represents, through relative forms, human nature in its ultimate manifestation as identical to the qualities and awareness of the Buddha. The Enlightened One, as represented in art, is thus depicted as ultimate perfection and beauty, both to arouse the viewer's appreciation and to spur him to seek the highest qualities inherent in his own nature.

The use of symbols in Tibetan art demonstrates a powerful means whereby insights, which cannot be grasped conceptually and which are normally inaccessible to our ordinary human vision, are charged with an illuminating energy. Symbols are meant to embody the innate presence of the Buddha—the self-originated, unborn, unchangeable essence of all beings. Like a diamond imbedded in a mountain, this primordial nature of Being is illusively concealed by a film of prejudice, erroneous spiritual conceptions and worldly bewilderments. The various Peaceful and Wrathful Buddhas, both radiant and awesome, at once exemplify man's highest ideals and stimulate in the meditator the dispersal of anxiety, anger, depression, guilt, dullness of feeling, inability to communicate, frustrated expectations—all the obstacles to freedom of body, speech and mind. The celestial bodies of Buddhas, seen as emanations of primordial energy become visible, embody a wealth of psychological and philosophical understanding of human behavior and human needs in all their variety, complexity and depth. Symbols, in the intensity of their implied intuitive meanings, become subtle catalysts whereby the meditator can break through mental and physical obstacles in the actual situations of human life and discover the opportunities and healthy attitudes that lead to a deepening of self-acceptance, light, beauty, and peace. But the primary 'utility' of Tibetan art is not necessarily what it presents or symbolizes, but simply and ultimately that it *is*—a manifestation of enlightened consciousness which enables

the viewer to see all that exists, including himself, as participating in the ultimate perfection of beauty and truth.

The creation of this art is in itself a meditation. Painters and sculptors, known as 'depictors of deities', are regarded as humble craftsmen rather than originators of new forms. The primary function of Buddhist art is not to express an individual vision or to explore new forms, but to awaken and enliven the intuitive awareness of both the artist and viewer. Beyond the mindfulness required of each brush-stroke, the execution of this art is highly stylized. As in the poetic creation of the bard, the artist visualizes the deities in meditation before and during painting, and follows elaborate instructions as to the appropriate time and method of drawing the figures in ink, mixing colors and applying paint. Each deity is associated with a specific spiritual practice, and the execution of a single painting may take weeks and even months as the various visualizations, mantras and rituals are performed. The paintings, seen as guides to perfection and perfection itself, are executed to correspond exactly to ultimate reality so that the painter and viewer might be invested with the deity's qualities and ways of being.

This art is therefore considered eminently sacred by the Tibetans, for it has great power to effect profound transformations in one's level of consciousness. In pointing to a 'divine' realm, thanka art clearly indicates the value and significance of human beings, particularly in that moment of appreciation wherein the 'message' of the art and one's own experience merges in the light of a deeply felt comprehension of universal insight. The thankas thus not only depict Bodhisattvas who serve the enlightenment of all beings, but the thankas themselves partake of that enlightening power to open the perception and awareness of the viewer, and are thus considered as sacred as the deities they represent.

There are five lineages of thanka painting in Tibet. Stylistically, Tibetan art reflects various degrees of Indian, Nepalese, Persian, Mongolian and Chinese influences. The clouds, the density or brightness of the paint, the number of displayed offerings, the ornamentations of jewelry, clothing, and landscape all vary according to the time and location of each individual painting. It is sometimes said that, because Tibetan art follows strict guidelines for imagery and proportion, the artist relinquishes the potential freedom of imaginative creativity. But this art, seen as inspired by the enlightened consciousness, allows the

Buddha Ratnasambhava—Gyantse Kum-Bum (Central Tibet)

artist to immerse himself in the consciousness from which the art springs, and yet to participate actively in the subtle and complex symbolism of the thanka's psychological imagery.

Further, paintings were created as an act of devotion, irrespective of whether they would be seen or not. More than mere decorations, they were prayers and meditations in line and color. For this reason, scroll paintings and frescoes were often lavishly encrusted with gold and minutely executed, but later they might even be placed in the darkest corners of the temples. Despite the minute execution of details, some fresco-figures are three, five, and even ten times larger than life, while others, no larger than a thumbnail, contain figures complete in every detail. Merely to trace these delicate lines accurately demands the most intensive concentration and permits the artist to relinquish his own (samsaric) identity and enter the bodies, personalities, thoughts, feelings, and innermost life of the Buddhas and Bodhisattvas, Lamas, Yidams, Ḍākas, Ḍākinīs, Rakśas, and the forty-two Peaceful and fifty-eight Wrathful Deities, each with different faces, colors, ornamentations and symbols. The artist thus enters an inexpressible *maṇḍala,* whereby the invisible becomes visible and appreciation merges with understanding.

The Tibetans' love of nature appears in their bright and joyful depiction of sky, clouds, valleys, rivers and animals which form the customary background to the central figure of the thanka. In particular, those paintings which illustrate the life stories of great teachers and saints–the Buddha, Padmasambhava, Gesar, Milarepa, the Eighty-four Accomplished Ones–often depict extravagant biographical scenes, showing for example, the Buddha's birth, his life in court, his renunciation, his enlightenment, his turning the wheel of the Dharma, and his Parinirvāṇa or passing away. A wandering story teller would often carry numerous rolls of thankas, perhaps those depicting the fable-stories of the Jātaka Tales, and point out the scenes on the painting with a stick as he sang or chanted the narrative. This technique of illustrated recitation circulated among monks in India, China and Japan, and long captions were sometimes written under each scene to identify the figures and episodes.

The sculptured images of Tibet, known as *rūpas*, are variously made from wood, metal, papier-maché and clay. The large temple images are usually constructed from hardened clay, which is sun-dried, gilded and painted. Smaller metal images are cast by the 'lost-wax' method, where the original form is first shaped in wax and then buried in packed earth. When wax is melted out, molten metal is poured into the resultant mold. Bronze and brass are generally used but sometimes a highly-prized silver-gold alloy is substituted. Copper images are hammered into proper shape, and decorated with turquoise and coral inlays. The Tibetan rupas are hollow, and in a ceremony called *Rabs-gnas zhu-gi-pa*, officiating lamas place mantras, relics, jewels, precious metals, and various consecrated material in the inner cavity which is then sealed with a copper plate and marked with a crossed vajra (✣). This multiplicity of forms and metaphors thus reveals the Tibetan predilection that, at some time and some place, there must be some path or practice, or some appealing visible manifestation of ultimate and inherent reality, which is suited to the consciousness of every sentient being.

Conclusion

Only a handful of Westerners–ambassadors, anthropologists, mountain climbers and private adventurers–have ever glimpsed the Tibetan civilization first-hand. And Western scholars, having little choice but to study Tibetan literature as a classical language, seldom participated in a living, seasoned relationship with the history, legends, religion and iconography of the Tibetan people. Without a comprehensive knowledge of Tibetan language, culture, philosophy and spiritual practice, subjective observations and misinterpretations led to the extreme view that Tibet was a country overrun by magicians or that their art displayed a rampant eroticism. Internal symbologies representing an elaborate investigation of human nature require time, explanation and participation. Thus, even though many people are now aware that the Tibetans developed a sophisticated culture of vast learning, the depths of their knowledge–demonstrated by their rich oral methods of teaching–have remained unexplored and inaccessible to the West.

Many changes have inevitably affected the life and ways of the Tibetan people. Some would even say that Tibet's misfortune is the Western world's unique and unprecedented inheritance. What matters, then, is that the continuity of Tibet's cultural and spiritual heritage, which is based on a living tradition and conscious connection with man's origins, not be severed.

Buddhism recognizes change as the nature of all life. The test of its versatility, adaptability and universality lies, perhaps, in the challenges which are offered by communication with the West. Here, may the strength and character of this ancient tradition give new birth to the timeless concern of all men.

References and Further Readings

An-che, Li. A Lamasery in Outline, *J. West China Research Soc.,* 1942, *14,* 35–68.

An-che, Li. Rnin-ma-pa: The Early Form of Lamaism, *J. Royal Asiatic Soc.,* 1948, 142–63.

Bell, Sir Charles. *The People of Tibet.* London: Oxford, 1928.

Chang, G. C. C. (Trans.) *The Hundred Thousand Songs of Milarepa.* New York: Harper & Row, 1970.

Das, Sarat Chandra. *Journey to Lhasa and Central Tibet.* London, 1902; New Delhi: Manjusri, 1970.

Ekvall, Robert B. *Religious Observances in Tibet: Patterns and Function.* Chicago: Univ. Chicago Press, 1964.

Ferrari, A. & Petech, L. *mKhyen-brtse's Guide to the Holy Places of Central Tibet.* Rome, 1958.

Govinda, Lama Anagarika. *The Way of the White Clouds.* Berkeley: Shambhala, 1970.

Harrer, Heinrich. *Seven Years in Tibet* (Trans. Richard Graves). New York: Dutton, 1954.

Norbu, Dawa. *Red Star Over Tibet.* London: Collins, 1974.

Norbu, Thubten Jigme & Turnbull, Colin M. *Tibet.* New York: Simon & Schuster, 1968.

Olschak, Blanche Christine & Wangyal, Geshe Thupten. *Mystic Art of Ancient Tibet.* New York: McGraw Hill, 1973.

Shakabpa, Tsepon W. D. *Tibet: A Political History.* New Haven and London: Yale Univ. Press, 1967.

Snellgrove, David L. *Four Lamas of Dolpo.* Oxford: Bruno Cassirer, 1967.

Snellgrove, David & Richardson, Hugh. *A Cultural History of Tibet.* London: Weidenfeld and Nicolson, 1968.

Stein, R. A. *Tibetan Civilization* (Trans. J. E. S. Driver). Stanford: Stanford Univ. Press, 1972.

Taring, Rinchen Dolma. *Daughter of Tibet.* London: John Murray, 1970.

Tucci, G. *Tibet: Land of Snows.* London, 1967.

Tucci, G. *To Lhasa and Beyond* (Trans. M. Carelli). Rome, 1956.

A Tibetan Buddhist Looks at Christianity

Lama Anagarika Govinda

Great religious and deep-rooted philosophical attitudes are not individual creations, though they may have been given their first impetus by great individuals. They grow from the germs of creative ideas, great experiences and profound visions. They grow through many generations according to their own inherent law, just like a tree or any other living organism. They are what we might call 'natural events of the spirit'.

LAMA GOVINDA, Foundations of Tibetan Mysticism

TO UNDERSTAND A TIBETAN BUDDHIST'S ATTITUDE towards Christianity we must first of all know what religion means to him. The nearest Tibetan equivalent for 'religion' is *chö* (Sanskrit, *dharma*), which signifies the spiritual and universal law, the principle that supports (*dhar*) all that exists. To live in harmony with this law is the highest aspiration of man and means to dwell in a state of truth and virtue.

To a Tibetan, therefore, religion is not so much the adherence to a certain creed or dogma, but a natural expression of faith in the higher destiny of man, i.e., in his capacity to free himself from the bondage of delusion and the narrowness of egohood in order to realize the universality of his true nature in the Enlightened Mind.

There are as many ways and methods to achieve this as there are types of human beings, and, therefore, the Tibetan regards the diversity of religions not as a calamity or a reason for quarreling and mutual enmity, but as something that is natural and necessary for the spiritual growth of humanity.

The Tibetan, who is highly individualistic, therefore recognizes and respects innumerable forms of religious practice and devotion, and, in fact, there are many different schools of Buddhism in Tibet—as different from each other as the various Christian Churches and sects—but there is no enmity or sense of competition between them. They live peacefully side by side and recognize each other's validity. By accepting a teacher from one school one does not exclude those of other schools. Indeed, very often the teachings or methods of different schools complement and help each other in the most effective way.

The individualistic attitude in religious matters is expressed in a well-known Tibetan proverb:

> *Lung-pa ré-ré kä-lug ré,*
> *Lama ré-ré chö-lug ré.*
>
> Every district has its own dialect,
> Every Lama his own doctrine.

According to this principle, people are free to accept or to reject beliefs or practices according to their conviction and to express their opinions freely and fearlessly. Religious discussions are always welcomed, and people who can give convincing expression to their ideas are highly respected. The art of public discussion was particularly fostered by the big monastic universities, like Ganden, Drepung and Sera.

At the same time the Tibetan is not so naive as to believe that religious truths can be proved by mere logic or settled by arguments.

Tibetan teachers always stress the fact that ultimate truth cannot be expressed in words, but only realized within ourselves. It is therefore not important what we believe, but what we experience and practice, and how it affects us and our surroundings. Whatever leads to a state of greater peace and harmony leads us on the right path.

IN TIBET A SAINT is regarded to be higher than a king, a man who is able to renounce worldly possessions, higher than a rich man, and a man who can sacrifice his own life out of love and compassion for his fellow-beings is honored more than a world conqueror.

Up to the present day the stories of the self-sacrificing career of the Buddha during innumerable previous lives on earth as a Bodhisattva are recounted at camp-fires, at religious and secular festivals, in homes and in hermitages, on lonely caravan-trails, and in crowded market-places—and they never fail to stir the emotions of even the roughest mule-driver or the most sophisticated townsman, because these stories are not merely matters of a nebulous past, but have their counterparts in the lives of many Tibetan saints who have inspired past and present generations.

Under such circumstances it will be easy to understand that the story of Christ and his suffering on the cross for the sake of humanity is something that appeals deeply to the religious feelings of the average Tibetan. But if somebody would tell him: "Now you must abandon all other saints and saviors and only worship this one," he would be surprised and shocked at such a demand. Because to him the proof of truth lies in the very fact that at all times and among all peoples enlightened religious leaders and saints have appeared, who brought the message of love and compassion and re-established the knowledge of that ultimate Reality, which Christians identify with God, Hindus with Brahman, and Buddhists with the state of Enlightenment, beyond words and definitions.

If Christianity could not make headway in Tibet, in spite of the warm reception which was accorded to early missionaries, then this had its reason not in a rejection of Christ or of his essential teachings but, on the contrary, in the fact that the teachings of Christ coincide with and are amply borne out by the Bodhisattva ideal and have been practiced in Tibet more than anywhere in Europe.

The second reason, however, was that those who tried to convey the teachings of Christ to Tibet were unwilling to recognize the great thoughts and saints of that country, and were more concerned with their own parochial outlook and man-made dogmas than with the universal message of Christ.

Nothing could illustrate better the Tibetan attitude towards Christianity than the following historical instances which amply bear out my contention.

THE FIRST CHRISTIAN MISSIONARY to reach Tibet was the Portuguese Padre Antonio de Andrade, who in the year 1625 was received with great hospitality at Tsaparang by the King of Guge in Western Tibet. The King paid him high honor and, in the true spirit of Buddhist tolerance, allowed him to preach his religion! To him, a

The central rock of Tsaparang Monastery with Palaces of the Kings (Western Tibet). Pen drawing by the author

man who had traveled around half the world for the sake of his faith was certainly worth hearing and deserved the greatest respect.

He was convinced that truth cannot harm truth, and that, therefore, whatever was true in the religion of the stranger, could only enhance, amplify, and bear out the teachings of Tibetan saints and of the Buddhas and Bodhisattvas. Was it not possible that in the countries of the West many a Bodhisattva had arisen, of whom the people of the East had not yet heard? So, out of the goodness of his heart, the King of Guge wrote the following letter to Padre Antonio de Andrade in the year 1625:

> We the King of the Kingdoms of Potente, rejoicing at the arrival in our lands of Padre Antonio Franguim (as the Portuguese were called in

India) to teach us a holy law, take him for our Chief Lama and give him full authority to teach the holy law to our people. We shall not allow that anyone molest him in this, and we shall issue orders that he be given a site and all the help needed to build a house of prayer.

And the King gave even his own garden to the stranger, a gift which under the conditions of Tibet, where gardens are scarce and a rare luxury, was more than a mere polite gesture.

But, alas, the King in his unsuspecting goodness did not know that the stranger had come not merely to exchange true and beautiful thoughts with those who were striving after similar ideals, but to repudiate the teachings of Buddhism, in order to replace them by what he regarded as the sole truth. The conflict was inevitable: discontent spread in the country, and the political opponents of the King rose against him.

While Padre Andrade, encouraged by his success in Tsaparang, proceeded to Lhasa in order to extend his activities over the whole of Tibet, a revolt broke out in Western Tibet, the King was overthrown, and with him the Guge dynasty and the glory of Tsaparang came to an end.

ABOUT A CENTURY LATER, in 1716, the Jesuit Padre Desideri arrived in Lhasa. He was given a beautiful house, provided with all the comfort of an honored guest, and was allowed to propagate his religion by preaching as well as through writing. In fact, he wrote a book in order to refute certain Buddhist teachings which created much interest. This is how Desideri recorded the event: "My house suddenly became the scene of incessant comings and goings by all sorts of people, chiefly learned men and professors, who came from the monasteries and universities, especially those of Sera and Drepung, the principal ones, to apply for permission to read the book."

Tibet in those days was certainly more civilized than contemporary Europe, where heretics and their books were burned and persecuted. One can imagine what would have happened in Rome if a stranger had tried to refute publicly the tenets of Christianity!

No wonder, therefore, that the representatives of Christianity were not able to appreciate the spirit of tolerance and to take advantage of the door that was opened to them by reciprocating in the same spirit. Thus, the great opportunity was lost!

Yet, we may hope that when the followers of Christ and those of the Buddha meet again on the ground of mutual goodwill and understanding, there will come a day when the love, which both Buddha and Christ preached so eloquently, will unite the world in the common effort to save humanity from destruction by leading it towards the Light in which we all believe.

Pilgrims and Monasteries in the Himalayas

Lama Anagarika Govinda

To see the greatness of a mountain, one must keep one's distance; to understand its form, one must move around it; to experience its moods, one must see it at sunrise and sunset, at noon and at midnight, in sun and in rain, in snow and in storm, in summer and in winter and in all the other seasons. He who can see the mountain like this comes near to the life of the mountain, a life that is as intense and varied as that of a human being.

LAMA GOVINDA, The Way of the White Clouds

THE HIMALAYAS ARE NOT ONLY the highest and mightiest mountains in the world—awe-inspiring by their mere vastness—but are also the meeting place of the most ancient and spiritually advanced civilizations of the world. Like a gigantic magnet, the Himalayas seemed to attract the best that each passing age and culture had to offer and thus to blend the wisdom and art of many nations and ages and to retain them in the shelters of protected valleys and in the fastnesses of its highlands.

Though the mountains acted as a barrier to physical forces and the worldly ambitions of kings and conquerors, they were no obstacle to the exchange of spiritual achievements and to the cultivation and preservation of ancient traditions. On the contrary, they acted as a restraining, selective and purifying factor, separating the chaff from the grain, the base metal from the gold and the trivial and superficial from the genuine. The mountains are therefore a challenge to the spirit of man. Only those who have the strength and endurance to stand up to it can survive in this world.

The challenge of the mountains is twofold. On the one hand, nature presents itself in such enchanting beauty and grandeur that creations of human origin appear to be dwarfed and insignificant in comparison. On the other hand, nature displays its ferocious and destructive forces which challenge the very existence of man.

But the more a man has to struggle against the adverse forces of nature, the greater is the intensity of his inner life and of his creative imagination. In order to balance the powerful influences of the external world he has to build up his own inner world. This, however, does not happen in an entirely independent or arbitrary way but according to certain laws, and the deeper a man looked within himself, the more it dawned upon him that these laws were the same which created the rhythm of mountains, the eternal song of streams and waterfalls, the fury of blizzards, and the silent beauty of snow and clouds. And it was this discovery which gave man the strength to accept the twofold challenge of nature and made the Himalayas the abode of saints and sages and the refuge of all those who were seekers of truth and beauty, of bodily and spiritual health.

The profound parallelism of body and soul, spiritual and natural laws, inner and outer forces, is nowhere more capable of direct experiment than in the mountains, and of all mountains nowhere more than in the Himalayas where thousands of years of human devotion have created an atmosphere and tradition which is unequalled by any other region in the world. It is an atmosphere of devotion, which is older than any organized religion or dogma, though many a religious belief may have grown out of it and many systems of religious interpretation may have been superimposed on it.

"In the oldest religion, everything was alive, not supernaturally but naturally alive. . . . For the whole life-effort of man was to get his life into contact with the elemental life of the cosmos, mountain-life, cloud-life, thunder-life, air-life, earth-life, sun-life. To come into immediate *felt* contact, and so to derive energy, power, and a dark sort of joy. This effort into sheer naked contact, *without an intermediary or mediator*, is the root meaning of religion" [D. H. Lawrence].

Broken ice at Ram-Tso (Central Tibet)

SUCH A RELIGION is truly universal, and if there is something that is characteristic of the mental outlook of the Himalayan people, it is this ancient and universal religion which flows like a mighty stream through all the various faiths and traditions. And it is this immediate contact with the elemental life of the cosmos (which in our intellectual conceit and shortsightedness we try to dismiss as 'primitive animism') which thousands of pilgrims seek year after year in the sacred mountains of the Himalayas under the guise of religious creeds and symbols.

Of all Himalayan pilgrimages, that of Mount Kailas* (which itself is situated in the Trans-Himalayan Range) is regarded to be the greatest and holiest by Hindus and Buddhists alike, and may therefore serve as a typical example. Whether Kailas is spoken of as the "throne of the

* Cf. Lama Anagarika Govinda, *The Way of the White Clouds* (Berkeley: Shambhala, 1970), p. 198ff.

gods" and the "Abode of Siva and Parvati," or as the "Mandala of Dhyani-Buddhas and Bodhisattvas," or as "Meru," the spiritual and phenomenal center of our world, the fact which is expressed in the symbolic language of different traditions is the experience of a higher reality which is conveyed through a strange combination of natural and spiritual phenomena, which even those who are unaffected by religious beliefs cannot escape. Like a gigantic temple, rising in regular tiers of horizontal ledges and in perfect symmetry, Kailas marks the center of the "Roof of the World," the heart of the biggest temple, the seat and center of cosmic powers, the axis which connects the earth with the universe, the super-antenna for the influx and outflow of the spiritual energies of our planet.

The great rhythm of nature pervades everything, and man is woven into it. His imagination is no more a matter of individual fancy; it becomes an instrument of those forces which govern the movements of suns and planets, of oceans and continents, winds and clouds. Imagination here becomes an adequate expression of reality on the plane of human consciousness. Here the gods that were buried in the subconscious regions of the human mind for thousands of years, until their memory had become mere shadows and phantoms, appear again before the pilgrim, and he hears their voices and sees their radiance and knows that he can never lose them again in all his life, because he has been face to face with the Eternal.

Thus, the pilgrim feels himself surrounded by many subtle influences, which in accordance with various religious traditions have been described as the presence of divine powers. Whatever their origin or their definition, there is no doubt that a strange transformation of consciousness takes place in those elevated regions and especially around those time-honored places of pilgrimage. One becomes sensitive and open to new realities; in short, the intuitive faculties of the mind are awakened and stimulated.

Thus, many of those who felt the call for a life of religious devotion and meditation took advantage of these ideal conditions: some as hermits in solitary caves and hermitages, others in small groups or in monastic communities. The development of the latter was particularly favored by the highly organized character of Tibetan Buddhism which exerts its influence over the greater part of the Himalayas and far beyond the confines of Tibet proper: from Ladakh in the west to Bhutan in the east.

While Hindu sanctuaries and those of local deities are generally confined to isolated temples and wayside shrines, according to the more individualistic and therefore less organized character of Hinduism, Buddhist monasteries, wherever they are found, have grown into a dominating feature of Himalayan life and landscape. They do not dominate as something that has been forced upon their surroundings, but rather as something that has grown out of them.

There is a deep inner relationship between those mountains and monasteries. They are the true embodiment of the spirit of the Himalayas. What mountains and monasteries have in common is greatness, simplicity, strength and aloofness. The sloping lines of mighty mountains are repeated in the slanting walls of massive architecture.

The inner relationship of man and nature is nowhere more strongly expressed than in those mighty citadels of faith, the monasteries of the Himalayas: "proudly isolated on summits beaten by the wind, amidst wild landscapes, Tibetan Gompas (monasteries) look vaguely aggressive, as if bidding defiance to invisible foes, at the four corners of the horizon. Or, when squatting between high mountain ranges, they often assume a disquieting air of laboratories where occult forces are manipulated. That twofold appearance corresponds to a certain reality. The hard conquest of a world other than that perceived through the senses, transcendental knowledge, mystic realizations, mastery over occult forces, such were the aims for the pursuit of which were built the lamaist towering citadels and those enigmatic cities concealed in the maze of snowy hills" [Alexandra David-Neel].

WHEREVER BEAUTY, SOLITUDE, AND GRANDEUR produce an atmosphere of awe and religious inspiration, there will be found a sanctuary, a hermitage or a monastery. Many of them were founded by monks and mystics who retired into caves in order to meditate in the stillness and purity of nature. Such caves were later enlarged, decorated with wall paintings and turned into temples, around which new dwellings were constructed or carved into the living rock until a complete monastery came into existence.

In other places, the disciples of a hermit built their huts around that of their Guru, either on the lofty summit of a solitary mountain or on top of an isolated rock-formation, out of which in the course of time grew bigger and statelier buildings. Where the conditions were favorable, temples and libraries, assembly-halls, courtyards, storehouses,

Lama Govinda and monks at the entrance to the main Temple of Nenying (Central Tibet)

and dwelling quarters for students and guests were added; and finally, complete monastic cities came into existence, in which hundreds and, in some cases, even thousands of monks were living.

A third type of monasteries are those which have been carved into the face of sheer cliffs. All their temples, living quarters, corridors, staircases, etc., are carved into the living rock, and only verandahs and windows, sometimes adorned with decorative carvings, are visible from the outside. Some of these rock-monasteries have elaborate facades with balconies, projecting roofs and other architectural additions which make the whole structure look like a swallow's nest hanging on to the rock high above the valley.

These monasteries are the chief sources of culture, the strongholds of civilization in the untamed wilderness of the inner Himalayas and far into the Trans-Himalayan regions. They are the fortresses of man against the hostile forces of nature. And yet, as already pointed out, they are the fulfillment of nature on a higher plane, as they express its spirit more than any other thing. This proves their greatness as architecture.

In spite of the primitiveness of the materials used, Tibeto-Himalayan architecture is most effective and often of monumental dimensions, like the palace of the former kings of western Tibet at Leh, or some of the bigger monasteries in Ladakh, Spiti, Lahaul, and other Himalayan countries. In the south-eastern Himalayas, similar architectural forms are combined with slanting and peaked wooden roofs suitable for the more humid climate. What, however, is common to all of them is their emphasis on solidity, strength, massiveness and monumental greatness. They try to emphasize the substantiality and weightiness of matter. This purpose is achieved aesthetically, not only by the use of slanting lines of walls and windows, but also by accentuating the edges of their flat roofs with dark red-brown cornices which form a heavy horizontal line (like the protruding edge of a lid), separating most effectively the white or light-ochre walls from the dark blue of the sky. When buildings rise up in a terrace-like fashion, as is mostly the case with big monasteries, these red-brown cornices are like the punctuation in a rising rhythm, and they set off one building against the other beautifully. The same device is used for the small roof-like cornices over every window and verandah and over the main entrances of monastic buildings for which this decoration is exclusively reserved.

It certainly can be said that this architecture has created a maximum of effect with a minimum of building material and technical aid.

It has created something so powerful and noble that it appeals to people of all races and times. It is, truly speaking, a timeless architecture, which the pilgrim of the Himalayas will always associate with the Eternal peaks and the profound peace of these far-off regions. He will cherish the memory of those mysteriously challenging citadels of faith in which the aspirations of the human soul have found such perfect expression, and he will keep their challenge in his heart like a talisman, until, perhaps, one day he will find himself on the way towards the realization of his ultimate aim.

PART FOUR

PRACTICE

Opening to the Dharma

Tarthang Tulku

Those who are unhappy or tormented by frustration,
Or engrossed in their happiness and wealth,
Or who are deeply attached to or bitterly
Set against anyone, be they near or far,
Should practice these corresponding mental attitudes:
The desire that there be happiness
And that there be freedom from suffering,
That there be no separation from joyfulness,
And that the mind operate in calmness.
Although there is no fixed order in their practice,
The beginner should at first develop equanimity.
When the mind no longer oscillates between
Attachment and aversion, one may then develop
Love, compassion and joyfulness.

LONG-CHEN-PA, Sems-nyid ngal-gso

We are constantly searching for some lasting satisfaction, and today there seems to be more grasping and craving in the world than ever before. But the samsaric condition means that everything is impermanent. We cannot rely on our feelings or thoughts, on money or any external substance. Even though we have no major war, increasing numbers of people are experiencing poverty and many natural resources are dwindling. There is an energy problem, and something as basic as food is a major concern in many parts of the world. The future is uncertain and unpredictable, and mankind's survival seems threatened. When even life itself is impermanent, where can we find refuge?

We may have very comfortable lives. Our body may be healthy and our mind clear, but in the future, we may not be so comfortable. Perhaps when we are older, we will be lonely and no one will care about us—we may not even be able to care for ourselves. We may be in pain and experience tremendous suffering. At that time, the Dharma becomes especially important, because no matter how old we are, it teaches us to investigate our life and to look at ourselves honestly.

Most of our problems are created by negative mental attitudes and feelings of bewilderment, separateness, hopelessness or meaninglessness which constantly tax our life energies. Emotional attachments and unfulfilled cravings only create further discontent. On the other hand, our own suffering can be our best teacher. It can awaken in us the desire to change our habitual patterns of behavior, to examine our dissatisfactions and frustrations. It is certainly possible to overcome repression and anxiety, to eliminate feelings of isolation and separation, and to develop warm and positive feelings for ourselves and others. Once we can see ourselves clearly, we can begin to see the beauty around us and to appreciate our lives on this earth.

The best way to develop ourselves as human beings is through compassion. For the Bodhisattva, the essence of Dharma practice and the whole purpose of being in the world is to enlighten other sentient beings. For him, no hardship or difficulty is too great. Nothing else is important. His compassion is all-inclusive because the teachings of the Dharma exclude no one.

Compassion begins with totally accepting yourself, just as you are. Learn to accept any inner agitation or discomfort. Open yourself to all life situations, even though you may have many disappointments, pains and frustrations. If we can feel this compassion for ourselves deeply enough, we can totally reverse and heal our negative karma. But compassion is not feeling sorry for yourself. Self-pity stems from weakness. We are anxious or passionate or grasping or occupied with our ego—something is wrong and we feel guilty. Instead, teach yourself to develop positive feelings. The more you can be kind to your own body and mind, the more you can understand and extend this compassion to others. According to the Buddha, even one single act of open and unreserved compassion can be more effective in relieving pain and suffering in the world than anything else you might accomplish.

Meditation and compassion are like the sun and its rays and are the best method for healing emotional and mental dissatisfaction. Meditation—if carefully practiced—can return our body and mind to its natural flexibility and help us to develop trust and openness. Our success in meditation depends on our ability to communicate with our own heart.

In the heart there is warmth and very positive, joyful feelings, so that compassion rises freely from within. Once we become receptive to our own inner voice, we begin to feel calm and relaxed, and our problems do not seem so serious. Something beautiful continues to endure no matter how difficult our life situation may seem. Life becomes a fresh experience every moment. We learn to truly take care of ourselves and to extend this light and knowledge to others.

So it is very important to contact ourselves within the meditative state and to make our awareness clear and sensitive. When we become relaxed, everything comes alive. We taste, we hear, we see more clearly than before. Our six perceptions are totally awakened. Even though we may have very busy lives, we can definitely find this inner warmth. Just completely relax and let go of everything–even for a few minutes–and become silent. Once you contact this deeper energy within your heart, you can extend it to your present experience and use it to heal yourself. In this way, you begin opening to the Dharma by opening to yourself.

Questions and Answers

Question: I know practically nothing about Tibetan Buddhism. What is so unique about your brand of Tibetan Buddhism and what does it have to offer me or other people here in California?

Rinpoche: Buddhism may be summarized into three schools basic to Asian countries. First, there was Theravada, which now flourishes in Ceylon and Southeast Asia. Then in northern India, China, Mongolia, and Japan, Mahayana Buddhism took root, and later on, the esoteric practice, which is called Vajrayana unfolded. These three yanas or teachings have all been preserved in Tibetan Buddhism.

In my opinion, which may not necessarily be true, there are several things Tibetan Buddhism can contribute that are unique. One of the most important is the range of its psychology. Western psychology, although it is very practical in certain aspects, is not fully comprehensive. It has not yet discovered the full potential of the human mind. In this area, Buddhism has much to contribute and there is already a very healthy interest in Tibetan Buddhism on the part of some Western psychologists and mental health professionals.

In addition, although Western psychology has many techniques and interesting theories, it offers very little which can effectively transmute human problems in a sort of recycling of psychic energy. Usually when problems arise, a person either fights his problem or denies it or tries to avoid it. There is no way to deal with it directly or use the energy generated by emotional problems or neuroses. In those areas, particularly, I think Vajrayana, the esoteric part of the Buddha's teachings, can help tremendously. The key to most of the problems of human life on earth lies in understanding the human mind. We always feel our problems can be solved in some external way, but almost all of our problems are in reality manifestations of our human mind. So in dealing with these situations, we must directly understand the entire reach of the mind.

Question: I'm a Buddhist and a therapist. I want to know how to be a good Buddhist therapist.
Rinpoche: In therapy, the most important thing is compassion—not just treating the person to gain more understanding of his situation, but completely giving yourself, trying to open your mind fully to those with whom you work. Compassion is essential to Buddhist practice and therapy, not only to explain something to a person in a way that he understands, but to provide an atmosphere of openness and loving-kindness towards that person. Compassion is the major focus of Buddhism.

Question: What is the relationship between therapist and patient?
Rinpoche: In Tibet, there are four major schools; the earliest one is called 'Nyingma'. Like all the schools, the Nyingmapa has developed inner practices which are passed on through oral instructions. Also, there are many texts and a vast literature. These texts categorize all human beings under nine classifications. Each person at any given moment manifests a specific level of awareness. The master, teacher, or therapist is a person who can understand each level of human consciousness, through his own experience, as well as through having received oral instructions. He can then easily deal with any problem. He cannot mistreat anyone, and there are no gaps between him and another person. He can put himself totally in the place of the patient. In other words, he is not treating somebody else; in a way, he is treating himself. There is no discrimination.

Question: What assumption does the Buddhist therapist have to make about himself and about his patient?
Rinpoche: The Buddhist therapist must understand the human intellectually, plus he must understand himself and how his own mind works. Through this he is better able to deal with the consciousness, perceptions, cognitions, and behaviors of others. Whatever human behavior he may encounter, he has a deeper understanding. I think this deeper understanding comes from practices which involve spiritual or religious knowledge. Through them, he can understand how the total human mind works, how it reacts and what the consequences are. He can understand the emotional levels, the positive and negative levels. Then, when something internal arises, he understands how this works through his own experience, rather than according to theory. This

requires a great amount of inward study, inner depth. A really qualified therapist comprehends fully what mind is, but not just on the intellectual level. He is definitely required to have experience.

Question: How would you define health and disease and the phenomenon of healing?
Rinpoche: There are many different techniques in healing. One person may have developed the use of visualization, another the chanting of mantras or meditation. There are also various ways of healing through the use of various devotional channels. We tend to believe a healer is someone special, who is indispensable. He can heal me and thus solve my problems. But I think that the essential healing can be done by oneself. For example, if you have a physical or mental problem, breathe deeply and relax completely. You can experience a revitalizing feeling on this first level. This is just the elementary level, but as beginners we need to feel the sensations that accompany real relaxation. Once you are completely relaxed, both physically and mentally, there is a feeling of calmness; and that calm relaxation inwardly increases a very subtle energy, which you yourself can develop and continue to increase. This healing energy can be useful in dealing with our everyday problems or conflicting emotions. Once you sense this feeling, you eventually reach a state where you no longer have a restricting self-identity. The tenseness of the ego is gone, you don't feel you possess a self, and you become a part of the relaxation. The relaxation feeds you, it transforms you, and you experience the state of what is sometimes called 'Samadhi' or bliss. This healing we can generate from our own mind and physical body, which is different from someone who has particular healing techniques.

Question: How does that relate to what you spoke of before—the difference between *solving* a problem, which is therapy perhaps, and using the energy to transform the problem, which is the aim of Vajrayana?
Rinpoche: As beginners, we are all in the process of finding inner truth. We may begin slowly and gradually, step by step, to transcend all negativities. Immediately perhaps, we can't do it. However, we can definitely learn something from our problems and difficulties. At that particular moment, just relax. Energy itself becomes transformed.

Question: How do you treat people diagnosed as schizophrenics?
Rinpoche: The best way to treat people is not to make them suspicious of you. I think the best treatment is by not creating extra problems. The more you label the problem, the more it is increased. So the best way is to treat them as normal. In other words, a good psychologist will not act as if there were something wrong or different about the person.

Everywhere and with everyone problems exist all of the time. There may be different characteristics, but the basic human problem is the same everywhere. The more I learn of other problems, my problem automatically dissolves. If I can respond compassionately to another person's problem, communication becomes a sort of healing link that operates in both directions. The more we understand other people, we respond more compassionately. This is the beginning of openness. The more open you become, the less problems you have. You are dedicated to all sentient beings, which is part of the idea of the Bodhisattva. Knowledge of the other increases self-knowledge, and self-knowledge increases compassion.

Parents are also very important, and Buddhism asks us to consider how much struggling most of our parents have gone through in order to give us the best they could offer and to see us through childhood. We easily forget this–we only take selfishly, without giving back anything. The more you make similar observations and the less you dwell on your own problems, the more your compassion grows. Buddhism further teaches that you are the parents of all sentient beings countless numbers of times, and they have been your parents. As one realizes this, each relationship becomes based on feelings of love–not calculated love, but a natural friendliness to all beings, a natural openness based on a human understanding of interrelationship. I think this is one of the most important Buddhist activities.

Buddha activity means compassion. And what is the purpose? Let's say you become enlightened. Does that mean you completely retire? Or that there is nothing left to do? We say that until all sentient beings become enlightened we have a purpose. In fact, the purpose of my becoming enlightened is for the sake of all sentient beings, not for the sake of myself. Gradually, the whole idea of self-motivation disappears, and one sees that when you have no 'self'-motivation and 'self'-interest, then all of your problems get solved–there no longer exists any individual problem.

Question: Do you see any difference in various kinds of psychotherapy in terms of which has more compassion?
Rinpoche: I think the person who is the best therapist is one who has gone beyond therapy himself. He should no longer think in terms of therapy. If the person is no longer a 'therapist', then he is a good therapist. That means he has great compassion. Some schools of thought may place more emphasis on compassion than others, but even though there are different schools and different traditions, it rests finally with the individual–some are more developed and are more actively compassionate than others.

Question: What advice would you give to someone who came to you saying, "I'm very depressed, life has no meaning for me. I'm thinking of killing myself. Why should I live, why should I go on?"
Rinpoche: Well, I can teach you not to think like that. I can teach you that tomorrow is different than today, and that in the past you have constantly gone up and down. Therefore, you should not be discouraged with your life. If you are depressed now, you can be learning something about yourself–you can increase your self-knowledge. And I might also give you some advice about self-observation, and perhaps try to find out exactly who you really are. Maybe I would ask the question, "What is the problem, really? Is it really very serious?" If so, perhaps we can talk more, but usually the problems are really not that serious. Most of us just *think* we have a problem.

Question: How did we tie ourselves up?
Rinpoche: By not being aware. It's possible we really love our frustration–we don't want to give it up. Maybe it's all we know. Human beings are very contradictory. We don't like to have suffering or pain, but on the other hand we do not want to give it up. Once you give up suffering, you can listen to your own awareness. This will guide you and tell you how to continue.

If you try to relax for a short time every day, then a sort of sensation or feeling will begin to arise which gradually turns into something very wonderful, like a healer. In this way you can heal any negativity or any kind of daily problem or conflicting temperament. When thoughts of resentment or discomfort rise, you yourself can heal them. More and more you can eliminate your internal enemies. For example, we call anger or frustration an enemy, but all of our negativities can become part of the relaxation. In other words, genuine relaxation releases energy which can be used to heal ourselves.

Question: What is the cause of rising indignation in relation to an external object and what are the factors that would lead to not expressing that indignation?
Rinpoche: My perceptions are automatically recorded through my senses and through my conditioning. My subjective activity reacts, responds and communicates with objects, so there is always an interrelationship in which the reaction is instant, automatic. Ordinarily, people cannot cope with this easily or cannot immediately transcend or change it. However, there is a way you can deal with it directly the moment it comes. If, in that present moment of experience, you can go directly towards the meditative state, then there are no longer any subject-object relationships you need to find out about, for these are all results of intellectual speculation. The important thing here is that you do not need to know very much about causes, either internal or external. These are simply explanations offered by the thinking mind. Very practically, when the situation arises, just sit there and be the way you are, and completely cope with that experience of how you are in the moment. This is a task requiring skill. All samsaric problems, no matter what they are, are very useful. Were there no problems there could be no Nirvana, no Bodhisattvas. So solving samsaric or human mental problems is a learning process based on accurate knowledge. Whether internal or external, this direct experience is the best source of knowledge.

Question: How do you let go of the ego, melt down and dissolve self?
Rinpoche: Ego has many different interpretations, philosophically as well as psychologically. But it may not be necessary to melt down the self if you understand it fully. The self is part of the working process and is, in a way, necessary to enlightenment and to whatever goals you may have. In religious or philosophical terms, what we call the ego is something to be denied or done away with, or something to be transcended, but I think the first-level ego—not the selfish ego, but the self-maintaining or self-nurturing awareness—needs to be kept alive, even though Buddhism emphasizes that ego is the root and cause of Samsara. In a way, the ego is our projection. You learn about yourself from it. It's

like your own growth. The more you watch the ego, the more you learn . . . and through this it becomes transformed. So in the beginning, ego should not just be wiped out.

Question: Is it karma that is reborn or is it the consciousness?
Rinpoche: Karma is the process of developing–sort of the product. It is stimulated, cultivated. But the consciousness, the cause, is reborn. The continuation is the consciousness, which has many flavors, sometimes at an unknown level. It covers a lot of territory. Some Buddhist philosophers explain the whole entire universe as a projection of consciousness. In other words, this *is* the consciousness.

Within ourselves, we perhaps make dialogues–this is subject, this is object. For example, at night in a dream, I may have problems, something I don't like–I see it, I grasp it, I deny it, I discriminate, or whatever. Separate things happen within the dream. In the morning I wake up. The subject *was* there, but now I am here. Still, this is all one dream. There is no separate subject and object. Our waking consciousness is similar: once we get beyond the human consciousness level, both subject and object become unified. There is no separateness left. This is a theory, but there are practical aspects. You have to gradually develop into that stage–one can't just quickly jump to that state.

Question: Can you say something about the practice of Vajrayana Buddhism?
Rinpoche: The practice of Vajrayana Buddhism is a very big subject. But if you do meditation, develop your concentration as much as you can, and gradually move it within every thought, thought itself is a practice. But our immediate question becomes, "What do I do with my thoughts?" You can meditate within thought. Don't beat the thought itself, and don't try to ignore it. Just sit inside the thought. Expand it, and the thought itself becomes meditation. This is more or less the basic foundation of the Vajrayana idea. Any thought, any feeling, any discrimination you may have, expand it. From this, the thought has its own particular field or space, and you can expand it completely.

Question: When I visualize, is the image in the space in front of me?
Rinpoche: You don't hold the image outside. Awareness-seeing is not eye-seeing. If you look at your room, your house, or your friend, you see a very clear and colorful visual image. Likewise, when you have a memory, you have a distinct impression of seeing something. These images can be very vivid and alive. By seeing inside, without involving your physical eyes, your visualization becomes three-dimensional . . . more colorful, feelingful, sensitive, and light. Gradually, these impressions increase in intensity. Keep the visual image and this subtle feeling of awareness balanced. That is the very essence of visualization practice.

Question: Could you tell me in your words the feelings you get by Nirvana?
Rinpoche: Nirvana is very complicated, because Buddhism is very complicated and sophisticated, and it is not easy to make it into something simple. But the idea of Nirvana is the idea of full enlightenment, which means to be completely free from all bondages or any kind of problems on the physical, mental, or emotional levels. Interpretation of the term Nirvana is difficult because we always project our viewpoint. Whatever we say, it is subjective–it is the way we feel it. This is usually the way we philosophize. So according to that, Nirvana is complete freedom from Samsara, which means, free from all bondage.

Question: What is your main goal in life?
Rinpoche: My main goal, my really deepest main goal, is to help, to be of service to someone. I may not always be successful in my service to others, or I may not know the best way. But if I successfully reach that goal, then I will be of service to everyone.

Question: What are your specific ambitions in the operations of the Nyingma Institute?

Rinpoche: First I want to establish the Abhidharma, which is the basis of Buddhist psychology. As much as possible, I want to make Buddhist psychology available to the West. More teachers can offer more training and help with translations, such as the small book we recently published, *Mind in Buddhist Psychology*. These activities can spread much knowledge about the Buddhist understanding of mind and consciousness. After that, I will emphasize Madhyamika, which is the meditative philosophy. Everyone has vague ideas about enlightenment, so I want to provide a better description of the state of enlightenment. Also, what is Shunyata? What is the Absolute? In this second stage I want to put more emphasis on these questions. The third stage is the Prajnaparamita. This describes more about what 'Buddha' really means, the significance of Buddha's enlightenment. The second one is partial. The third one, Prajnaparamita, is total, as Buddha really saw—what Reality *is*. Everything is part of Buddha activity, Buddha-nature. So I wish to explain these things using accurate terminology. Then eventually there will be Vajrayana practices.

I do not really want to convince the West how great Buddhism is. My aim is to present certain basic ideas of philosophy, while emphasizing the practices, and then unify both the philosophy and the practice. I would hope that Buddhist understandings could be integrated into your own culture and traditions to give them more strength. For example, I know many priests and psychologists for whom Buddhism has increased understanding and interest in their own culture. The more you know about Buddhism, the more you go back to your own culture. It works better both ways.

Question: My friend has what our society would call a beautiful life—a comfortable apartment and a well-paying job. The whole economy is turning downward, so one feels a tendency to hold on to such things. At the same time, there is an urge to pursue the spiritual life and give up this kind of life, which at this time would seem to be a crazy thing to do. What about this?

Rinpoche: It doesn't matter what you have—whether you're wealthy or whether you're poor—you need to appreciate it. Enjoy it. Be completely satisfied. Whatever you have, whether it be a small portion or a big portion, you must learn to appreciate it.

The human mind is very interesting. We think, "This is my whole hindrance . . . if I give this up then I will have no more problem." Or, "I can have a wonderful job." But when I reach that place, internally all the same activities are still going on. Without grasping or trying to attract attention, just use whatever you have. Enjoy whatever things you have and transform them into meditation. It's possible to expand emotional-physical sensations to the point where you go beyond them. Whatever you have, enjoy it to the fullest. Do not use it selfishly, and don't make guilt feelings, but just live within the meditation.

Question: What sort of feelings do you have about sex and sexual morality?
Rinpoche: I think the best sexual morality is complete relaxation.

Question: Were there any great women spiritual masters in the Tibetan tradition?
Rinpoche: Yes, quite a few. In Tibet, there are a number of historical women, such as Padmasambhava's consort, Ye-shey Tso-gyal, who concealed many secret, documented teachings in order to preserve them. This is called the Terma tradition–various teachings and treasures which are hidden all over the world. There are a number of other very prominent women teachers, or women reincarnations, such as Ma-chig-lag, who developed an important following.

Question: In a book I was reading, there's a place in one of the prayers at the very end where you pray that you will be incarnated in the body of a male . . . and it says that that is better. I don't know, that doesn't seem like . . . the concept of better or worse. . . .
Rinpoche: There is no better or worse. According to the Tantras, male and female are represented symbolically. The Adibuddha is called Samantabha*dra* and Samantabha*dri*, both male and female. The male often symbolizes form, all existence, and the female represents Shunyata. Sometimes Prajna is represented as the female, and skillful means (*upaya*) as male.

Physiologically, the female is more complicated than the male, and undergoes greater biological changes. This is perhaps reflected within consciousness, which means that positive and negative reactions may fluctuate more actively. If you have a comprehensive understanding of these energies, you may channel or balance them. Being a female, however, definitely does not limit the potential to become enlightened. Sometimes it seems that being a male is easier, if only because the mother's role of taking care of others is time-consuming and socially involving. But that is not necessarily a drawback. For example, to the Bodhisattvas, Shunyata is a mother principle, represented by the Prajnaparamita. According to Mahayana Buddhism, all the Buddhas are born from within this Buddha-mother. The Buddha, in order to be enlightened, arises from Prajna.

The Theravada categorizes the female as liquid or water, which implies that emotions are flexible and difficult to control. It characterizes the male as earth, more grounded. In ancient times, Buddhist monks had certain rules. If a woman gave the monk an offering, he could not take it: from a male, he could. Why? Perhaps it was felt that monks would be attracted to the female, through desire and attachment. Externally it may seem like a prejudice, but certain rules were intended to protect *sila*, or morality. On the other hand, Mahayana texts and the more esoteric texts of the Vajrayana do not discriminate between male and female. Tara, for example, is one of the most important female Bodhisattvas. Sometimes Avalokiteshvara, the Compassionate One, in certain traditions such as the Chinese, is represented in the female form. Also, certain Tantras are known as the Mother Tantras. Male and female each have their own character, and each is symbolically represented at the center of the Mandala. From ancient times many different countries or traditions, such as the Greeks, refer to mother principles and father principles. Buddhism, I think, is more the mother principle.

Question: Isn't the desire to be more aware, to be more clear, a way of rejecting what is happening . . . ?
Rinpoche: Yes, for many beginners, that's true. For example, certain psychologists say, 'this is the way to do it' . . . and perhaps the literal teachings say, 'that is the way to start'. But when you really go into the center of the thought, the thought itself becomes awareness. When you touch these subtle states of mind and then look back, you can see certain differences between this side and that side—you can see how and where your meditation has evolved. As we emerge from the ego's shell, we may have many emotions and problems, and then start to meditate and begin to see them clearly. That much is good. But also understand, the one who sees is still tied up with ego. As long as mental concepts belong to some*one*, ego develops much strength.

We're actually talking on two levels. We say we should not have any grasping, attachment or desires. At the same time we say that we should not reject, deny or ignore our attachments—we find it difficult to escape them. Our talking is like one mouth with two tongues, yet without contradicting itself. For example, the Vijnanavadin say that everything 'is'. Here is a huge mirror, and everything is reflected in the mirror, and we're seeing the images . . . the seer and the seen are both in the same place, within awareness. Perhaps you receive the highest teachings, such as the Nyingma or Absolute Perfection teachings, and they say, you see something, and it seems seen, but the viewing and the object seen, are at the same time inseparable—the seer, the seeing and the seen: there is no difference. The object and the subject are instantly one . . . they are not separate.

At the very beginning of proper meditation practice, thought itself no longer exists. We can learn to go into the thought, and when the thought itself becomes meditation, it is no longer 'thought'. There isn't anything left to hold on to. If I try to grab space, I cannot get anything, because there isn't anything that originally exists. But in the first state, I do grasp. First, there are thoughts and then meditation, and then you shouldn't lose that thought . . . but it's so subtle . . . you have to learn. Mind experience is much subtler than any knowledge, because there are no concepts, no thoughts. Once you know this subtle inner path, then meditation becomes much easier, then you understand what we're talking about, what we're trying to understand, what becomes meditation, what the real teaching means. Then the teachings come alive. Whenever we want to grasp something somewhere else we cannot really be fulfilled here and now. So in this way, just sit and become your meditation . . . be whoever you are in this present moment . . . without trying, without too much expecting, but with feeling. Then everything just naturally falls into place.

In this way we deal with thoughts gently. Thought is actually like a wild elephant. If we deal with thought roughly, it becomes more uncontrollable. But if we deal with our thoughts gently, they become our friends and bring many pleasant feelings. That enjoyable feeling—without guilt and without attachment—can be our meditation.

Encourage Yourself

The Vajrayana or Diamond Path opens up a hidden treasury of self-knowledge within us. It turns every aspect of every situation into a process of training, learning and understanding. The Vajrayana is especially effective because it does not depend on any one technique alone, but includes a rich variety of approaches, methods and exercises. There is not just one way to gain Enlightenment, because the aliveness of the teachings or the meditation practice is not separate from all objectives and all energies–everything works together simultaneously as part of a whole and perfect Mandala.

Most of the time however, we deal with situations mentally. Even if we live for a hundred years, we can never exhaust thinking, talking, projecting or imagining things. The mind endlessly reinforces memories, discriminations and countless dualities which govern the responses of our body. When there is too much mental pressure–thinking, studying and inner agitation–we may even experience severe pain, headache and tension. Finally the mind becomes totally exhausted and the rest of the body collapses.

While our mind is the source of thoughts, our nervous system embodies our feelings. When our feelings are restricted, our muscles become tight and our heart becomes closed. Once the heart is closed, and once the more subtle life energies are blocked, our feelings become weak and imbalanced. Sometimes we feel this way or that way, but most of the time our mind has already formed a concept, such as 'this is positive' or 'this is negative', 'this is wrong' or 'this is right', 'this feels good' or 'this does not feel good'. Once thoughts take the initiative to determine our actions, then our feelings and emotions just follow along. Even if our inner feelings conflict with our thoughts, they cannot fully influence the outcome, because they do not have that much power. So often, our inner voice–our intuitive awareness or positive attitude–is completely subdued and controlled.

This process goes on continuously. As soon as an image arises, the mind instantly discriminates, but the emotions are much slower, thicker and heavier. By the time an interpretation, judgment or decision has been made, the emotions are just beginning to stir. Similarly, some of the stars which are now dead emitted their light a long time ago, but we can still see them. The same with emotions. The emotion is often felt most strongly later on, after the experience has already been processed by the mind. Since the emotions take no specific form or shape, we become confused and cannot express exactly how we 'feel', because the image, the original experience, is already gone. The emotions are like water. In one way, water is very soft and flexible, and in another it is very powerful. It can flood valleys and destroy everything, or slowly wear mountains away. Similarly, emotions use up tremendous energy. When they disagree with our thoughts, concepts and images, they can create dissatisfaction, inner arguments and conflicts, and produce unpredictable physical imbalances. If the emotions and intellect support each other, then life seems meaningful, balanced and healthy.

All of this occurs within the thought itself, for the mind is filled with a constant stream of thoughts, day and night, never resting. Perhaps one thought is slow, another fast, and sometimes there may be gaps between the thoughts. Sometimes a single thought develops gradually and then splits into two separate interpretations. One thought may be, 'This is beautiful!', but in the next moment our interpretation may reverse. One thought creates and multiplies other thoughts endlessly. From within, thoughts seem to be progressing, to be going somewhere, to be reaching or creating something. You imagine you are resolving a problem or 'dealing with' your feelings. But one thought produces another thought, which produces another thought, and on and on. You can see different forms, have different ideas and feelings—each superimposed on the original thought.

All of these mental events work together in a very complex way. Our positive attitudes always seem to depend upon the relative strength or weakness of our negative attitudes. If negative influences are very active, the positive side becomes very depressed. There is no light, no awareness, no power or energy. Nothing is interesting. Our feelings are totally withdrawn, completely collapsed. The more positive energy we lose, depression becomes darker and darker, until there are no perceptions and no images, just a sort of numbness.

Feelings of deep negativity or depression can arise after a death or be caused by a physical condition, by disease, or by too much mental worry and anxiety. Negativity is also self-creating: we may suddenly become withdrawn and wonder why this is happening. Simply, humans

have a certain quantity of energy, and each time the mind uses energy to produce a thought, the energy freezes rather than flows. The more thoughts, concepts, ideas and images you have, the less energy is available. So the head and muscles become tighter and tighter, the body cannot relax or get relief, and finally it shuts down. Once everything is tight, depression increases. Because we hold certain negative images in our consciousness, the nervous system responds and reacts according to the intensity of these images. If an image becomes fixed and never changes—for example, a specific memory—we always maintain the same feeling and response to that initial experience, so that finally we have no flexibility. The longer we maintain a certain image pattern, the more difficult it becomes to change its effect upon our personality. From childhood, certain feelings are locked in our hearts, and we repeat the same habit patterns for so many years that they dominate our life style. Everything in our life operates according to these patterns, whether for good or bad, and eventually they become very difficult to change.

If we can physically relax, the tension and feelings within our heart can loosen. One method to become calm, positive and balanced is not to be concerned with the future and not to dwell in the past, but to extend the present moment. When we meditate, we can concentrate on sound or on taste and can expand our awareness. We can meditate on thoughts or within emotions or on different external forms. We can use any situation, wherever we are. At that time, just *be* in that present situation—not in the past or future. Otherwise you may tightly hold on to some idea of how meditation should be, how your life should be. You may say, "Now I should not think." But as soon as you create this thought, another thought comes. Or you say, "I should not *try* to do anything." But you become restless. The same thing happens when you interpret your experience intellectually or when you 'pretend' to be meditating—you may only be feeding the self-image. This pretending and delaying may never end.

If you are not aware of what you are doing, you may just waste a lot of valuable time and energy. Here and now, this is your life. Whether you accept it or not, that is up to you. But once it's gone, you can never, never again get it back. That is it. Finished. Yesterday was. Whatever opportunities you have, whatever you own in life—body, mind, energy, awareness—whoever you are at present, whatever you are collecting, you have to use it right now. In the next minute it is lost. You are already another person. The deception is that we 'feel' as though we were the same person. You may say, "I am 25 years old. I still have 40 or 50 years to live." But actually, you cannot predict the future and you cannot recapture the past. Even though you have recollections and memories, they are only images superimposed onto your present experience. So whether your life is meaningful or not depends on how much you value your present situation. Otherwise all you will have left are your excuses, explanations, reasons, words and weakness—but nothing else. As long as you create intellectual explanations to pretend or to cover up, you are just deceiving yourself and playing games. Ultimately, you have to confront yourself directly and honestly work out—physically and mentally—what you want for yourself. If you want to meditate, for example, you have to do it at this very moment and not 'prepare' for the future. The same is true for changing your negative life patterns. The only way is to do it.

We may think, "I don't want my body to be so tight, but I don't want to work on myself any harder." Why? "Because I'm afraid. Because I don't like to feel pain. I'm afraid of pain and suffering. I'm afraid of confronting something." But watch yourself—how long have you been afraid? As long as that fear continues, you can't do anything. Physically and mentally you collapse. Fear only creates more fear, so you tightly hold yourself back until you have no warmth. You need to confront these things in yourself. Ultimately you cannot escape or hide. The weaker you become, the less you will want to confront anything.

Whether you are working or studying or meditating, do it openly, directly, and without excuses.

Let's say you are sitting in meditation. You may say, "There is 'nothing'. I have no explanations. I am fully participating." No. You are playing games–whether this way is meditation or that way is awareness, or, "This is maybe something I'm seeing," or, "I'm getting something, achieving something." These inner dialogues of proving this or that just waste long periods of time, without any real openness or strength. On this samsaric level, it makes a big difference whether or not you orient yourself to be healthy-minded. Even though it may be painful to look at yourself, ultimately it will be easier. Whatever difficulty you have, try to confront it directly. Even though you may not like to concentrate for a long period of time, meditate regularly for a short while each day. Then informally, extend your meditation into every moment–into your anger, pain, desire or grasping. Whenever a difficult mental situation arises, stay within it, listen, sort of chew it and taste it within meditation. Each situation can become more healthy and refined. But if you are afraid before you even begin, you will just delay this entire process. Therefore, it is very important to take the first step. Even though you cannot immediately transmute or transcend the difficulty, just confront it directly rather than holding back or trying to escape. That specific moment of confrontation may not be pleasant or very easy, but once you begin to watch your mental and emotional processes and break down the initial obstacles, you may find your whole life-atmosphere becoming smoother and lighter. The difference in your attitude will be like night and day. Each day you can grow, learn something, understand something, and benefit both yourself and others.

It's very important to try to change your personality early in life. After 40 or 50, it becomes more difficult. So, as much as you can, try to meditate, to practice relaxation exercises, and to concentrate on breathing and visualization. These methods help you to break mental concepts and fixations, especially the concept that you don't really want to be involved. When laziness, weakness, excuses or rationalization are constantly repeated within the mind, they generate a kind of callousness or frigidity, and a feeling of avoiding something 'terrible'. It is *not* terrible. Even fear can be used to awaken, recognize, change and relieve the tension. But you must do something yourself and not expect someone else to do it for you. How much are you learning from this experience? How much can others help you? It's absolutely important to risk taking responsibility for yourself. You need to grow and develop for your own sake, so you must deal directly with yourself.

We definitely have karma, so we must definitely pass through these things. Someone knowledgeable, who has suffering or pain or depression, does not run away. Where can he go? There is no place we can go to escape. The ultimate answer is that we must take responsibility right away. Even though the first time is the most difficult, try to make the present situation healthier, and then future conditions will steadily improve. I'm sure that even Lord Buddha–if we interpret his six years of ascetic practice from a human point of view–did not find it easy. Everyone has to go through certain difficulties, obstacles and problems. There is no such thing as a person being completely free from karma. There are no exceptions. Everyone has to participate in this functioning of karma. We cannot avoid it. The practice is hard and life is not easy, so sometimes we may imagine that there is another place where there are no problems. But still, the ultimate solution is that we must face our problems directly, in every given moment.

Why do we have problems? Because we believe there is a 'no-problem place'. We have that kind of a concept. Therefore, the contrast between who we are and who we would like to be, we call 'problem'. If we don't imagine there is a 'no-problem place', if we do not have that kind of fixed idea, we may never suffer. But we believe that somewhere something is wonderful, something is beautiful, something ideal and stimulating. What is non-existing is created through artificial images and yearning. "Oh, I saw it–it was beautiful, happy, wonderful!" These are only emotional sentiments, lasting for just a short time. Afterwards the feeling or the ideal completely changes. This happens not only in one individual or in one society, but in all societies and all mankind. These projections of 'wonderful things' are secretly permeating our thought patterns and feelings–we believe in them, always yearning, always looking somewhere else . . . for some other relationship, some other job, some other place. You cannot find that 'place' anywhere, unless you examine and work on yourself, and find it within.

It is also useful to be physically active, so that your cells are energized to live a longer life. If you sleep and stay in one place for a long time, you become weaker and weaker, and life becomes physically stagnant. But if we as human beings strongly believe that we are more advanced than any other form of life on this earth, then we have to discover the real potential, meaning and value for our lives. You can question what you have done in the past and what you can do in the future. Look, project, plan, think about, and understand how your life will be–how it will look when you are sixty years old, what kind of person you will be. For some, perhaps, life will remain the same as now, but for others, life steadily becomes more interesting. This process of self-growth and health is just like walking. Even though you do not walk very fast, you grow stronger the longer you walk. But it is important to move slowly and genuinely. Gradually your goal seems closer–closer to your life, closer to your work. The more carefully you work to open your feelings, the more you feel alive, balanced and healthy. Your progress will give you strength and confidence, so that whatever happens you won't change your goal, your interest or your wisdom for anyone. You need to be just that kind of dynamic, clear-minded person. You must have confidence in yourself–you need to stimulate your positive attitudes.

If you listen to negativity once, twice, three times, it repeats itself endlessly so that you become weak and cannot protect yourself. You seem to be faced by disturbances and conflicts–dangerous animals in all directions. How do you protect yourself? Once you can understand the freedom and health within your own experience, then life becomes very interesting, never boring or dull–life is never wasted. You learn to enjoy everything . . . every mouthful of food.

It is very important to concentrate on what these things mean. Don't feel like, "Oh, I can never do those things. I'm not that kind of person. I can't do it." This is just fooling, cheating yourself. This is worse than when others cheat you. Others can cheat you several times, but you can cheat yourself a whole lifetime! You only fool yourself when you make excuses and explanations, and are envious, guilty or afraid. You can go on and on like this with no progress. So make up your mind to achieve what you want your life to be, what is important action for you to do. Once you have that goal, try to continue and don't give up. Once you fail, who can help you again the next time? No one will tell you. No one will encourage you unless you yourself are determined. Who else really cares?

Therefore, encourage yourself–not because you believe in Buddhism or meditation, but because it is so important to take responsibility for your own life: prepare yourself in these essential understandings so that no matter what situation or condition you become involved in, you may easily pass through it. You will have to promise yourself, make a commitment to yourself, be determined, and accept yourself. Without strong determination you cannot succeed in anything–your life will not be healthy, you cannot accomplish your job or goal, you cannot succeed spiritually, you can never become a lama or teacher or scholar, you can never become an effective worker, and you may find yourself at the bottom of everything, in the corner . . . no one knows you, which is not ultimately important, but you spend the rest of your life in a hopeless situation suffering and accumulating more karma. It is not too late now to take responsibility for cleaning up negative karma. If you have enough vigor, if you have strength and courage, and if you develop awareness and a positive attitude, you can do it. Otherwise, you will always be casual and numb, always the same–eating the same food, living in the same place, following the same pattern, never changing, never finding anything interesting, always working on the same problems or job. Life will continue to be very uninteresting, frustrating and dull, and you will never genuinely enjoy anything. This does not mean that you have to perform great deeds, but that you should just make whatever you are doing meaningful to you and valuable to your growth. Even the simple things you do, like cooking or serving, can be done by living according to the six perfections.

Once there was a small monk called Phags-pa-sgur-chung-pa, who didn't know anything. So his teacher said, "You do the cleaning in the temple." So he spent his whole lifetime cleaning, cleaning, cleaning. One day he said, "rDul-spang-sa-ngo, dri-ma-spang-sa-ngo," which means 'the dust will go and the smell will go'. "Dust goes, smell goes." And he repeated this constantly as he cleaned the temple. Finally, he thought, "What does 'dust' really mean?" And he understood within that the real dust was his own kleshas or obscurations. So he concentrated on these words more and more until he realized the pattern and became an Arhat, which means that even if a person spends a lifetime working at a simple, lowly job, such as dusting or cleaning–if he has *that* understanding–his life can be something meaningful. Therefore, it is not the type of work that is important, but *how* to work–the motivation, the concentration, the mindfulness with which the work is done.

If you are not in tune with what you are doing inside, there may be no meaning or value. Maybe you don't like what you are doing now, or you are frustrated, or you do not understand its value and you do not care, or you are uninterested and just passing the time, or you are just playing games for ego purposes. Depending on how constructively we work, the results follow . . . and the rest of our lives follow. This life offers a very great opportunity, and you are very fortunate in having this unique existence. You are not sick, poor or hungry. You are not in pain, you don't have that much suffering, and you have a healthy body. You have experimented with many kinds of things, and now you are learning the Dharma. You don't have too much to worry about. Even if you have some worries, you are not experiencing the conflicts that exist in other countries or places where there is much heavy suffering. Everywhere, it seems, there is worry and concern, planning for the uncertain future. Working in the factories is difficult, living with parents is difficult, and living alone is lonely. Whatever and wherever it is, there always seem to be many problems.

Now you have a unique opportunity. You can read books, you can learn meditation, and many positive opportunities are open to you–so you should not waste time. If you cannot meditate for a long time each day, then do it informally. I'm sure there are a couple of minutes you can find to sit quietly, to practice, to work on yourself, and to grow in meditation. It is important for you to take care of yourself and to understand and appreciate what a balanced life means–not just for one day, but moment to moment, in each situation.

Compassion and Self-healing

We have been talking about warm feelings . . . making yourself comfortable, quiet, peaceful. You can share these feelings with all beings who have mental or physical pain, with whoever is in samsaric bondage. Feel you are giving to them, helping them, making them happy. This feeling is a kind of gift, first to yourself in the form of complete self-acceptance, and then to your parents, your countrymen, and to all beings in this world. Deeply and genuinely feel this compassion, especially for those who are ignorant, dissatisfied or deluded. Offer this love and openness unreservedly and without prejudice to all beings in every realm of existence. The more you open your heart with positive feelings, the more you will begin to understand the Buddha's unlimited compassion.

Soon we hope to have a country center in the mountains or some quiet place where we can meditate for longer periods of time and further develop both formal and informal meditation practices. But then, Bodhisattvas also work in cities. Wherever there is suffering, wherever there are people, you can work, share, and help each other. We have a short time together in this century and in this life. Since you supposedly know something about the Dharma and how to develop your own health, it becomes your responsibility to help others. If someone is suffering or not aware, or does not have this knowledge, he cannot help because he does not understand. But whoever has some knowledge or compassion can share this with others. Even if you can't help completely, at least think about your own sufferings: just as you have problems, so do others. Others have the same human situation, the same problems, and you can exchange your own solutions with others. Also, you cannot improve the world if you make enemies with anyone–with parents, friends or government. Try to accept ignorance–even if others do wrong or continually make mistakes. They may not even realize their own lack of understanding or the source of their problems. In this world there are very few without suffering, so always remember to be compassionate.

One of the best ways to learn and one of the best teachings, I think, is suffering. Suffering is the best teacher. I'm not encouraging you to create more suffering . . . I'm sure you already have enough! So just use whatever suffering is already present. The real suffering, the pain that we feel—physically, emotionally, intellectually, psychologically—this is our raw material. Escaping suffering is only temporary. Sooner or later we have to face our own dissatisfaction. Then our understanding becomes more than just a passing idea or some elaborate philosophy.

The teachings say many things: this is best, this is not best . . . but you can't believe any of these things until you watch and see exactly and precisely just what you are experiencing . . . how your life is really going. If you thoroughly understand your own suffering, you can lead yourself out of many uncomfortable situations through your own clarity and awareness. Once you understand, once you have gone through this very basic experience, then it is easier to change your life. Then compassion for yourself and others becomes really possible.

Once you have accurate meditation instruction, once you understand all the problems, doubts, and fixations, then you need to meditate. Meditation is something you do for yourself—for your own balance and health. All I can do is direct, point, and give advice—this is an assumption, or this seems better. I can give suggestions, but the inner quality you need to investigate for yourself . . . and then meditate every day. Each time, try to increase or prolong your meditation. Begin by becoming completely silent, beyond thoughts and distractions . . . even if you can only get away for thirty minutes each morning and evening. Then be completely silent and physically relax . . . breathe openly and slowly and don't pay attention to externals.

Motivation is also very important. As you meditate more, motivation becomes voluntary, but you can easily become sort of numb or dull, and even though you are sitting there you can become very bored. This is more reason to meditate very loosely, but at the same time very energetically. When you were younger, say 15 or 18, you may have had many questions . . . what is the meaning of life? who am I? . . . and at that time you might have experienced a certain anxiety to find the answers. Later on, you may have become more involved with work and personal relationships, you may have had many experiences, and then the questions return: what are you doing here? for what purpose are you doing these things? Meanwhile, you may have forgotten your original questions. Perhaps you have been involved in business or you have attempted to enjoy the many things life offers, or you have had much suffering . . . your relationship fell apart, there's no future in your job, and everything seems lifeless and hopeless. Then ask yourself these questions again, because ultimately whatever you do in this life depends on you. Your best protector and your best friend is you yourself, your own meditation, your own inner health and growth, your own spiritual path.

So now the question comes, what is Buddhist philosophy, what is Buddhist teaching? What does meditation mean? Buddha's teaching is a way of living, a life style . . . how to deal with everyday situations and how to live and work in a practical and positive way. Even though you may not necessarily become enlightened in one day, Buddha's teaching is not for later but for right now. Now be comfortable, now be positive, now fully enjoy whatever you are doing. Otherwise our life just goes up and down, and meanwhile we remain confused, engulfed in chaos and endless struggling. The teaching itself is a way of life, a pattern for living on a practical level without going to extremes. The Buddhadharma challenges us to change our patterns of suffering so we can find just what we need every moment.

It seems that meditation is the most effective method to overcome all suffering, agitation, anxiety, worry and inner turmoil. If the mind becomes quieter and less confused by daily situations, then this in itself is something very significant, and you will most likely experience many more positive changes as the weeks, months, and years follow.

One of the early teachers in Tibet said that all knowledge is like the stars at night—there are so many that you cannot count them. So it is better for you to count only the important ones—what is your life, what is the healthiest way to live—and then begin developing your insights gradually, day by day. Right now, you may have many insights or ideals that you are not ready to accomplish, but if you progress gradually, step by step, little by little, your motivation will increase. Once you gain this inner confidence and certainty, it will become as indestructible as a diamond, and no one will ever be able to take it away from you.

Within your own experience, you will begin to see that first you provide the effort—the effort to investigate, the effort to become more aware, the effort to meditate. Then you will soon find that investigation brings clarity, awareness brings satisfaction, and meditation just naturally comes . . . like the morning sun. Once you begin with full and complete dedication, everything begins to fall into place. Even dis-

couragements lose their power to upset you. When you feed yourself this way, you no longer need to depend on anyone. You yourself become your own teacher. I can point out certain things, or push you to examine yourself or point out where the danger lies. Even the Buddha himself said that he can only show you the map, but you yourself need to take the initiative. You should not think that there is an easy or magic way. If it does exist, then you will have to find it on your own.

All of Buddha's teaching comes to the conclusion that you are essential, you are responsible. You cannot expect someone else to reach enlightenment for you. You cannot delegate that final authority or expect that you will reach enlightenment overnight. The Buddhadharma teaches you to begin on the basic level of your experience. Wherever you are, whatever situation you are in, this is the appropriate time to begin to make your life more simple, smooth, balanced–not too many extremes . . . not too happy and never sad. If you are stimulated for great changes, they may occur, but the most steady work is the best. If you practice properly, if you truly become aware, if you follow the basic teachings wholeheartedly, then you need not worry about the results or your progress.

There are many things to teach. Buddhism abounds in methods and techniques and advanced philosophical and psychological practices. But these come naturally in the later stages. First of all we must learn to take care of ourselves in the best possible way in every situation . . . a healthy body and a healthy mind. What is a healthy mind? No confusions, no disappointments, no disillusionments. What is a healthy body? Balance, not emotionally stuck, sick, or painful. These are basic. Everything the Buddha taught has its foundation in knowing how to take care of yourself properly. It means that you can teach yourself, you can heal yourself, you can guide yourself. With this confidence, you can become totally independent, self-sufficient and find lasting satisfaction.

So right now, at this time, we already have a great opportunity. Use whatever you have. And if you don't have what you need or want, don't worry and don't be too anxious to have more. Just try to appreciate whatever you have–your body, your mind, your material things, your sensations, your feelings, your knowledge . . . whatever you are doing. Be kind to yourself. Take the time to reevaluate what a fortunate opportunity you have and look at the tremendous pain and suffering and confusion of others. You don't need to repeat your past errors . . . and some day you may be able to help others. Whenever you are depressed or feel hopeless, or desperate, use the energies within your meditation. And at other times, when you are extremely joyful and positive, do not become too attached. In other words, whatever happens, up or down, use your experience to learn, to become more aware. Once everything becomes meditation, you can find this balance, this peace and this contentment. Life will not seem too difficult and you will continually become more open to appreciate all that you already have and are.

Author Notes

TARTHANG TULKU was born of a royal family in Golok, eastern Tibet, and was recognized to be an incarnation from Tarthang Monastery. After extensive scholastic and meditational training, Rinpoche traveled throughout Tibet receiving instruction from important gurus in all of the major schools. From these masters he undertook training in the Vajrayana and initiations in Maha-, Anu-, and Ati-yoga, and carefully studied the works of prominent Nyingma lamas. He was reunited with his root guru, Khentse Rinpoche, in 1959, and later served as a Professor of Buddhist Philosophy at the Sanskrit University in Benares. In 1968–69 Rinpoche traveled through Europe and arrived in Berkeley where he established the Tibetan Nyingma Meditation Center and, in 1973, the Nyingma Institute. In the tradition of Long-chen-pa and Lama Mi-pham, he carries on the Dzog-chen Nying-thig lineage of the Nyingma school which traces its origin to Padmasambhava.

HERBERT V. GUENTHER, Ph.D., is head of the Department of Far Eastern Studies at the University of Saskatchewan. He has held distinguished positions at two Indian universities and is eminently versed in the major Buddhist languages, philosophies and traditions. His books and translations have provided a major contribution to the understanding and accessibility of Tibetan Buddhism in the West. These include *The Jewel Ornament of Liberation*, *The Life and Teaching of Naropa*, *Buddhist Philosophy in Theory and Practice*, and *Mind in Buddhist Psychology* (with L. S. Kawamura). Through his close association with Tarthang Tulku, Dr. Guenther has been working with texts of the Nyingma tradition, and his most recent translation is Long-chen-pa's *Ngal-gso skor-gsum*.

LAMA ANAGARIKA GOVINDA spent many years living and traveling in Tibet, and has been initiated into all the schools of Tibetan Buddhism. Born in Germany in 1898, he helped to organize the Buddhist movement in Europe and founded the International Buddhist Union. Author and artist, Lama Govinda has published numerous works detailing a rich understanding of Buddhist teachings and their application in personal experience. His writings include *The Psychological Attitude of Early Buddhist Philosophy*, *Foundations of Tibetan Mysticism*, and *The Way of the White Clouds*. The lama and his wife, Li Gotami, have made their home in the foothills of the Himalayas, where he is the spiritual head of the Arya Maitreya Mandala, a Vajrayana order.

ANILA LI GOTAMI GOVINDA, whose photographs of Tibet appear throughout Part Three, is an internationally recognized photographer/artist and a one-time Associate of the Royal Photographic Society of Great Britain. Li Gotami traveled with Lama Govinda through Central and Western Tibet during 1947 and 1948, documenting in photographs, drawings and fresco-tracings the rich treasury of Tibetan sacred art.